R.H. Vogel

THE FULBRIGHT EXPERIENCE, 1946-1986

THE FULBRIGHT EXPERIENCE, 1946-1986

Encounters and Transformations

Edited by

ARTHUR POWER DUDDEN

and

RUSSELL R. DYNES

Foreword by J. William Fulbright

Transaction Books
New Brunswick (U.S.A.) and Oxford (U.K.)

Library of Congress Catalog Number: 86-25047
ISBN: 0-88738-141-3
Printed in the United States of America

Library of Congress Cataloging in Publication Data

The Fulbright experience, 1946-1986.

   Collection of essays by participants in the
Fulbright educational exchange program.
   1. Educational exchanges—United States.
2. Educational exchanges. 3. Intercultural
education. I. Dudden, Arthur Power, 1921-
II. Dynes, Russell Rowe, 1923-
LB2376.F83   1987   370.19′6   86-25047
ISBN 0-88738-141-3

Contents

To
J. WILLIAM FULBRIGHT
United States Senator from the State of Arkansas
and
Educator to the Nation and the World

We must try, through international education, to realize something new in the world—a purpose that will inspire us and challenge us to use our talents and material wealth in a new way, by persuasion rather than force, cooperatively rather than competitively, not with the intention of gaining dominance for a nation or an ideology, but for the purpose of helping every society develop its own concept of public decency and individual fulfillment.

—J. William Fulbright

The Fulbright Alumni Association dedicates itself to supporting and strengthening the Fulbright Program, and programs of similar objective, to insure that future generations will be sustained and enriched through its opportunities. Further, the Association intends to mobilize the experienced wisdom of students, teachers, scholars, artists, men and women in business and government service, and others, who themselves benefited from the Fulbright and similar exchange activities, to contribute through their interaction to resolving the awesome problems confronting mankind by stimulating fresh ideas, new analyses, constructive proposals, and cooperative initiatives.

—Statement of Purpose, FAA

We recognize that the experience and support of former Fulbrighters can help to maintain the high quality of the Fulbright Program in the future; we shall assist the formation and activities of Fulbright alumni associations within our respective countries, and we shall encourage their cooperation with the Fulbright Alumni Association of the United States of America.

—The Salzburg Resolution

Acknowledgments

The editors gratefully acknowledge the following publishers and publications for permission to use previously published materials:

Richard Arndt, "Questioning the Fulbright Experience," from a lecture delivered at the American University in November 1983. Published under the title "Rethinking International Education," in *International Education: The Unfinished Agenda* (Indianapolis: White River Press, 1984) as part of ITT Corporation's Key Issues Lecture Series.

David L. Paletz, "A Personal Memoir," originally published in *American Studies International* 20 (1982):30-36.

Otto N. Larsen, "The Evolution of an Ethnic Identity," originally published in *The Bridge*, II:2 (September 1979), pp. 22-36; reprinted in *The American Dane*, XLII:9&10 (September, October, 1979) and *Sociological Microjournal*, XV (1981)

Ray Marshall, "Reminiscences About Finland," *Finnish-American Academic and Professional Exchanges: Analyses and Reminiscences* (Helsinki: Foundation for Research in Higher Education and Science Policy and United States Educational Foundation in Finland, 1983), pp. 103-5.

Michael M. Gunter, "On Turkish Students," originally published as "Academe in the Third World: The Experiences of a Fulbright Lecturer," in *International Studies Notes*, IX:3 (Fall 1982), pp. 4-8.

Foreword

A few months ago the editor of *Foreign Affairs* wrote that "the overall situation today is as threatening and truly portentous as it has been at any time since World War II." The world is in disarray and we are in a state of perplexity and bewilderment. It is obvious that the themes of traditional policies are not working. In the past such circumstances often brought on revolution, but in this nuclear age it is not revolution in the streets that is called for, but revolution in our thinking. Shortly after the war, Albert Einstein put the matter as follows:

> We must never relax our efforts to arouse in the people of the world, and especially in their governments, an awareness of the unprecedented disaster which they are absolutely certain to bring on themselves unless there is a fundamental change in their attitudes towards one another as well as in their concept of the future.

In this collection of essays by participants in the Fulbright Educational Exchange Program we have convincing evidence that the transnational educational experience is an efficient and effective way to change the attitudes of people toward other people with different customs, religions, and political systems. The principal source of our apprehension about the future is the ongoing and increasing antagonism between the two superpowers. The best antidote for the poisonous relations between these two giants bristling with nuclear missiles is a large dose of cultural exchanges in place of the disastrous escalation of the arms race and its extension into outer space.

Higher education, especially cross-cultural education, exists to help students and scholars learn, not only for themselves, but for all of us. They will understand how life today and tomorrow might be better, and, in these ominous years of nuclear gloom, how life itself is in fact to remain clinging to this planet. As they acquire an understanding of what the two great powers are concerned about and why, they will recognize that in this nuclear age competition and hostility must give way to cooperation if both powers—and the world—are to survive. This new manner of thinking is the purpose to which the exchange program is dedicated.

J. WILLIAM FULBRIGHT

Introduction

The Fulbright Program of international educational and cultural exchanges between the United States of America and other countries—involving students, scholars, teachers, and artists—is regarded almost universally as a rare triumph for achieving its stated purposes while contributing substantially to mutual respect, peace, and understanding among its participants and supporters.

Today, forty years after it all began, former U.S. senator J. William Fulbright, Democrat of Arkansas, is celebrated at home and abroad for initiating the exchange process that bears his name. Fulbright, then a freshman senator, introduced his bill in September 1945 to authorize the utilization of the proceeds from sales of surplus war property for "the promotion of international good will through the exchange of students in the fields of education, culture, and science." His own rewarding experience at Oxford University as a Rhodes scholar and memories of the troublesome issues raised in Congress and public opinion between the United States and the European belligerents over the reparations and debts of World War I, induced him when World War II ended, as he later explained, to attempt a novel approach to healing the latest wounds of war: "It was a combination of these two thoughts which led me to introduce the legislation to try to make use of the results of that war to improve the cultural relations in an area in which we could do the most for promoting better international relations."

> I had to say to my colleagues, "Look, I'm not asking you to give your taxpayers' money to educate people abroad." They never would have. They wouldn't even give them money to educate them here in those days, much less abroad." See, this was a long time ago. . . . You had to approach it that way. I said, "These bills are all owing to us what you can't collect." I don't think I could have got it enacted any other way. Anyway, it was enacted, with very little said, not enough to arouse the parochialism and chauvinism of our own members of Congress. One of them told me afterwards, one of the senior members, "I didn't know about the bill, that I see now has been passed. If I'd have known about it I don't know if I'd have allowed it to pass. You know, it's a dangerous thing to send our young, beautiful American girls and boys abroad to be subjected to those *foreignisms*." And he believed it!

At any rate, the Fulbright Act passed both houses of the Seventy-Ninth

1

Congress by the end of its final session, and President Harry S Truman signed it into law on 1 August 1946. The act's title was purposely innocuous: ". . . to amend the Surplus Property Act of 1944 to designate the Department of State as the disposal agency for surplus property outside the United States, its Territories and possessions, and for other purposes." The "other purposes" constituted a peculiar postwar blend of housekeeping and peacemaking. It would be prudent housekeeping for the nation to divest itself of surplus war properties by sales for nonconvertible currencies instead of futilely demanding repayments in scarce U.S. dollars. As to peacemaking, the transactions were formulated to use part of the proceeds of the sales to endow international education by enabling U.S. citizens to study, teach, or undertake research in other countries, while affording the citizens of those countries the opportunity to travel to the United States and learn and understand more about Americans. Isaiah's directive to beat swords into plowshares would find its expression in this measure. Yet Senator Fulbright himself would have been hard-pressed in 1946 to anticipate the development of the Fulbright Program into a worldwide system of international educational and cultural exchanges, as it has done, or the wide variety of achievements destined to be accomplished under its heading. He could scarcely have imagined that his own surname would come to signify a particular kind of prestigious scholarship in a great many languages; nor that holders of these grants would henceforth become known to themselves and each other as "Fulbrighters"; nor that a Fulbright Alumni Association comprised of former American Fulbrighters would endeavor to carry on the work he has begun, together with similarly constituted and like-minded organizations in more than a dozen other Fulbright nations.

So it was, then, that the post–World War II academic exchange program came into operation. There were delays in negotiating agreements with other governments to set aside funds to underwrite the exchanges. To find the dollars necessary to pay the stateside costs of grantees coming to the United States, as well as the costs of the selection process at home, took time at the outset. The answer came from the private sector. American universities proved willing to award fellowships, assistantships, and visiting lectureships to the foreign applicants selected. The Carnegie Corporation and the Rockefeller Foundation agreed to sponsor the cooperating agencies for the first six months so that the exchanges could get underway. A symbiotic relationship was born at that time between America's private institutions and agencies and the U.S. government that has managed and operated the nation's academic exchange program down to the present.

Still more time elapsed before a full-scale enterprise developed that satisfied the injunction of Secretary of State Dean Acheson in April 1947 to take the fullest advantage of the opportunity offered by the Fulbright Act to improve common understanding among the peoples of the world. The Fulbright Act applied at first only to the Lend Lease countries of World War II, although exchanges with Latin America could also be instituted under the Good Neighbor program of hemispheric cooperation begun in 1939. The U.S. Information and Educational Exchange Act of 1948 (also known as the Smith-Mundt Act for Senator H. Alexander Smith of New Jersey and Representative—later senator—Carl Mundt of South Dakota, who joined in sponsoring it) extended to the rest of the world the same broad powers and authorizations for funds to undertake educational exchanges like those enacted earlier for Latin America. The Department of State, through its Bureau of Educational and Cultural Affairs, which was advised by the presidentially appointed Board of Foreign Scholarships, could now begin seeking appropriations to conduct exchanges with most other countries, even those with minimal surplus property sales as well as those having large frozen assets, and to pay contractual costs and certain dollar expenses of incoming grantees.

With the signing of binational agreements the exchange process finally got underway. The first participants—47 Americans and 36 foreign nationals in exchanges with China, Burma, and the Philippines—set forth in the fall of 1948. Additional agreements with New Zealand, the United Kingdom, Belgium and Luxembourg, France, Italy, the Netherlands, and Norway were also signed. Eight hundred and twenty-three Americans and 967 foreign nationals traveled to and from each of these participating countries in 1949–50. Seventeen additional countries signed agreements with the United States before December 1952. For the academic year 1952-53, the number of Americans entering the exchange program grew to 1,253 and foreign nationals to 2,210 under binational programs. The exchanges began to function abroad through binational commissions or foundations and their secretariats, whose major responsibilities expanded to receive and disburse funds, submit annual program plans, conduct local competitions and recommend candidates for awards, certify the acceptability of the Americans nominated, arrange institutional affiliations and local hospitality for them, sponsor seminars and workshops in such fields as American studies, arrange orientation meetings for foreign and American participants, and report on the program's progress. One of the most significant developments of this binational network was the growing willingness of other governments to join with the United States in financing the exchange program. By 1971, at the quarter-century mark, Fulbright exchange programs were operating through forty-five binational commissions abroad and in fifty-six additional countries and territories where direct government-to-government arrangements supervised the process.

The numbers of participants rose accordingly. By 1971 the total number of grantees had reached 104,021 since the program's inception. Foreign grantees coming into the United States outnumbered Americans by then 67,842 to 36,179. Students comprised the leading category with 41,103 foreigners and 17,821 Americans. Teachers followed with 13,224 foreigners and 6,923 Americans. Next were research scholars—9,608 foreigners and 3,883 Americans. In the only category dominated by U.S. citizens, university lecturers added up to 2,763 foreigners and 7,552 Americans. There were also 1,144 foreign nationals who had been engaged in a short-term social work training and study program in the United States. But drastic cuts made by Congress for FY 1969 in appropriations for educational and cultural exchange, as applied by the Department of State to make the American grantees bear the brunt of the cuts, curtailed the growth rate severely.

Since then the Fulbright Program has reasserted itself with measurable successes. Wars and revolutions, domestic politics, inflation and budget cutting have complicated this effort, yet the number of countries participating rose to 120 by 1983.

Forty-two binational commissions (Belgium and Luxembourg share a single commission with headquarters in Brussels) and 77 governmental offices in noncommission countries were operating the exchanges under the program's agreements and guidelines. No fewer than 29 of the countries with binational commissions were sharing the costs of the Fulbright Program themselves through direct financial contributions to their commissions totaling over $10.5 million annually. Participating governments and host institutions in many countries including the United States provided significant assistance to the grantees more or less indirectly through supplemental grants or salaries, waivers of tuition, housing, and other benefits including counseling and medical services. By the spring of 1985 a grand total of 152,371 Fulbright grantees had been exchanged between the United States and other countries, comprised of 52,957 Americans and 99,414 other nationals. The ratio was continuing of approximately one American for every two foreigners involved.

Present legislative authority for academic exchanges originates from the Mutual Educational and Cultural Exchange Act of 1961. Also known as the Fulbright-Hays Act, it was introduced by Senator Fulbright in the Senate and by Representative Wayne L. Hays of Ohio in the House. The Fulbright-Hays Act consolidates all earlier laws while adding new features to support American studies abroad and promote modern foreign language and area studies through teacher exchanges and curricular development programs in schools and colleges in the United States. The Fulbright-Hays Act is the basic law for all U.S. government-sponsored educational and cultural exchanges under which exchanges are carried out between the United States and other countries all over the world.

The principal U.S. government bodies concerned are the Board of Foreign Scholarships (BFS) and the Bureau of Educational and Cultural Affairs of the U.S. Information Agency (USIA). The BFS consists of twelve members appointed by the president of the United States from academic, cultural, and public life to three-year terms subject to their confirmation by the Senate. The intent of Congress in creating the board was to establish an impartial and nonofficial body to be assured the respect and cooperation of the academic world. The BFS sets policies and procedures for administering the Fulbright program. It also approves the selection of all grantees and supervises the conduct of the exchange process both in the United States and abroad. The USIA provides administrative staffs for the program, negotiates and upholds agreements with foreign governments, maintains liaison with American embassies and consulates on exchange affairs, and, in Washington, seeks the assistance and cooperation of other U.S. government and private organizations as necessary. In countries where no binational commissions exist, USIA's cultural affairs officers administer the educational exchange program from the U.S. embassies processing applications from students and other candidates while providing orientation and supervision to American grantee participants.

To operate the Fulbright Program, the USIA routinely contracts for the services of several agencies. The Institute of International Education (IIE) assists in the exchange of students supervising foreign student grantees in the United States and screening American student applicants for awards to study abroad. The IIE also supervises the Hubert H. Humphrey North-South Fellowship Program which brings mid-career professionals from developing countries to the United States. The Council for International Exchange of Scholars (CIES) similarly operates the exchange of lecturers and research scholars by conducting the applications process and preliminary selections of American candidates and by supervising the placement within the United States of scholars and lecturers from abroad. The Office of International Education Programs, formerly in the Office of Postsecondary Education, U.S. Department of Education, conducts the exchanges of teachers directly under USIA auspices. Other organizations carry out similar responsibilities for the Fulbright academic exchange program, but with a focus on a specific country or geographic area. The International Research and Exchanges Board (IREX) of the American Council of Learned Societies conducts the scholarly exchange program with the Soviet Union and other Eastern European countries. The Latin American Scholarship Program of American Universities (LASPAU) and Tufts University conducts exchanges with American Republic countries for training university faculty members. American-Mideast Educational and Training Services (AMIDEAST) puts together study programs for graduate students for the region under its oversight. The Committee on Scholarly Communication with the People's Republic of China, National Academy of Sciences, arranges exchanges on a unique bilateral basis between the two countries. Additional Fulbright-Hays grants are available for research and training to improve U.S. education in modern foreign-language and area studies, which are administered by the Office of Postsecondary Education as an integral activity of the Department of Education. In every instance the final selection of Fulbright and Fulbright-related awards is made by the Board of Foreign Scholarships which strives, as it always has, to be guided by quality and ability to its choices. The board's choices become Fulbright grantees, individual men and women Fulbrighters once (or more if they win a subsequent award) and forever afterward as they will be known.

The experiences of these Fulbrighters afford the truest measures to date of the Fulbright Program of international educational and cultural exchange during its first four decades. The Fulbrighters' personal encounters with alien cultures and circumstances in their host countries transformed their lives and careers significantly and permanently, as our authors attest and demonstrate in the following pages.

Taken together these forty-seven selections from fifty authors (three essays are coauthored) convey the variegated flavor of the Fulbright experience and its effects on individuals of studying, teaching, or undertaking research in another country. The writers who once were Fulbright grantees came from disparate backgrounds with surprisingly wide ranges in their qualifications. Some countries and disciplines are described more than once by different Fulbrighters from diverse spatial, temporal, or experiential vantage points. About some of the authors more is known than about others. Certain essays are more self-revealing of their makers than the remainder. Unavoidably the quality of the essays spans a wide range of interests, information, insight, and literary style. Generalities contend against particulars. Objectivity confronts pedantry in a number of instances, enthusiasm even veers toward polemics. There is more than a hint of foreign-tainted English in some of the essays, whether from the selections by foreign Fulbrighters who came to the United States as grantees or by American Fulbrighters whose first language is other than English. Undoubtedly there are errors of fact, certainly there are biased judgments, which is not surprising given the disparate backgrounds and educational specializations of the essayists as well as the range of countries and disciplines they represent. Readers may gain an impression of randomness both of order and significance, as though there were gathered together a large roomful of Fulbrighters eagerly exchanging their experiences with each other, while we were eavesdropping just as eagerly. The effect is a vivid sampling of the varieties of the Fulbright experience.

We proceed through these personal reminiscences to learn what Fulbright encounters and their effects are all about. We learn firsthand about the cultural shocks of making immediate adjustments to other cultures as experienced by self-styled wandering scholars. Their personal growth is attested as having occurred in strange places and novel ways. Their lasting satisfaction from having created something new can be located in the Philippines, in Ireland, or even in St. Louis, Missouri, among other places. One academic discipline, psychology, for example, was constructively put by three of its practitioners to the demanding test of rethinking about its fundamentals in Ireland, Turkey, and Argentina by the strangeness of non-American circumstances and value systems, while elsewhere a perceptive sociologist could be driven by his Fulbright experiences to learn enough from the mistakes of others to reflect at large about American innocence and guilt abroad. It is not surprising that foreign environments stimulated new research in Greece, Russia, and China. More surprising perhaps, and heartwarming at the same time, several essayists supply clear indications of the Fulbright educational exchange functioning as a two-way street in tightening the bonds of affection and understanding between other nationals and citizens of the United States and bridging the wide distances across the Atlantic and Pacific oceans. Then, to cap it all, the sixth Apollo astronaut to stand on the surface of the Moon relates his spectacular lunar exploits to his one-time Fulbright experience as a geology student in Norway.

The compilers of this collection of individual experiences believe that its message unequivocally testifies to the great significance and extraordinary value of the Fulbright Program for our own nation and all nations of the world. The recollections and insights the authors relate illuminate some part or feature of almost every other Fulbrighter's own encounters. Our categories emphasize particulars, but these are not intended to classify, restrict, or discolor any essayist's personal message or convictions. Intentionally the authors of our essays have set their thoughts and words down on paper, which have neither been homogenized nor explained away for diplomatic purposes. This book conveys the Fulbright experience as Fulbrighters have experienced it.

Without doubt the educational and cultural exchanges conducted under the Fulbright and similar independent programs of high quality lead to the enhancement of individual capabilities to comprehend and respect other cultures and the citizens representing them. As William Hale of Pawnee,

Kansas, wrote recently to Senator Fulbright expressing his personal gratitude for his 1983-84 Fulbright research grant, which he spent in India:

> On more than one occasion, I met former Fulbright grantees in India, who graciously offered their utmost assistance to me since I was one of them. Undoubtedly though, the most important doors opened were in my own mind. Being abroad, I was able to experience firsthand how America was viewed by the rest of the world, and to see more clearly how our country affects the world and is affected by it. Now I have the direct experience that events and ideas may be viewed from many different perspectives in addition to our own, and that each of these may be valid and meaningful.

Our own experiences—one in Denmark as a historian and biographer, the other in the United Arab Republic and India as a sociologist—internationalized both our careers along various avenues we could not possibly have otherwise explored, even, for instance, to the point of our putting this book on the Fulbright Program together. The essays we have assembled attest that a largely benevolent process of cross-acculturation takes place in most Fulbrighters, and it radiates outward from themselves thereafter as they gain the power and skill to influence others in like fashion.

We believe that the contents of these essays demonstrate the premise and promise of the Fulbright Program. We believe that you will agree.

ARTHUR POWER DUDDEN
RUSSELL R. DYNES

PART I
EDUCATING AMERICA

Introduction

We start with two essays: one by a distinguished diplomat, Richard Arndt, and the other by a distinguished historian, Robin Winks. Because of their lifelong involvement as participants, administrators, and observers of the Fulbright Program, each provides the necessary overview for what is to follow. The essays which follow these are like snapshots in which the authors focus on some aspect of their own Fulbright experience. That experience is usually specific and even narrow. As such, it allows us to savor the grain of that experience, much as we enjoy the textures Ansel Adams captured in his photographs.

But a narrow focus lacks the depth of field necessary for the panoramic view of the Fulbright experience. The necessary vision is provided by Arndt and Winks who have been involved almost from the beginning of the program. They both started their involvement as students, on different sides of the world, one in France and the other in New Zealand. Their subsequent careers took different routes in different places, but their rich experience provides an understanding of the beginnings and evolution of the program and some of its accomplishments.

Richard Arndt's student experience led him, in good academic time, to become a cultural diplomat, a rare and often endangered species. Until his retirement in 1985, he had served as cultural attaché at U.S. embassies in Beirut, Colombo, Tehran, Rome, and Paris. He also served from 1972-74 in the Department of State's Bureau of Educational and Cultural Affairs. He served as director of policy, plans, and evaluation in the U.S. Information Agency's Bureau of Education and Cultural Affairs and, before his retirement, as program coordinator of the Office of Near Eastern, South Asian, and North African Affairs. That long and productive career provided not only time for observation about the evolution of educational and cultural exchanges, but also time for reflection on the meaning of such programs. Arndt places the Fulbright Program in the historical context of the longer tradition of educational and cultural exchange in America. He also raises important issues about the program in terms of the larger context of American "foreign" policy. These are issues which individual Fulbrighters seldom think about since most see the program in individual and professional terms. When they do think about that role, they are

11

uncomfortable and usually critical. Arndt raises the issue of the ups and downs of support for the program by the U.S. government. Individual Fulbrighters also seldom think about that, except in periods of crisis. Arndt's thougtful treatment of the riots, evolution, and the nature of the program provides the depth of field necessary for the outlines of that larger picture of the Fulbright experience.

While Arndt supplies the outlines for the structure of the program, Robin Winks anticipates themes which will reappear throughout the subsequent essays. He entitles those themes a "tissue" of clichés. As he indicates, the student Fulbright fellowship marked an important beginning to his distinguished academic career. The international dimension of that career, with Yale University as his longtime base, and where he is now master of Berkeley College, also has taken him to many places. That career included two years as cultural attaché at the American Embassy in London, where he negotiated a new Fulbright agreement with Margaret Thatcher, then minister of education. Winks's sprightly style in piecing the tissue together provides an introduction to recurrent themes ahead.

1

Questioning the Fulbright Experience

Richard T. Arndt

Thirty-seven years ago, I began a long association with the Fulbright Program, first as a participant and later as an administrator. In these years, thousands of American and foreign Fulbrighters have moved through my life, and I have learned that no two of them have had the same experience. For this reason I propose, in the space here allowed, not to recount my own particular Fulbright odyssey but to dwell instead on some of the qualities which make the four Fulbright decades, and especially the first two, so meaningful in the cultural, political, and social history of the United States. After some forty years, we are surprisingly far from a depth assessment of the Fulbright years. Before we get to answers, it is well to ponder the questions. I shall be content if I raise a few important ones.

All discussions about Fulbright begin with autobiography. In 1949, I found myself on a ship traveling to France with the first contingent to that country of American Fulbright graduate students. That year in Dijon began my association with the program. Returning to the United States in 1950, I entered an 11-year period of graduate studies and teaching, for the most part at Columbia University, where I worked with other American Fulbrighters, and with Fulbright and various other foreign visitors. In 1961, I entered the process itself when I began an intimate 24-year association as one of USIA's cultural attachés, administering the program in five countries and in Washington, D.C. I have been thoroughly "Fulbrighted" in this quarter century as a cultural diplomat pursuing the elusive ideals of international education; and I can look at the Fulbright Program, as it were, from "both sides of the desk."

"What is a cultural attaché?" I am often asked. Most Fulbrighters encounter a cultural diplomat, perhaps in an arrival orientation session in their host country, but few know much about them. In some smaller countries, association with the cultural attaché and staff can be very close; but in the very small countries there is no cultural attaché, since all of USIA's one-person overseas posts are headed by public affairs officers. And in large countries, where Fulbright commissions administer the program, grantees may never even meet their diplomatic guardian angel. I may be forgiven therefore for taking a moment to reflect on the increasingly rare species *addictus culturae*, if only to lay bare my biases.

Whatever the Fulbright Program or international education is or means, cultural diplomats are chief among its front-line servants. Their role is not simple. Charles Frankel referred to the cultural attaché as "the man in the middle." George Kennan wrote this to one of us: "I know of no profession which must more sorely try the souls of its practitioners than yours." Ambassador Kennan, one of the most cultured and cultural of American diplomats, knows that my former colleagues and I, with our weary souls, sometimes project a certain amount of confusion when we try to generalize from experience. At least four dangers affect a cultural diplomat's ability to understand the meaning of his own experience, and these dangers will color what I see and say.

The first we may call the "Rip Van Winkle effect." Diplomats live abroad for long periods of time, say ten years at a stretch, with only short visits home. And cultural diplomats live abroad with a special kind of intensity that may disorient them to American life on return. The more profoundly we sink into another culture in order to understand it, and that after all is our job, the greater the risk of losing sight of home base (in its excessive form we call this "clientalism"). Some less charitable souls accuse us of naiveté, dupery, cowardice, and even treachery, of "surrendering to the enemy in the war of ideas." I prefer to believe we follow Spinoza in trying to understand. Yet as we move from country to country we rarely have the scholar's luxury of specialization, so our understanding is an odd and unpredictable mixture of general and specific.

Like Rip returned from his long sleep, we carry doubtful virtues. We learn and experience a great deal abroad, even if we are correspondingly out of touch with the fabric of day-to-day life in America—there are books, news items, new vocabulary, political trends, pennant races, intellectual controversies, TV specials, and films we shall never know. Still, we take comfort from our novel viewpoint, enabling us sometimes to see things from the perspective afforded by distance in time and space. Comparative judgments can be disconcerting, and we can be uneasy company. Our friends, even our Fulbright friends, wisely treat us with marked distrust.

A second flaw in our vision of things inheres in the phrase "scholar-bureaucrat," often applied or misapplied to us. Scholars are taught to ask questions, to keep an open mind, literally to play with ideas, knocking disparate thoughts about in new contexts so as to bring forth new questions and thus new light. Scholars use wit and irony; they learn from Montaigne to doubt all statements and from Machiavelli to distrust the motivations behind them. For scholars, thought takes time and time is in ample supply. But cultural diplomats are bureaucrats, and they avoid questions. They learn to have opinions, or "policies," at the ready. They know how to back them with the facts that come to hand in the available time. Wit and irony, based on imagination, are out. Play, in a carefully counted 40-hour week, is noted as sick leave. Skepticism may be appropriate, if confusing, when dealing with subordinates, but supervisors see doubt as weakness, negative thinking, or disloyalty. Put these two conflicting approaches to the world into one person and each can compound the other's weaknesses: The scholar's questions confuse the bureaucrat; the bureaucrat lacks time and staff to answer them; the scholar's anxiety at what he does not know mounts higher. This relentless cycle can scramble good brains in no time at all. In short, to be a scholar-bureaucrat is probably impossible, and to be accused of being one most often means being neither.

A third problem faces cultural diplomats. A diplomat by training is an advocate. His job is to promote the national interest in a fairly uncertain field, that of international law and foreign relations. But a cultural attaché's functions lie closer to those of a teacher. In one way or another, we invest our time and resources in educational acts which, certainly over time and possibly in the short run as well, can and do promote national interests, properly defined. But a teacher cannot lie, or at least must not seem to. Sisela Bok has reminded us of the myriad sly forms which lying can take, and one of our great American diplomats left his memoirs under the title *Lying in State.* Given the choice between one of the many forms of lying in the short run and maintaining a reputation for the honesty and, yes, scholarship which in the long run will make words credible and even persuasive, the cultural diplomat prefers the truth. Choosing the truth can indeed try the soul. For the purposes of this essay, this particular ex-diplomat will not quote a recent president and promise never to lie. That would be presumptuous, given the difficulty of ever achieving anything so simple as the truth. But I can say I shall not lie knowingly.

A fourth element of confusion: knowing too many Fulbrighters, knowing too much about the Fulbright and other exchange programs, too much even to know where to begin. For one thing, the Fulbright Program of *academic* exchanges is a major tool, but it is only one of many available to the cultural diplomat. He or she is expected to fashion some kind of coherent contribution to the bilateral relations of the United States with a given country, using these tools. (I recognize the shock inherent in the discovery that a Fulbright scholar can be viewed as a "tool," but I promised not to lie.) Thus the four Fulbright decades are part of a larger picture, a longer history. The formal cultural relations program of the U.S. government antedates the Fulbright Act by only eight years, but its informal antecedents in our missionaries and the philanthropic movement give cultural relations considerable seniority over Senator Fulbright's latter-day contribution. The cultural diplomat is immersed in this longer tradition and sees the Fulbright Program in perspective.

While we know too much, we also know too little. It is ironic that Fulbright alumni and other observers of the program, before the appearance of the present volume, have distinguished themselves by a fairly profound silence on the subject, so that a cultural diplomat, with a lot to understand, has little help in figuring it out. Why have so few found the program and other elements of the American presence abroad to be worthy of scholarly research? Anywhere from 6 to 10 million Americans have lived abroad during the last three decades; yet journalists, scholars, filmmakers, critics, and novelists only rarely have attacked the meaning of that significant fact. Unique questions arise from the choice of millions of Americans to live abroad, from their presence and impact, from the impact of other cultures on their lives as Americans and on American life, from the perceptions others have of us, from those we have of them. Why has the Fulbright Program, with perhaps 40,000 U.S. alumni, attracted so little critical and scholarly interest? How can we provoke interest and attention to the subject so that we may begin to focus thought and research on the meaning of America's crucial experience abroad?

The contributions of my companions in this volume, I have no doubt, will demonstrate my thesis: No single Fulbright experience resembles any other. Or perhaps it would be safer to bet that the obvious similarities will turn immediately into a few home truths: e.g., that we learned to experience cultural difference, or that we learned to look at our homelands more objectively from the comparative viewpoint afforded by our time abroad, or that we underwent some undefined "life-changing experience." Each Fulbright experience is affected by so many variables that we cannot begin to list them all: the grantee's previous training, experience, expectations and hopes; accompanying spouse and children, as opposed to a solo experience; the host country and its particular historical moment at the time of the grant; the encounters inside the scholarly specialty and, more important and unpredictable, those outside the work proper; and the process of returning home and readapting to the old context, among other factors.

What similarity is there between a carefully prepared research grant in a European country and the resourceful improvisation required by research in so many Third World nations? Or between a teaching assignment and a graduate student year? Or a teaching assignment in industrial chemistry and one in Islamic civilization? A facet of my own experience abroad: In three countries, I watched efforts to gather foreign Fulbright returnees into some kind of association, only to discover that participation in a U.S. government-funded academic experience is rarely enough to bind people who are separated by class, caste, and professional commitments, or economics, politics, and geography. What does this tell us?

Questions like these come easily to mind as I reflect on the Fulbright years, and each suggests several more. My purpose in this essay is to propose some ways of looking at our Fulbright experience, ways that may help us understand better, in the years to come, what has happened since 1946, when the wily senator convinced his tight-fisted Congressional colleagues they might just as well spend abroad, for do-good purposes, the money they could never collect anyway.

All questioning should begin with a look at the Fulbright Program in the light of American cultural history, generously defined. As an official government effort in international education designed to build "mutual understanding," the program came on the scene after a century and a half of American ambivalence about other nations. And it took place despite the burning conviction that government (read: politics/power) should stay out of education, scholarship, and research. How did we accept so readily a federal intervention of this kind?

Michael Kammen has named us: We are a "people of paradox." Our nation was born in a state of two-mindedness about the rest of the world, and it has remained so. All nations are ambivalent about others but in the case of the United States the paradox was designed into the fabric of our life. We had to reject Europe if we were to begin to define our own identity and a Jefferson, living amidst his homegrown inventions and his imported European cultural treasures, would warn us more than once about the temptations of Europe. Despite its cultural wealth, Europe and especially its politics represented all that was to be feared. Outside Europe, in the eighteenth-century equivalent of the Third World, there were other lands. These lands Americans treated either as space to be conquered and settled, like our frontier; as territory to be liberated from European domination and kept free for our own purposes, like Latin America; or as geography to be relegated to exotica, hence to explorers and scholars, and thus ignored except as entertainment.

Our foreign policy, as Arthur M. Schlesinger Jr. has observed, has always steered a careful course between geopolitical, balance-of-powers, nationalist realism, and the idealistic rhetoric of one version or another of making the world safe for democracy (our kind, of course). Some Americans worried from the outset about the social and economic development, and the souls, of selected less fortunate foreign brethren; others of us drove the hard bargains of the Yankee trader. American isolationism, given new importance and form after the soft-speaking Theodore Roosevelt discovered the subtle joys of big-stick international meddling, posed its own paradox: Isolationism draws strength both from the ignorance of the know-nothings and from the sophistication of those who fear the consequences of too-rapid modernization in traditional societies, or "cultural imperialism," as it is sometimes called.

We Americans are proud to be considered "practical idealists" or "realists . . . with ideals," in Mrs. Kennedy's phrase, and we live comfortably with this self-image. Yet both phrases are contradictions, oxymorons expressing the paradox of American power and lying deep in the idea of internationalism.

We have been persistently ambivalent about non-American cultures from the beginning. Other cultures, primarily Europe, seemed first to threaten our efforts to become American. Later, waves of less familiar European and non-European immigrants posed a different kind of threat. Only recently have we been able to turn our immigrant origins into the fuel for an ingenious search for ethnic identity in the context of a pluralist nation. Only in recent years have we endeavored to celebrate rather than persecute difference.

As Americans, we sought our identity in action, in *our* actions, thus in the here and now; and our philosophers devised a pragmatic style to justify our ways to God. As the "here" reflects our disinterest in geography, in the elsewhere, so the "now" reveals our distrust of history, whose role in locating America in the unfolding of civilization still has too little value to ensure it a central place in American schools. Even when we do history, at certain universities, for example, dressed in the priestly garb of "Western Civ," we tend to ignore our non-Western roots and tributaries.

In cultural terms, are Americans more ambivalent about other nations than are the citizens of the rest of the world? Perhaps not so very much; but in our open, pluralist, and information-flooded society, our ambivalence is more visible. Most nations leave foreign affairs to a tiny elite and allow the natural hostilities toward other countries and cultures to play freely through national attitudes. In countries like these, only diplomats need "international education." Americans, on the other hand, have been convinced that foreign relations are too important to leave to professional diplomats; we depend on an informed public to feed our democratic process. So we turn, in our natural American way, to the educational community for help in informing our people, in broadening access to and participation in foreign policy. The Fulbright Program was designed in part as a response to that need. I wonder whether the 40,000-odd American Fulbright alumni in the United States today think about their experience in this light. If so, would they agree that it has helped advance mutual understanding on a national scale?

In social and political terms, Americans still fall victim to national para-doxes. We celebrate the individual against the state; we defend the auton-omy of the press and the university and leave both, along with public transportation and most communications, to the tough mercies of the private sector. No tenets of American life are more religiously defended, even when these vital institutions suffer from malnutrition. We celebrate free enterprise, free speech and expression, rugged individualism. Yet abroad we pass alternately for conformists or kooks. Seen from Europe, our airports, shopping centers, housing developments, newspapers, and television coverage look amazingly the same. Our politics produce two consensus parties, barely distinguishable in ideology and adaptable in pro-gram, depending on the nearness of elections. Our media convey impor-tant news at a level of superficiality we would never accept in coverage of a football game. In foreign affairs, our political parties confound overseas observers by concentrating almost exclusively on domestic issues. What is more parochial than an American political party, more provincial than the assumption that our elections will turn solely on the state of the economy come October? We are, as a nation, ill-equipped to understand foreign politics, and foreigners have equal trouble with ours. The difference is that *we*, as a nation, do not seem to mind not understanding. Our contradic-tions may bother us less than they do our French friends; but we may agree they make it harder for us to understand our Fulbright experiences in other cultures.

Another element of confusion: All Fulbrighters are teachers, students, or both. Thus most of us consider ourselves authorities on education, as the educated tend to do. But there are major ambiguities in the idea of educa-tion. In the land of the self-made, American education was long in acquir-ing the kind of value that most other cultures gave it—in many languages "education" and "culture" are the same word. America's universities first aimed at the very few. Study was fine, if there was time, but institutional education was not needed beyond a few basic skills. When Emerson ex-horted us to recognize that an American could be a scholar, could take pride in an American intellectual style, it became possible to confront our European past, to make the "grand tour" without attracting hometown gossip. Later the Puritan-tinted minds of a Hawthorne, of a Melville, and ultimately of a Henry James articulated for America the deeper costs in social dislocation and spiritual confusion consequent on the discovery of our European connection, of the intellectual and spiritual debt to our own past; and even as they did so, they Americanized the nineteenth-century European theme of the alienated artist-prophet unheeded by his audience.

By the 1830s our missionaries had already begun their noble and under-chronicled saga to bring the truths of Christianity to the wretched of the earth, through the so-American tools of education, especially in medicine and agriculture. Their experience reflected the American ideal of education as mission. When the Civil War unleashed giant new industrial energies, it was relatively simpler for this sense of mission to permeate an American mass education movement, than to spread, to expand, and become a manifest destiny at home and abroad.

The nineteenth-century overseas educational activity, undertaken in suggestive parallel with the growth of the European colonial system, was carried out in the normally paternalistic language of the schools. The sense of American mission heightened this tone; and even while rejecting the patrician British style, we edged over into the vocabulary of empire. The educational vision of our missionaries *mutatis mutandis* was couched in a language not unlike that of Macaulay's famous "Minute" on India's educational system as a function of administrative order.

At the same time, we were discovering at home an uncomfortable dependency on Europe. The great American universities—including the Land-Grant model with its unprecedented triple mission of applying knowledge as well as generating and preserving it—saw no choice but to look to Europe for their development. The federal Office of Education, from its creation, had a specific charge to draw what was required from Europe to help build our research universities. So our students began to flow to Europe, perhaps 2,000 right after the Civil War. Not long after, foreign students, not from Europe's elite but from lower in the social scale and from outside Europe, began to come to our shores—5,000 in 1911, 10,000 in 1930; and probably close to 400,000 today.

By the beginning of this century, Americans involved in education abroad were poised between the giving and the getting of education, which are very different matters. If, as one stimulating definition suggests, imperialism is a phenomenon produced by the impact of higher-technology on lower-technology societies, then the language of the bestowing of education and the language of imperialism tend necessarily to share their vocabulary. In the getting, Americans channeled European high technology as justly, as democratically as possible through our pragmatic universities into the most mundane aspects of our daily life. But in the giving, with our endless generosity and our desire to let the whole world in on our utopian secret, we paid scant attention to the way our high technology might impact on others—if the product was pure, the marketplace could surely handle problems like justice. In the getting, we could afford to be selective, and the natural democratic elitism of science and technology took over; but in the giving, we did what we could, where we could, and we assumed that the benefits would diffuse by themselves. The getting of knowledge requires humility. But the giving may presuppose a generous and gentle form of arrogance.

The education/training dichotomy likewise reflects the European elitist versus the American democratic context, a paradox we find today in the ongoing American discussion about the whole man, the great books, the liberal arts, and the core curriculum approaches, as opposed to various more implemental styles of training, or in the discussion about higher academic achievement in American public schools designed to reach 100 percent of the eligible population. In this last case the paradox, pointed by ideological manipulation, has been turned to political use, a dangerous development in a nation that has always been comfortable with its pluralistic paradoxes and thus ill-equipped for casuistic tugs-of-war. How many alumni owe to their Fulbright experience the awareness that most of the world pays a lot more attention to ideas and their structuring effect than we do, that the kind of consistency which Emerson and Whitman dismissed so lightly represents a major quest for most of the world's intellectuals?

It is a common Fulbright experience in the Third World to find ourselves accused of cultural imperialism, perhaps because as Americans we easily slip into a didactic posture. Even in Europe, have we always resisted the temptation to complain about things we know we do better? It is a common perception, even among foreigners who understand and love us, that fervent belief in our own American myths may make us difficult friends at best. Those neochauvinists who would have us proudly proclaim our values as flatly superior to others' are no less uncomfortable than those apologists who declare any and all foreign values acceptable and even preferable to ours. American exceptionalism, based on the certainty that we are unique, induces us all to want to explain. Who among us has not felt the temptation of lecturing our foreign friends about the superiority of American driving, toilet habits, central heating, or even political process, government, and justice? I suspect I am not alone in having yielded to this temptation. Only our paradoxes can explain behavior which, if not arrogant, is at least ill-mannered.

Let us look at history of another kind—that of events, and recent ones at that. The background of the Fulbright Program itself extends well back before its beginnings in the aftermath of World War II. For brevity, I suggest we begin in 1919, after World War I. Now the world was surely safe for democracy; the war to end all wars had been won, and we assumed a role of leadership among nations. Fritz Stern has put this moment succinctly:

As history goes, American leadership is a relatively recent affliction. In part, our global responsibilities were thrust upon us—by the weaknesses of former allies and by the threat of new rivals. For the first century of our national existence, we were a continental power—and even after our imperial adventure in the Spanish-American War, we retained an essentially insular outlook. Until 1917, we were blessed with the reality of privacy. We traded with the world, we learned from it, but we were not responsible for it. Incautiously we ditched the burden of responsibility in 1920, by 1944 it proved inescapable.

The effects of this moment on American society are endless. By 1918, large numbers of Americans had for the first time been internationally socialized by being transported to Europe and then returned home. Questions about keeping them "down on the farm, after they've seen Paree" arose all too naturally. The new-found hospitality of grateful citizens in postwar France, Italy, and Britain, and even in a resentful Germany, eased the problems encountered by American students in those countries. Rhodes Scholars began to be a part of our educational and political landscape. A generous exchange rate enabled a new generation of Americans, some of them scholars, some tourists, and some celebrants of lostness, to emulate Jefferson by touring Europe and bringing home bits, pieces, and memories of its culture.

In 1919, the marriage in America of education and internationalism was consecrated, with the founding of the Institute of International Education. The IIE, brought into being by American universities and foundations, reflected the growing need for a national clearinghouse to coordinate the getting and giving of knowledge with regard to other nations. Today it still handles all American and foreign Fulbright graduate students.

Overseas other educational institutions were burgeoning. In Paris, we founded two hostels for American students and a Carnegie-sponsored home for scholars. Another endowed center in Paris, complete with swimming pool, would help students spend their leisure hours in wholesome activities. A similar healthy, near-monastic orientation kept the Fellows in the American Academy in Rome, founded twenty-odd years before but growing rapidly now with the help of J.P. Morgan, safe on their high Janiculum from the fevers below. At Oxford and Cambridge, visiting professorships in American studies were founded, as was a chair at the Collège de France. And the American philanthropic foundations, restoring old monuments like Reims Cathedral and Versailles while building new ones like the Dental Faculty of the University of Rome, created a climate without precedent for the interchange of European and American elites. By 1930, there would be more than 5,000 American students abroad, plus the tourists, business executives, artists, and émigrés.

Wilson's failure to sell Congress on the League of Nations had been political, not cultural. In cultural and commercial terms, the die was cast.

The energy of the rampantly internationalist city of New York was already beginning to spill over and out into the rest of the nation. It was no accident that the IIE was located there.

In formal diplomacy, the effects of this new awareness of education were also beginning to be felt. Earlier, the indemnity paid by China for damages in the Boxer Rebellion had been allocated to educational exchange, as were the repayments from Finland's World War I debts to the United States. An incident in Iran in the early 1920s would repeat this precedent. We moved from a gentleman-staffed foreign service to an institutionalized system with a corporate memory, thanks to the Rogers Act of 1924, creating the Foreign Service. The service would soon discover, as the French had already done, the cultural dimensions of diplomacy. But even the French did not formalize their separate overseas cultural service until the 1920s; the British Council was not founded until 1935, in response to Nazi programs.

In the United States it was only in 1938 that the State Department yielded to the obvious (with the extreme reluctance natural to any federal agency—especially one staffed by an educated elite). Urged by the universities, the foundations, and the IIE, the State Department agreed to provide an office for the benign coordination of overseas educational and cultural activities. The period 1938–50, so ably documented and analyzed by Frank Ninkovich in his remarkable *Ideas of Diplomacy*, would soon see this office led out of its passive role into activist programs by the wartime energy of young Nelson Rockefeller, who believed with the British that a dynamic cultural program was an important weapon for countering Axis power, especially in Latin America.

If World War I began the international socialization of Americans, World War II carried it further: more Americans went abroad, and they went to many more countries; expanded media coverage and the powerful Hollywood machine brought the war close to every American. Afterward, an American like young Senator Fulbright approached the postwar period with a Rhodes-generated sophistication flowing from close observation of the lessons of the 1920s and 1930s.

Some kind of United Nations was taken for granted and so was UNESCO—perhaps too much so, it now seems. The Marshall Plan, pouring into Europe an average of $3 billion annually, along with thousands of Americans, was an amazing success, even if it left its share of illusions about the power of money, good intentions, glib expertise, and technical assistance. The parallel success of German and Japanese "reeducation" (itself a thought-provoking word) fed other illusions about quick cultural and educational fixes.

Were our illusions more sophisticated than those of the 1920s? Did anyone in the late 1940s believe that *this* war had ended them all, or that the world was safe for democracy? The war drums of its colder cousin could already be heard, and there was thunder in China. So it was perhaps natural that the newly dynamized government cultural programs, now linked to the foreign affairs interests of the United States, should not revert to prewar benignity but carry their new-found vigor into the battles of the Cold War era. The sense of mission does not die easily in America, and the early postwar period, naturally strewn with the language of the Crusades, marked the beginning of a new one. However sophisticated, Americans of the 1940s and 1950s were still missionary idealists.

In 1953, from the land of Machiavelli, Luigi Barzini felt strongly enough to warn us against idealism and simplistic solutions:

> How can Americans quickly adapt themselves to the permanent war, which has to be prepared, threatened, feared or fought, hot or cold, every day of their future life? . . . The temptation is always with them to rush into whatever there is to be done, do it, and get it over with. Who will tell them that the flames will never be extinguished and they will never go to bed?

Brash young America knew better than to heed this kind of tired old European cynicism. We scoffed too at Europe's insistent stress on the effect on us of our Puritan ancestors. A recent definition by Professor Heikko Oberman of Tübingen University exemplifies Europe's perception of the dangers of unacknowledged American Puritanism. He asks:

> To what extent did the American enlightenment, somewhat different from the French, combine secular knowledge with religious obligation to form a "civic religion" unknown in Europe? Was there a genuine American Puritanism whose concept of freedom, coupled with a missionary mentality, produced its own value hierarchy and urged the assumption of supranational responsibility for spreading freedom to the rest of the world?

Whether the American mission was focused on heathens or hunger, Nazis or Communists, it still looks like a mission to friendly and neutral observers. If idealism and a sense of mission, part of what makes us unique as Americans, lie at the base of the Fulbright experience, can we analyze our life-changing experiences without an awareness of this subtext?

World War II brought education into international politics, into proximity with programs in information and propaganda. At the end of the war, we find three symbolic actors: General William J. Donovan and his Office of Strategic Services, Elmer Davis and his OWI, Archibald MacLeish and his cultural programs. These three forces would ultimately regroup and form the CIA on the one hand and USIA (with State's CU) on the other; and the USIA configuration would persist, with various reforms and reshapings, until today. There seems to have been no thought of returning to the passive coordinative stance of cultural diplomacy adopted in 1938.

International education entered two decades of stunning growth after the war, soon escaping from the context of the diplomats. The GI Bill allowed veterans to stay on in Europe; many even studied. The Marshall Plan and German and Japanese reeducation had important training dimensions at home and abroad. Senator Fulbright's ingenious way of settling war debts without disrupting national economies opened a new era of exchanges, turning rusty tanks and surplus clothing into scholarships; and the Smith-Mundt Act of 1948 broadened the program's reach. First-generation American Fulbright returnees multiplied the investment as they contrived hundreds of year-abroad programs, which even today sponsor perhaps 10,000 American students annually in France and Italy alone. And in the 1940s and 1950s, secondary-school programs like the American Field Service, the Experiment in International Living, and later Youth for Understanding began their growth. The Fulbright Program became a small flagship for a large and proliferating armada.

In 1957, shocked by the Soviet ability to launch a basketball-sized satellite, Congress passed the National Defense Education Act, authorizing among other things federal funding for university foreign language and area studies programs, and bringing the U.S. Office of Education into the game, dedicated to its traditional purpose: the enrichment of U.S. education. The great foundations, ever out front, expanded their own important commitment to international education. In 1961, the Third World became part of the curriculum when the Peace Corps posited three separate purposes: helping others, shaping the American image abroad, and informing Americans about the world. Later in 1961, an expanded Fulbright-Hays Act was passed. The International Baccalaureate, in the 1960s, began its efforts to produce uniform international secondary school-leaving criteria, a major step toward free educational interchange at secondary and tertiary levels.

In short, the period from the end of the war until the mid-1960s was marked by tremendous optimism, unexamined assumptions, and a growth worthy of the wildest dreams of those who saw the Fulbright Program as a sower of seeds. These factors flowed together in the International Education Act of 1966. Extending the motto of the University of Wisconsin, where education reaches the boundaries of the state, and proclaiming that the responsibilities of American education covered the entire globe, this noble document fell flat: The IEA never received a penny of appropriated funds. Its demise coincides with the end of an era of burgeoning both for the 20-year-old Fulbright Program and for its myriad offshoots.

It is useful and revealing to examine this vibrant 20-year period. In these years international education, sparked by the Fulbright Program, took shape as a concept, boomed in the United States and abroad, and assumed a particular American style. Let me throw out a few descriptive thoughts, listed almost as they come to mind and without any pretense of their telling the complete story of this complex period. Each item suggests the kind of interpretive questions political scientists, economists, historians, and even philosophers might ask about our Fulbright experience and what it generated:

- The numbers were large, but how large? It is not inaccurate to speak of a proliferation. In absolute terms, no nation ever imported, before or since, so many students, researchers, and teachers with the possible exception of the Soviet Union; certainly no nation ever exported more.
- Why was there so little central coordination, so little attention to aggregate numbers? A thousand flowers bloomed, but many faded unseen. Abroad, it was not long before a country like France, where higher education is a function of the state, began to wonder why thousands of Americans should fill scarce places in its universities at no cost when French students in the United States paid heavy tuition fees. And Pakistan began to worry about the deculturation and deracination of their young people during the deeply emotional, family-based experience of the American Field Service year.
- How sensitive were we to the fact that most of these exchanges took place in a private sector American framework that foreign governments found impossible to match and hard to deal with? It was difficult for Americans, accustomed to moving easily from Kansas to California, to understand why foreign nations seemed so stodgy, bureaucratic, and frustrating. In my own case, impatience focused on the French police and my identity card. Important political and economic niceties, to Americans, seemed to reflect foreign orneriness, incompetence, and occasional malice.
- What about the canard of cultural imperialism? The tone, vocabulary, and style of this expansion, conscious or not, had a hegemonic tinge to it, lodged in the persistent notion of education as mission. Was intellectual leadership not a natural consequence of political power? asked Perry Miller in an article that reached me in Dijon in 1949. Few Americans ever dreamed of ruling the world, but accusations of cultural imperialism, not only from the predictable enemies, dupes, and disinformed but from sensitive friends, began to be heard.
- Similarly, what effect on us did the discovery of the highly articulate and sophisticated rhetoric of anti-Americanism have? A nation whose self-image stresses its generosity to others, its two military "rescue missions" in Europe, takes to heart the discovery that it is not universally loved. The British had long before learned least of all to expect love, but for Americans it was a wrench. Further, our emotions blinded us to the

different strands woven into the complex fabric of anti-Americanism and impeded analysis of the phenomenon. How many of us saw it at first as a combination of hurt national pride and fear of change, as well as manipulation by interested parties with political motives?

- A certain lustrous quality, epitomized by the early participation of scholars like Daniel Boorstin, Charles Frankel, Saul Padover, Leslie Fiedler, Leo Marx, Henry Nash Smith, and hundreds of others, had given way, even by the late 1950s, to a stream of solid but less glamorous scholars funded by a more parsimonious budget. At Columbia, for example, the rule of thumb in the 1950s was simple: A faculty member with a Fulbright could only afford a one-semester research sabbatical abroad, but with a Guggenheim could make it a full year.
- Responsibility for federal funding of international education during these years was dispersed through several federal agencies, with only the merest coordinative structure between them. Charles Frankel counted fifteen separate agencies with diverse interests in overseas educational and research relationships. What effect did this dispersal have?
- Despite continual Congressional carping, total government investment, all considered, was small. The real quantitative impact came from the ignition of private energies, meaning primarily the universities. At its high point in 1966, the budget for the Department of State's Bureau of Educational and Cultural Affairs barely edged over $50 million, while the Office of Education was struggling hard to get its international budget up to $20 million even in the 1980s. How can we calculate the real value of these investments?
- Many of the important funding breakthroughs in Congress were dressed in the language of the military: Fulbright was funded by surplus military sales, for peace we needed a corps, educational legislation was first geared to national defense and in 1985 to economic security. When he heard the NDEA might be renamed without the word *defense*, one university area studies figure exclaimed, "My God! Now we'll *never* get any money!"
- While the exchangees and their administrators produced a mountain of humdrum publications and reports, why did the process itself generate so little serious research and analysis? What did appear, as Ninkovich notes, was a "somewhat anemic and inbred literature." Meanwhile, federal administrators, trying to make the most out of too little, skimped on research and evaluation.
- Americans discovered, on returning home, a disheartening lack of curiosity about the quality of their experience. As J.K. Galbraith tells it, response to his return to Harvard after his years as ambassador to India was typified by the colleague who begged him to tell all about it, " . . . but not now."
- The dynamic style of many federal education programs overseas, particularly those with their home in USIA, persisted. Why was it so un-

thinkable to go back to the benign and coordinative prewar style? What was the program's relationship to foreign policy? Is it possible that programs defined as part of our foreign affairs support system tend to become ends in themselves rather than seeds or links in a process? And if so, how have the universities learned to live with these conditions?

• There was real progress in university language and area studies, but as Harlan Cleveland would point out in 1980, the area studies programs were surprisingly insular, often separate from the rest of their universities. One typical pattern, an outwardly expanding language program, often incurred stern opposition from social scientists and historians.

These snippets, thrown out literally at random, suggest how much there is to examine. Elusive questions of the program's relationship to foreign policy concerns began early to be raised but they were silenced for the most part with wordy nonanswers. It was obvious that proximity to power would exert strong pressures on the Fulbright Program, pressures to deliver certain kinds of policy-relevant results. After the acerbic discussions of the late 1930s, was no one concerned about this dilemma?

The political dimensions of the Fulbright Program are worth a book by themselves alone. For example, it is useful to consider the quality of each experience as a function of the nature of the relations between the United States and the host country. We can see broad categories, if we extrapolate from the different kinds of bilateral relationship. In terms of what Americans and foreigners expected from each other, there were perhaps three kinds of exchange relationships in the two decades after World War II: getting, giving, and confronting (like all categorizations, mine admits the usual exceptions).

With the major nations of Europe, we were still in a predominantly "getting" stage, at least in the 1950s and 1960s. European universities were still too proud to admit need, and Americans tended to look up to Europe's history of humanistic scholarship, sitting, for example, at the feet of F.R. Leavis. Even a field of acknowledged U.S. expertise like American studies or American literature found hard going in Europe, because of budgets and the politics of university appointments. Today it is still nearly impossible for an American to hold a tenured position in a foreign university, while foreigners teach in America, where we readily admit our need, by the thousands.

The second category of bilateral relationships, based on giving, took place with the developing countries. Here we were not students so much as teachers, at least in the first instance, and their students came to the United States to get what they could not get at home. Only our future area studies practitioners went to the Third World to learn and even then they often brought their highly polished American methodologies.

A third group is typified by exchanges with the Soviet bloc countries, where the mode was confrontational and the style wary and exploratory. There the purposes were tentative and partial, the tone suspicious, the product highly limited. But the Soviet model, whatever its characteristics, typifies nothing.

Setting aside the highly politicized and atypical Soviet relationship and the recently revived program with China, the Fulbright Program was and probably still is poised between giving and getting. Each bilateral relationship has its own history and character, but by and large each is still either a giving or a getting process, each covering a subtle mirror play of national pride and ambivalence. Every American Fulbright alumnus must carry inside him/herself some reflection of these interesting paradoxes.

These first two postwar decades of Fulbright exchanges, then, were marked in the United States by proliferation and abundance, but by little coordination, planning, or evaluation, by an indifference to international administrative and political niceties which was already causing nascent bilateral irritations, by persistent cultural ambivalence, by an implicit and ever-subtle kind of hegemonic utopianism, and in Washington by an absence of personnel utilization strategies, by a failure to institutionalize gains, by scant guidelines on how private and public funds might work together, and by no formal Congressional commitment to continuity over time, except through the heroic efforts of a single senator.

By 1945 it had been obvious that the role of world leader, whether or not we wanted it, was ours. Surely it was not much later that we began to realize that international leadership was better understood in the context of a growing interdependence, as Henry Kissinger was to point out at the end of the 1960s. Yet there is little evidence of a national educational policy consensus during these two postwar decades, little to indicate that our nation knew that preparation for life in a newly interdependent world, through education, was closely related to survival. Fulbrighters were not policies, not statistics but individuals: What were their perceptions of the international political picture during and after their Fulbright experience?

To aggregate the Fulbright years between the war and the failure of the IEA, even in so random a way, is to reveal many things. One is the gradual institutional acceptance of the idea of globalizing international education, i.e., educating ourselves about the world and the world about us, while educating the world. We are not surprised, in the postwar period, to see programs designed (even in an unplanned economy) to enrich our universities, to build competence and professionalism, for example, in foreign affairs—hence the rise of international relations programs in our universities. Nor are we surprised that American universities saw it as their duty to welcome foreign students. What is unusual, though perfectly consonant with our spirit of mission, is the growing awareness and articulation, even in the hermetic climate of legislative mandates, of two other aspects of the Fulbright Program: the need to educate Americans generally about foreign cultures and nations, and a sense of American educational commitment to educate others.

By late 1961, almost fifteen years had elapsed since the first act was passed. The products of a dozen active years of exchanges were back in the United States and in positions of growing importance. The Fulbright-Hays Act of 1961, a restatement of the original act and of Smith-Mundt with some added elements, captures the spirit of the early 1960s. It is worth a look by any Fulbrighter interested in knowing more about what was happening.

The act's statement of purpose outlines four explicit goals and three lines of action. First, it proposes "to increase mutual understanding between the *people* of the United States and the *people* of other countries" (my stress: the people, not the elites, the influentials, or the leaders) and to do this through exchanges. Second, it proposes to *strengthen* the ties which *unite* us to other nations (my stress: acceptance and growth of interdependence). Third, it proposes to promote international cooperation for educational and cultural advancement (presumably a commitment of support to UNESCO). And fourth, in summary, it proposes to aim for international relations that are "friendly, sympathetic, and peaceful." In the context of the legislative rhetorician's art, this is an impressive statement. It is significant that other than the fourth point no mention of foreign policy goals occurs in this text, though the idea had been specific and explicit in the Smith-Mundt legislation thirteen years earlier.

The means allotted to the second goal provide a puzzle. The act will strengthen our ties to others (again, my stress):

> . . . by demonstrating the educational and cultural interests, developments, and achievements of the United States *and other nations,* and the contributions being made toward a peaceful and more fruitful life for people throughout the world.

Assuming that this prose is no accident and that an ever-wise Congress meant what it said, we see embodied here an important idea: Americans need help in understanding others, and at the same time we accept an educational responsibility to educate others. This language, drafted by Fulbright alumnus Michael Cardozo and contiguous in time with the Peace Corps's third goal, would later be formulated as USIA's "second mandate" (as of today, long inoperative). It builds on a time-honored goal of American education, the idea that would underlie the IEA.

From this period another puzzling monument remains, of the most permanent kind: bureaucratic structure. Rather than create an agency or expand an existing structure to administer the Fulbright-Hays Act, it seemed natural in the Washington culture to continue to parcel out the program to existing bodies, mainly the State Department, USIA, AID, and the Office of Education. What Congress had put together, Congress allowed to be rendered asunder by executive decision. The gerrymandering of this act, done surely without malice and in the cool spirit of political realism, divided major responsibilities for cultural and educational affairs between four principal agencies, each defined by its own criteria, purposes, mandates, and self-image.

AID took what could be comprised under then-current definitions of technical assistance. The Office of Education took charge of building the strength, in the tradition of its NDEA programs, of American university language and area studies. The State Department's (later USIA's) Bureau of Educational and Cultural Affairs handled the Fulbright Program and all exchanges, including some minimal responsibility for foreign students in the United States. USIA was given the tools required for "telling America's story"—books, libraries, English teaching, visual arts, etc.

How did bureaucratic structure affect the Fulbright Program? Did the parceling out of this act water down its impact? Did Washington turf wars, jurisdictional disputes, and cut-throat budget games subtract predictably from what Congress's language seemed to have intended? For those of us interested in defining the American side of the Fulbright Program in practical terms, it meant, for example, that the projection of American values overseas through educational exchanges was handled separately from the enrichment of the American learning experience, or that foreign students in the United States might study under the auspices of three different agencies, each with its own purposes and terms. No coordinating committees or interdepartmental groups, however vigorous and well-intentioned, could put this Humpty-Dumpty back together. Even the carefully designed custodial bodies, like the Board of Foreign Scholarships or the peer-review networks fostered by the Council on International Exchange of Scholars, found harder questions before them.

How can we explain the sharp reverses of 1967-68? The story of the abundance of the two postwar decades is not complete without a look at its decline. The nonfunding of the IEA was the first sign. Then funding for the State Department's Bureau of Educational and Cultural Affairs declined over two years by almost 50 percent. Meanwhile, in the private sector, the great foundations began to pare, then to slash the size of their international commitments.

Historians may someday want to focus on the reasons for this generalized retreat, at the same time, across such a broad front. Charles Frankel, a key participant, found sufficient explanation in an increasing Washington preoccupation with Vietnam. Others have suggested that interagency rivalries and turf battles, perhaps exacerbated by budget drains to Vietnam, were major contributors. Some see government backlash against universities and intellectuals critical of American actions in Vietnam. Some believe that central figures in Congress like the famous congressman John Rooney, saw an overcommitment that needed to be brought into focus. Others point the finger at personalities, e.g., dwellers of one office or another of the White House. Still others see rising domestic priorities in education crowding out international activities, a reaction against perceptions of elitism. Perhaps some noticed a slight leftward tilt among the American returnees from overseas education. Some suggest, one hopes facetiously, that the IEA failed because it had no military language in its title. Equally facetious is the idea that, after putting a man on the Moon, America's problems were perceived to disappear. Some argue that the "effectiveness" of exchanges (meaning their contribution to U.S. foreign policy interests) had never been proven by appropriate research and evaluative mechanisms. Others see the beginnings of a crisis in national values, one that persists in the 1980s, as the precariously balanced idealist-internationalist worldview of the 1940s, 1950s, and 1960s began to tip toward a realist-nationalist stance.

Whether the end of the boom in the mid-1960s reflected a new mood in America, the costs of war, bureaucratic ineptness, competing priorities, ideological clash, or personal malice—this remains to be sorted out. One suspects that, like most turning points in history, it was a little of all of these, and a lot more as well.

If I have focused on the first two decades of the Fulbright Program, it is partly because my Fulbright experience took place then and because it is primarily alumni from those early years who will contribute to this volume. It is also because those days of prosperity are more easily examined at our present distance. Another reason to which I confess: I am not yet capable of recollecting the emotions of the more recent decades in the necessary tranquility. I hope therefore that this essay will serve as a gentle prod, or perhaps as a wistful challenge, to those who have lived through these four Fulbright decades. The questions are complex and interesting enough—it is time to concentrate our minds on the meaning of our experience. It is no longer enough to shout that we believe in Tinker Bell. It is time now to begin to discover what it is we believe.

2

A Tissue of Clichés

Robin W. Winks

One's thoughts about the value of the Fulbright experience invariably consist of a string of clichés. How could they not, when so many people have had the same experience and, by and large, arrived at the same conclusions? Being a Fulbright scholar changes one's life. The Fulbright experience, whether when young or in middle age, makes one more aware of one's own culture through the productive shock of comparison with other societies. Frequently the work done as a Fulbright student has been instrumental to the development of one's career. Often what one has learned as a senior Fulbright scholar has reinvigorated one's interest in a discipline, has altered a career in a significant way. All these remarks and more will have been echoed, originated, sightly amended in virtually every essay in this book. Thoughts become clichés in some measure simply by being true for enough people.

When one is asked to think a little beyond the clichés, however, those thoughts are often revealed to operate only across the surface. Precisely how was a career altered? Exactly how was one's life changed? I have been to dozens of conferences at which Fulbright alumni gather, ritualistically attest to the importance of the Fulbright experience in their lives, anecdotally tell of their putative adventures in some foreign land, and go home again, apparently renewed in their belief that they have done for the past what the past once did for them: renew their commitment to something often called "international education." Not once have I heard a paper or attended a talk that changed in any fundamental way my perception of what the Fulbright experience has meant to me.

Frequently, however, I have come away from such conferences with the sinking feeling that the Fulbright experience—indeed, any overseas experience as student or teacher—has given birth to a body of people content to express themselves in the jargon of "international education." (Since education is unique, particular, highly individual, emerging from a single mind and its encounters with reality, I do not believe that education can ever be international. But this is not the place to argue that case.) People speak of "cross-cultural impact," of "interfacing," of "interdisciplinary studies." To the extent that I understand what such jargon means, I am certain one need not go abroad to learn. I experience a "cross-cultural impact" every time I stand on a street corner in some small town in Oklahoma, Idaho, or Southern California and see how that street corner, for all the ubiquitous presence of the fast-food chains, differs from the street corner near my home in Connecticut. I never interface with anyone, though at times I do talk to them, and learn from them, and they from me. I have yet to master one discipline, and though as a historian, of necessity I dabble and read in other disciplines, I do not fool myself into thinking that I am working at anything like the same level of competence in those others. And if I were, it would not be because I spent a year in New Zealand as a Fulbright student and some time later a year in Malaya as a Smith-Mundt professor. Thoreau was right: One can do all this kind of traveling in one's back yard.

Of course I did learn much overseas, not only as a Fulbrighter but in other capacities, that I could not have learned in the same way at home. Again, what one learns is often a tissue of clichés, no less true for that: On the whole the American people are very fortunate. No, they do not, contrary to their self-image, work harder than others. (No one works harder than a Chinese in Malaya.) But they do enjoy a standard of living, an access to reasonably good health and reasonably well-based education, not available to most of mankind. They are, as they believe themselves to be, a different people, though not at all for the reasons Americans so often cite. They are also an irritating people in their provincialism, in their strong tendency to read their own culture as normative and to expect other peoples to want to conform to the American standard. So what else is new? Cultural insularity is true of virtually every society I know, in all of the more than 100 countries in which I have lectured. Nor would I have it otherwise.

The fact that one cannot always count on hot water, find a "Big Mac" when one's children demand it, or even be completely safe in one's home, when living in other countries, leads some Fulbright scholars to talk about the "hardships" of their experiences. I once walked out on a paper at one of the Fulbright alumni conferences when a speaker had, for the fourth time, told his audience of the hardships he had put his wife and children through while doing research and a little teaching in an Asian country. I do not think he knew what a hardship was, and I am quite certain that his children did not, and that they had missed the opportunity to learn. Even having a wisdom tooth extracted by primitive methods in an Indonesian village is a learning experience, or so a scholar ought to find it, and if it is merely a hardship to be recalled with displeasure, perhaps the person who finds it so ought not only to forget about having been a Fulbright scholar, but should give up being, or thinking of himself, as a scholar of any kind. Being a scholar means taking oneself outside oneself; living with a scholar means the same; and this can be done at home as well as abroad, though perhaps it is easier to do when one knows that the University Health Clinic is just down the road. The watcher from the shadows—for such the historian, at least, is—ought not to complan because it is cold where he stands. He may, of course, choose to come out of the shadows and participate in the scene he observes, provided he does not fantacize that he is engaging in a cross-cultural experience. He is merely setting aside the objectivity and distance that, for a time, made him a scholar, and he is, just perhaps, becoming merely a human being without disciplinary designation. However, neither shadow nor sunlight has any relevance for the notion of hardship.

All this is rhetoric, of course, inspired simply by my somewhat puritanical observation that we have lost our understanding so well expressed by a quite remarkable dean of Yale College, William C. DeVane. He held that every task given us, every assignment, new committee, new lecture, new hardship (what! how can academic life even be thought of in such terms?) is a new opportunity. But enough griping about griping.

I was a Fulbright student to New Zealand in 1952. The program was still in its infancy, nothing like the bureaucracy it became in later years, but full of sunshine and promise. The application process was even then as slow and screwed up as it became, though perhaps more so, later on. I was an undergraduate at the University of Colorado, emerging from the first of several cycles of what I like to call "creative drift": coming to college to major in forestry, in order to go into the National Park Service, shifting to geology, then to journalism, finally to history with a minor in anthropology. Having lived in thirteen towns in my first twelve years of schooling, I assumed that moving on was what people naturally did, so it did not even occur to me to fear a new environment. Having introduced myself into so many schools over those years, I was also interested, without quite knowing it at the time, in how people perceived "the stranger," and in how those who were strangers thought about, and thus presumably learned about, new societies. A course, as a junior, in the history of the British Empire had interested me in the way race relations had developed between different White settler groups and native peoples, and having been nearly everywhere in the United States, and having read a good bit of other histories and literatures (Pablo Neruda was my poet for the junior year, and that summer was devoted to reading the unabridged Toynbee, something I would never find the time to do again as a "professional" historian) I knew that the United States was not one country but several. I also felt that all the Turnerian stuff I was being taught about the American frontier and its uniqueness was certainly untested and therefore quite possibly wrong, if not in substance then in nuance. So when the coordinator (advertiser was the better word at the time) for Fulbright applicants, a professor of classics I hardly knew, spoke to me in the hall one day and suggested that I apply for a Fulbright, and told me of some of the places where one might study, I thought "Why not?" I applied to New Zealand, with a project on the Hau Hau, a Maori movement by which the native peoples of New Zealand (or at least some of them) sought, rather like the Ghost Dance of Wavoka and the Sioux, to drive the White settlers back into the sea. This combined my interests nicely: a frontier experience, a potential for comparison of White settler/native interaction in different settler societies, the chance to learn an exotic language, the probability that most research would be in the language I knew best, and not incidentally, the likelihood of traveling around the world, for it seemed to me that if I could get to New Zealand, I could probably go the rest of the way at the end of the year.

And then I heard nothing for months. Despite several changes of major, I had also gone to summer school every year, for in those days the best courses at the University of Colorado were summer courses, and I graduated at mid-year. Having heard nothing more, I went into a combined history-law degree program in January 1952, and then, in the last week of February, received word that I had been awarded a Fulbright Scholarship to New Zealand and should be ready to leave within a week. I did not know enough at the time to ascribe the long period of silence to bureaucracy, or something mysterious (now called the "application procedures"), and in any case, I was used to fairly fundamental changes in location on little more than a week's notice. So I told my parents I was off to New Zealand, bought a raincoat, and took my first airplane trip: from Denver to Salt Lake City, to San Francisco—where an informative and friendly New Zealand consul general loaded me up with a good bit of practical information—and then to Honolulu, Canton Island (and the last sight of the American flag for several months), and the Fiji Islands, and finally Auckland, where power outages meant that I had to grope my way in pitch-dark streets, illuminated infrequently by the headlamps of passing motor cars, to a hotel that, because it was after 9:00 p.m., was already locked up. The next day Eric Budge, director of the Fulbright Program, met me, and we went together by train, snaking down across the North Island to Wellington, where I was to enroll at Victoria University College, a unit of what was in process of becoming the University of New Zealand.

Eric Budge was the center of the Fulbright Program, as over the years I came to learn was true of his colleagues in other programs in dozens of other nations. I have often thought that the directors of these programs, chairing difficult binational commissions, sometimes suffering in silence when some politically appointed ambassadors, who knew almost nothing about education, much less education in the country to which they had been posted, mucked about, arguing about the legitimacy of projects they could hardly understand—that these long-suffering directors deserved far more recognition than they were receiving. Budge met me in Auckland, I think, because he had got wind of the fact that someone was arriving who had never been in an airplane, or outside the United States, and that the someone might need succor when he staggered off from his trans-Pacific crossing, courtesy of British Commonwealth Pacific Airways. So he eliminated the last leg of the journey and comforted me with a train. He could not have been expected to know that I had never been in a train before either.

And so, there was Wellington, in its natural setting surely one of the most striking cities in the world. There were the New Zealanders, about as provincial as I was, and therefore as comfortable as the proverbial old shoe. There was Weir House, cold, powerfully dark at night, where I had to stand on a table top in my room to reach an overhead light socket in order to plug in my electric razor, shaving each morning by feel. There was the history and anthropology faculty of Victoria, brisk, even brusque in the English academic manner, full of wisdom I wanted. There was a country of incredible beauty, a people—the Maori—of unending fascination, and a task that, though constantly redefined, never failed to attack me, into the field and back to the desk. I studied with Mary Boyd, who knew everything there was to know, it seemed to me, about the Pacific islands and the interaction between their indigenous peoples and the encroaching Europeans. There was Peter Muntz, who taught European history and the philosophy of history, and wrote poetry. There was J.C. Beaglehole, the grand biographer (though not yet) of Captain Cook. And Harold Miller, the librarian, also a historian, who had written the only short history of New Zealand I could find to read before I left Colorado. And Winston Monk, whose little book *British in the Western Mediterranean* intrigued me, but whose course in American history intrigued me even more.

In formal educational terms, the most useful experience I had in New Zealand that year was Winston Monk's course. I sat in on it out of curiosity and soon discovered that Monk had only been to the United States once, during the war, and then only to Norfolk, Virginia, with a hurried leave to New York (or was it Washington?). I knew precisely where Billings and Anniston, Providence and Spokane were, and he did not, so I was a little scornful at first, in the way of callow youth. But slowly I began to realize that I was learning American history as I had never learned it before. Until then the books of Ralph Henry Gabriel and Henry Steele Commager, and the courses of Colin Goodykoontz and Robert Athearn at the University of Colorado, had meant the most to me, as I had tried to decide what being an American meant in historical terms, but now Monk's course joined that list. He came to the American experience from so different a perspective, one I thought wrong then and still think wrong in important particulars as I look back on it, but nonetheless he came to America without the conventional wisdom, the assumption that America represented the good, the future, the triumphant, in all that it did. He made me a bit cross at first, and then he made me think, so as to refute him, and finally he gave me a sense of unending excitement with how we may learn about America by studying other cultures. I learned then that he who knew only his own country knew not his country, and that whatever label my scholarship might bear at some future time—the history of the British Empire, the comparative history of race relations, ethnic history, imperial history—it would, in some way, be about the notion of American exceptionalism, about how other societies perceived the United States, about the exercise of American power. I would, I thought, go into American diplomatic history and just possibly enter the American diplomatic service.

Informally, all of New Zealand was a campus. I and three other Fulbright scholars drove all over the North Island, to Lake Taupo, and Rotorua, and far up to North Cape, and down to the Bay of Islands. I hitchhiked all over the South Island, to its tip at Bluff, through mountains, often in snow as winter came on, sleeping on the floor of police stations and newspaper offices, or in the washrooms of campgrounds, waking each morning to the coldest, brightest, greenest of worlds in the North, to the coldest, brightest, often whitest of worlds in the South, sleeping bag and Allen Curnow's collection of New Zealand poetry on my back, Maori grammar under my belt. Ever after I would have a deep sympathy, even respect, for my Yale students who had the good sense to take a year off and, perhaps even as a much-maligned hippie, chose to go wherever what they could carry on their backs would take them. I saw far more of New Zealand than any New Zealander I met.

Most important, I met a woman and married her. (Such a sentence reeks of ego. So too did Avril Flockton "meet and marry," and hers was the courageous act, leaving her country at the end of the year to be taken off to a vast continent three flying days away.) We met at an Easter outing of university and arts students to the Marlborough Sounds, slightly less than a month after I had arrived. Here was this pixy, so bright, bouncing about, telling people what to do. On the second day of the outing, a group of students, professing sympathy for my expressed desire for a green salad, a fruit salad, for something, anything, that went beyond meat and potatoes, placed before me a handsome platter filled with sliced fruit and greens.

When, as I put my fork into it, it walked off my plate, a live starfish its base, she whooped with the others. I proposed on the third day, and she took two unconscionable days to think about it, and then said yes. We were married five months later, and I hammered out a good part of my thesis at a so-called honeymoon cottage up at Raumati, above Wellington. One of my fellow Fulbrighters, Charlie Reich, a geologist, was best man at the wedding; he is the only member of that Fulbright class with whom we have remained in touch.

The riches of the Alexander Turnbull Library, some good fortune while traveling on the East Cape, the intervention of an open-minded member of the Department of Maori Affairs, the steady flow of that Fulbright stipend—£432 for the academic year—and the lucky fact that, as a high-school student I had excelled at typing (and was probably the only person from my school to have been offered a typing scholarship, which went unaccepted, to the local state college) meant that the research project proceeded apace. The Hau Haus led me to the Ringatus, a syncretic Maori response to the multiple impacts of conflicting Christian mission groups, and curiosity led me to the *poutikanga*, roughly president, of the Ringatu Church, where a day spent helping him, afloat in a tiny boat, drag squid out from underneath rocks, suppressing my squeamishness (more about the depth of the water, since I could not swim, than about the tentacles of the squid, though I had no affection for them either), led him to dig out from under his bed the records of his church. There was my thesis, and it was hammered out across the months. In much expanded, altered form, the manuscript on the Hau Haus with a section on the doctrinal ties between Hau Hauism and Ringatuism added, would, eight months after returning to Colorado, become a second Master's thesis, and a published article from it was, I suspect, instrumental in winning me a fellowship to work on my doctorate at The Johns Hopkins University.

What had the Fulbright Scholarship to New Zealand in 1952 meant, then? A degree. A book, for I was overwhelmed with the desire to try my hand at travel writing, and in the three months left to us before we flew to San Francisco, and with the help of my wife, I battered away at a book of travel essays which, to my amazement, Whitcombe and Tombs, New Zealand's largest publisher, not only accepted, but advanced me money against, so that Avril and I had a second honeymoon, uninterrupted by writing, in the Fiji Islands. It had also meant an awareness that I wanted to study the United States by studying other nations; a certainty that I could write; and a conviction that one could only learn to write by writing—cliché piled upon cliché!—and that the scholar's greatest skill was applying the seat of the pants to a chair for hours at a time, undeluded by notions that good health required eight hours' sleep, or that two hours without a cigarette, a walk about the room, a talk with one's friends, was a hardship. It had meant an interest in what one might call the sociology of knowledge; an intention to enter the diplomatic service; reasonable knowledge of Maori and enormous respect for the Maori people, untainted by the romanticism of any notions about noble savages; some friendships that have never faded; some articles. More than anything else, someone so quick, so bubbling, so interested in everything and everyone, that I was taken outside myself in a way the classroom could never do: a wife.

Being a Fulbright student in New Zealand was, in the true sense of the word, a wonderful experience: full of wonder. That wonder broadened to the world: there was no place I did not want to go, and as Avril shared (or nearly shared—prescient, she looked at the map of America and said that Bridgeport was not high on her list of places we need visit soon) that willingness, we went everywhere, anywhere. Travel became an addiction. Then on to graduate school and a doctorate in diplomatic history, with the comparative element firmly set in place—I wrote on Canadian-American diplomatic relations, which automatically meant Anglo-American diplomatic relations, during the Civil War, and wrote rather more about Canada than diplomatic historians who feel it is American policy they are essentially explaining, would do—and an intended career abroad. But those were the days of Senator McCarthy and an intimidated Department of State, and Avril was not an American citizen, and who could tell, even in pre–David Lange days, New Zealand might drop an atomic bomb on our West Coast, and so I took a job at Connecticut College for Women (as it then was). A year later the history department at Yale decided to run the grave risk of hiring its first ever non–Ivy League Ph.D., and with commendable daring called Johns Hopkins and asked that they deliver, COD, one newly-minted Ph.D. I had been awarded a distinction, happily quite rare in those days before grade inflation, and so Hopkins informed me that I was mistaken in my notion that I had just accepted a job with the U.S. Naval Academy (unlimited free travel on naval planes if for legitimate research purposes!). I was on the Yale faculty. And somehow Avril and I liked it, especially since one grows best in the company of people who are smarter than oneself, and so we stayed.

Though not entirely. There was a grant for research in England. There were summer school teaching stints in Alberta, British Columbia, Washington. There were one-term visiting slots at the American University in Beirut, Sierra Leone, and South Africa. There was a long tour of universities in India, an equally long tour in the Pacific Islands, another in East Africa. There was a visiting professorship to the University of Sydney for a year. There was a year on leave as a Fellow of the Institute for Commonwealth Studies at the University of London. There were two challenging, extremely educational, wonderful years as cultural attaché to the American Embassy in London—Avril having become an American citizen in 1969—and there I learned about the Fulbright program from inside, sat opposite Margaret Thatcher negotiating the new Fulbright agreement, and traveled all over Eastern Europe (and later to Iran) on behalf of the program, paying a spiritual debt. But none of this was as a Fulbright scholar, though it all was no doubt reinforced by the experience in New Zealand.

The only other "Fulbright experience" (more properly, a Smith-Mundt experience) was as a visiting professor of American history (and the boot-legging, in an added teaching load, of an inaugural course on colonialism) at the University of Malaya. Here, as before, chance played a role. John Bastin, a very young, wildly able Australian who held the chair of history at the University of Malaya visited Yale, and I happened to fall into con-versation with him, as we walked. He wanted someone to come out to teach American history, but feared there would not be enough takers in a university that was yet to graduate its first class, so he wanted someone who would teach a more "mainline" subject (as viewed from Malaya) as well, though the added course would be without compensation. I told him, within the next twenty yards, that I could do it, but how? He suggested I apply for a Fulbright, and that all might come out right in the end. This time the wheels turned as oiled, quickly, with enthusiasm, and shortly Avril and I were on our way to Asia, our daughter, then twelve months old, strapped to my back. We were settled, after three weeks in a pleasant hotel, into housing in Petaling Jaya, near the university, and I moved in happily with a group of scholars, colleagues, soon friends, from whom I learned constantly. John Bastin and I did a large book on Malaysia together for Oxford University Press. I finished another. I taught furiously, to interested, interesting students, we traveled all over Southeast Asia, I took an intensive course in Malay (to small effect), we ate everything that came our way.

What of this second "Fulbright experience"? It reinforced much that I had believed about studying America from abroad, while giving me my first real handle on the colonial experience as seen by non-White societies. I learned a great deal about ethnic conflict, came to respect and/or admire the Chinese, Indian, and Malay cultures of the peninsula. Another cliché emerged with even greater strength: that students learn from the Fulbright professor only in equal measure to the extent that the professor intends to learn from them. More clichés about two-way streets, and giving as much as one gets, and hanging loose, being relaxed, seeing oneself as an ambas-sador for one's country (a bit pompous, that one, if one thinks through its implications), all were further legitimized.

Sometimes I think that *we*—I stress *we*, for this was an experience shared by three, with equal pleasure—learned most from eating. It is true that we are what we eat. Lévi-Strauss and others mean more than calories, of course, or even culture. Reactions to food tell us a good bit about ourselves. I have sat next to ambassadors who picked at the local delicacies put before them, perhaps fearing they were unclean, filled with great dollops of bubonic plague and human spittle. If it is a sheep's eye, or a fried worm, and if the local culture is eating it, I figure you eat it too. If you worry much about whether the water is safe to drink, you will only get fat on beer. Our infant daughter, carried by her amah to the front gate, would greet the Chinese food vendor as he arrived in his cart, and would gobble down strange, murky, and mysterious substances. I like to think that her tolerance now for other cultures, languages, came from all those visits to the food peddler at the foot of the drive, when she ate God knows what at the hands of an amah who knew no English and could never tell us what goody had been served up that day. (Of course, one can take a good thing too far. Though I ate it, I recall with genuine disgust the dish of orange-colored lard I was served in northern Nigeria, and daughter Honor will remark from time to time that something is nearly as awful as the frogs' backs she once struggled with in Spain. Avril thinks sopapaillas are too greasy. Otherwise, the sky's the limit.) My eating *and* drinking, that is, for a serious fascination with wine and the alcoholic inspirations of any number of societies, has grown over the years into a near-professional hobby.

I also learned, in that second Fulbright experience, about how heavy-handed our diplomatic representatives abroad could be. One day, about a month into my teaching, I received a call from an officer at the American Embassy to the effect that he wanted to see the syllabi for my courses, preferably outlines of the lectures, preferably even more, full texts of the lectures. Why? After some hemming-and-hawing, he said he had heard I was teaching about Marx. Not teaching Marx, but about Marx. I explained that a course on colonialism that did not mention Marx might be thought to be rather odd. He told me, quite brusquely, that I was not in Malaya on the taxpayers' money to teach about Marx. I told him to go to hell, and since a few years later he was posted to Saigon, I believe he probably did.

Then the ambassador called. Could the Winkses come to lunch? Of course. At lunch he casually asked how my courses were going. Well, I said. He understood I had had a little contretemps with one of his people. That was so, I said. The ambassador graciously apologized, and then said it would be of interest to him to know how the students were reacting to the material, especially to American history. I told him I would be happy to tell him about how Malayans reacted to American material, and later I did. He probably got what he wanted, and with tact, and I knew I was, in a sense, providing what a paranoid generation in the late 1960s would think was intelligence information, but I also thought that letting our representatives abroad know how foreign students felt about America was perfectly legitimate. There is a line between spying on one's students and learning from them and trying to help one's own country relate to them in mutually comprehensible ways, and most of the diplomats I have met know where that line falls. A good bit later, during the years with the embassy in London, I came to have enormous respect, and often affection, for our diplomats abroad. Most of them understand their country pretty well, and academics could learn a good bit from them, if they would. The experience in Malaya was not typical, though it happens often enough to be disturbing.

There have been no further "Fulbright experiences" in the formal sense of the word, though every new experience abroad is simply another branch of that tree. There has been no Fulbright year since our son was born, but he shared the years in London, the time in South Africa, and the summers in British Columbia and Washington, and I think his interest in any number of things comes at least in some measure from those times among other cultures. Still, I wish he too had the pleasure of a Fulbright year, for he seems a little finicky about his food—he turned down some fried snake the other day—and I hope the program, which has educated America, perhaps not enough but a good bit, will still be thriving when he graduates from college.

That is the real meaning of the Fulbright experience. It is not some American cultural colonialism, the spread of American ideas abroad. Most cultures are resilient enough to absorb what they wish from their visiting American academics, and then to continue being the cultures of integrity that they were. Rather, the experience, in a collective sense, has done something to educate America. Each returned Fulbrighter has brought back a little from abroad. Even those who complain, who speak of hardships, who give slide shows to friends and students and poke fun at the scenes they show—they too, if listened to carefully enough, can educate us about ourselves. We need to learn, and the Fulbright program has been a rare learning experience for America.

We and our educators need to learn that education cannot be quantified. When I was with the embassy I engaged in an annual exercise, the "proof of effectiveness," which was seriously self-contradictory. Every now and then educators, legislators, and diplomats want some proof that educational exchange programs are effective. One suspects that this collection of essays is meant to serve the same end. Truth is, as most educators know, one cannot prove the effectiveness of education, of cultural programs, or of Mozart in soothing the savage breast: One must take most matters in education on trust, or even faith. Proof of effectiveness relates to body bags. To target analyses for bomber command. To stars on performance boards in automobile showrooms. It does not relate to education or to the Fulbright experience. We either believe the Burkean idea that education pays because it leads to a stake in society, or we do not, for we certainly cannot prove it. We either believe that an educated electorate will elect able representatives or we do not. We either believe that exposure to Dante, Thomas Mann, and the sounds of a tonal language being spoken will inform and broaden, or we do not. And since we do, we ought not to devote much effort to arguing the obvious. The reply that the effectiveness of educational exchange is not so obvious to our congressmen is best met by the simple injunction to elect congressmen who understand the value. We either learn to live with ambiguity or not, and if not, by my definitions, we have learned very little about education, whether we stayed at home or taught abroad.

When first invited to contribute an essay to this celebratory volume, I waffled about, thinking that whatever I wrote would contribute nothing to the covert argument about the effectiveness of educational exchange programs, and exceedingly little to an understanding of the Fulbright experience. To me that experience was as palpable as Archibald MacLeish's "globed fruit," but like his idea of a poem, I thought it ought not to mean, but be. I suspected that whatever I could write about so important an experience was bound to be a tissue of clichés. And then I found myself seated next to an American businessman, a retired automobile executive, on a bus tour in Budapest, and I wondered about his obviously profound unhappiness with being there. After a gray day in a gray city, he leaned over to me and confided, "Can't stand this place. All full of Communists." And I thought, well, why not write my tissue of clichés anyway? As I read back over what I have written about my Fulbright experiences I see my early reluctance was right. A tissue of clichés it is. But no less true for that.

PART II
LEARNING ABOUT OTHER CULTURES

Introduction

The very essence of being a Fulbrighter is changing cultural contexts. The importance and persuasiveness of culture becomes obvious when confronted with an unintelligible sign or a different meaning for a common term. For every Fulbrighter, it means dealing constantly with new subtleties. For others, going to Third World countries, the differences are far from subtle. They create puzzles and not all of these puzzles are solved, only endured.

Not all experiences by Fulbrighters are positive, as James Becker recounts in his "Inquiry into an Incident on the Via Porta di Castro." But even unpleasant incidents teach us lessons about the world. So does embracing completely that which is strange and different. Alfred de Zayas describes his role as a German "student" in joining a fencing fraternity.

The experiences of Marshall Fishwick as the first Fulbrighter to go to Bangladesh was unique, but in many ways, his reflections would be shared by many others. Most Americans express contradictory attitudes toward tradition. They are impressed by the stability, and perhaps the severity, of tradition. After all, America is young and our traditions are likely to be repetitious of last year's activities. While the depth of tradition impresses, it is also obvious that it is restrictive and in many ways, cruel.

For many Fulbrighters—Chad Walsh as an example—the experience is profound, leading not just to appreciation of their Fulbright country but an awareness of the darker side in every society. That appreciation and awareness of his host country, Finland, left him a "changed and different man."

That potentiality for change which a Fulbright offers is reflected in other ways. David Paletz suggests that his experience in Denmark forced him to think about American society, about the media, and about its influence on American political life. For others, such as Peter Rose, a Fulbright in England was the start of a long international career which has included comparative work on racial and ethnic relations as well as research for the Board of Foreign Scholars on the Fulbright Program in East Asia and the Pacific.

3

Inquiry into an Incident on The Via Porta di Castro

James F. Becker

Even when the person is unscathed, there attaches an element of assault to the theft of personal property. Probably for this reason, too, the impact of the event receded in waves that now and again flowed back with surprising force. So it happened that some days after our fated stroll on the Via Porta di Castro in Palermo, the tide came sweeping through the cold upper hall of the museum in Syracuse.

The unexpected upsurge was provoked by a masterfully executed terra cotta, "Bandits and Their Hostages," from the nineteenth-century workshop of Bongiovanni Vaccaro.[1] The tableau is of two bound captives surrounded by armed and hard-eyed bandits. An old man, hands bound to the branches of a tree, and at his feet a young boy, both fully aware of the hopelessness of their condition. And there, shaking once again the flattened strand of the viewer's psyche, seated in the foreground, is the leader of the band. A rifle across her knees, she is a powerful if portly matron in the garb of a country squiress. The devitalized captives' contrast with the fierce competence of their captors, combining with the unexpected feminine figure with her camouflage of gentility, raise the scene to a level of pathos far above the sentimentalism to which contemporary ceramics so often cater.

The first recession of shock from the afternoon's banditry had come while we were standing in the courtyard of a precinct police station adjacent to the Via. The three victims of the assault stood chatting with a friendly policeman who, whether conscious of his role or not, was helping to usher us back from the nether world into the tolerable world from which we had been so rudely ejected.

"We have two serious problems in our beautiful city," he confided, "thieves like these"—and he nodded in the direction of a nearby woman and child, the woman talking animatedly to another policeman—". . .

thieves like these," he continued, "and the Mafia." The gentle coaxing of the kindly officer to consider once again the larger predicament aroused, for all its good intent, a somewhat perverse inclination to question the assertion. Are these really two separate problems? Are they somewhat bound together? And bound to all of us, perhaps?

We were beginning, too, to appreciate that the operation to which we had been subject had been classical in its conception and execution. The organizer and director of the action was a blond matron, hair badly in need of redyeing. Her reconnaissance post was an iron balcony some thirty feet above the street. Watching the local folk below her, she must have viewed with satisfaction their clearing the street, moving surreptitiously into doorways on her command, while the three walkers strolled unsuspectingly toward the site. The tourists were preoccupied, as others had been before them, with the extraordinary sights and sounds of this ghetto of poverty, struggling to put the scene of decayed handicrafts and petty trade into relations far removed from those of the narrow thoroughfare. As they approached the spot below the balcony, the final phase of the operation began. A hundred yards up the Via, the boys on the motorcycle began to drift down the narrow street, their idling motor almost silent.

The captain's lieutenant, a younger, black-haired woman in a leather jacket, leaned against the wall of a house just beyond the critical point. Orders had been issued and posts assumed since the time, a quarter of an hour before, when the trio had first entered the street, their approach heralded by yet another woman on a bicycle who, overtaking them, preceded them as they entered the slum. Of the three now approaching, it was the woman with the handbag slung over her shoulder who had been designated the target.

Vaguely aware of a vehicle approaching from the rear, the tourists fell into single file, the woman with the handbag in the middle between the two men. The cycle swerved next to her, the boy on the rear seat snatched the handbag, and, as the engine roared, the startled and uncomprehending trio watched the handbag, held aloft by its new possessor, round a corner and vanish.

So it was done, and in the stillness of the aftermath, there was a refusal to accept what had happened. There came a surge of anger, a few paces in pursuit, quickly abandoned for its evident futility. The refusal to accept the situation clashed with opposing, more realistic impulses. We stared at each other and at the fragment of shoulder strap clutched in the victim's hand. She might have been killed, most certainly injured, had that strap not broken. (More than once, subsequently, we were reminded of our good fortune. When straps failed to break, their luckless owners were sometimes dragged to a serious injury along the cobbles. "Only a few weeks before . . . ," the policeman recounted a sad affair.)

We sought to reassure each other, beginning to feel our own responsibility for what had happened, the ancient feeling of the need to conform with the edict of the gods. While occupied with an assessment of damages, psychological and otherwise, the lady in the jacket came up to us and addressed us sympathetically.

How serious was our loss? "Everything," was the reply.

Had we not been warned? Yes, we had been, and more than once. Conscience prodded the supine mind. The questions carried with them a demoralizing imputation of guilt that was not lost on these listeners. Why had we ignored the warnings? The pall descended with the query. How (I thought later) did the old man feel, his arms tied to the branches of the tree? Did he look forward to his demise in free atonement for failing so miserably his helpless grandson?

Suddenly, a motorcycle patrolman appeared at the corner nearby. He sat confidently, surveying the scene. Hope sprang up, but soon fell back. It was not easy to detain him even for a few moments of explanation from a more pressing appointment. Uninterested in details, he advised us to report to the police, indicating its location with a nod of the head. He, too, vanished down the same side street that had swallowed so quickly all traces of our burglars.

While we were so fruitlessly employed, the solicitous brunette was exchanging words in some unknown dialect with the blond on the balcony. She turned back to us, advising us to wait with her a few minutes longer and for a reason that we could not at first understand. Did we want our documents? she was asking. "Yes, of course," we replied. Very good, then, we must retrace our steps up the Via; our documents might be returned.

Taking this advice, we wandered distractedly in the direction indicated, coming shortly upon a group of curious women and children—or had they come upon us? It was by no means clear. A street vendor at the corner held out an apple. "Take it, it's free. No need to pay," he insisted. The crowd was growing somewhat larger and then, heralding his coming, its ranks parted to make way for a tousle-headed and grimy youngster of unmistakably Dickensian stock. He held out to us a greasy paper bag. The documents were returning to their owner. Inside the bag was a passport and a few worthless papers, part of the contents of the missing handbag.

Accepting almost gratefully this surprising offering, we turned back down the Via proceeding in the direction of the police precinct. At last, a cross street climbed heroically, carrying us out of the dank shade that in November marks the climate of the ghetto. Emerging, we found ourselves on the edge of a beautiful park, glowing in the afternoon sunshine. It was bordered by a row of handsome buildings, one of which turned out to be the police precinct. The brief walk in the sun had the effect of reviving our curiosity in regard to the real integuments of life in that neighborhood from which, we supposed, we were departing forever. We would, however, return once more, to gather data that would be useful for unraveling its mysteries. We knew only that hidden there were realities that our confused minds were as yet unable to plumb.

At the door of the station we discovered our now cycleless patrolman, the stiff edges of his pressed uniform standing out, like his dark glasses, signs of his life mission. Talking with a plainclothesman, he seemed not to see us as we passed. A clerk appeared to usher us into the courtyard, and from thence into an adjoining room, a large office where two obsolete typewriters were sporadically clacking. We sat before one of them operated by a sergeant in full dress. He prepared a large sheaf of papers interlarded with carbons, inserted them in his machine, and, with a series of questions, began pecking at the entrails of our story.

All this proceeded in an ambience of developing theatricality in which we were finding ourselves, as it were, downstage center. Along with the tapping background to our own rather abbreviated account, came a tendering of fragments of discourse on the virtues of public safety, including an itemizing of precautions that would have contributed so much to that good cause. Despite the kindliness of all this, there was developing a sensation of entrapment between attackers in the Via and rescuers in the police.

It was a feeling of compression, qualitatively very similar to my reaction some days later when I happened upon a pathetic account, in a well-known guide to Sicily, of a find in the vaporous caves of Sciaca:

> Two deep underground galleries were explored by a team of speleologists and archaeologists who, equipped with breather apparatus to overcome the fumes, managed to get down to a depth of nearly 200 feet, though this was still not the bottom. Down here they came upon a number of huge four-handled jars of copper age date (III millenium) and one group of three pots of particular interest, for one contained decomposed organic material (perhaps grain?) and was accompanied by a carefully selected collection of little bones, all exactly similar and thought to be the arm bones of very young children. Without doubt these were sacrifices made by anxious prehistoric people in an attempt to placate the terrifying gods of the underworld.[2]

Reflecting on this and on the events of a few days before, one could not help but wonder whether we "moderns" do not flatter ourselves in supposing that we are so far above and beyond the primitives, especially in certain human fundamentals. So much that transpired in Palermo that day had the feel about it of times long, long past; but precisely what it was that conveyed this troubling sensation would continue to elude detection for a considerable time to come. Even then, however, the feeling seemed somehow related to the deep well of fears that everywhere in today's society we cover over in layers of ritual procedures that sometimes do, and sometimes do not, help to preserve a general peace of mind.

At the police precinct, desultory typing put together our little charge, a record with the minimum of information compatible with the conventions. In the official distillation of the incident much energy had been expended in the production of residuals, and as a result, events took on a new guise. At last there emerged a single page with uniform borders, all in the "discreet Italian" of the normal bureau. Had the robbery been so frugal in conception and execution, that little purse must have remained in its owner's possession!

Nevertheless, the size of our loss and perhaps our ability to understand what we were being asked, helped to elicit a measure of sympathy from these officers. Maybe this is why the question arose, finally, would we like once more to visit the scene of the crime; we might see a familiar face, someone who could provide information that would be useful to the inquiry? Consulting briefly among ourselves, we agreed, although we soon discovered that there was room for only two of us in the back seat of the blue and white Alpha Sud. So only two of us set off in the company of two officers. We came shortly to the Via, descending it again almost to the original point of impact.

The overly sympathetic vendor had taken his apples and vanished. The Via was almost empty, but while crossing the intersection we glimpsed down a side street and saw, playing ball with his friends, the disheveled bearer of discarded documents, as recorded in the charge. Pointing him out to our escorts, they responded by leaping from the car and apprehending the culprit. Even as they did so, we realized that they supposed us to be fingering the thief. It was too late to stop them.

Hardly had they taken the lad in tow, that our entire convoy, the police car included, was surrounded by swelling numbers of neighborhood women who, seeing the plight of one of their own offspring, quickly found ways of expressing their disapproval. While they closed in on us steadily and with increasing menace, bits of vegetables and refuse began to drift down from above on the police and on their vehicle. The fortress of the Porta was better manned than anyone had supposed and, at the last moment, before he could be hemmed in completely, our driver plunged through the crowd, scrambling for the radio in the front seat. "We are only two here!" he hastily reminded the office as he asked for reinforcements.

Seizing the opportunity, we tried again to explain to him the exact role played by the blond delinquent. Understanding us at last, he entered the crowd to rejoin his companion. As he did so, we saw that the blond matron had descended from her balcony to lead the rising litany of protest. Whenever she spoke, faces contorted in fury, fists were shaken at us, and spittle began to sully our little Alpha, now tightly surrounded.

Armed with an improved comprehension of the role of the boy in his custody, the officer's explanations to the crowd had a momentarily calming, if not entirely abating, effect. It became again very shortly a contest, however. Under the priestess's leadership the litany ascended, swelling once again, and with it trash fell in greater volume than before. Suddenly, lights flashing, a second police car came dashing up the Via. Our reinforcements had arrived. The crowd quieted and turned to watch. It was a quiet born more of calculation than of either fear or anger.

From the blue and white auto stepped a slender, white shirted, and immaculately groomed official, dark glasses matching an olive skin over taut cheeks, cigarette dangling marvelously from the mouth, held so steadily between thin lips that its long ash remained intact as, with measured stride, he approached the center of the scene. The crowd parted to permit his entry.

The chanting ceased and all listened intently while information was exchanged among the principals clustered around this rather noncherubic lad in custody. The matron joined in to tell once again the tale of the boy's extraordinary discovery of the documents, hidden in a paper bag, lying on the street where this youngster had happened upon them. The contrapuntal conversation among the protagonists, the chorus responding, continued for some time, but it became evident that a diminuendo in tensions had occurred. In the end, leaving the boy behind, the police returned to their vehicles, the imperturbable "Bogart" embarking first, his driver backing down the Via at a furious pace. We followed shortly in our now decidedly less than virginal Alpha and also at a speed sufficient to prevent us from locating the sacred spot where we had parted so effortlessly with the neighborhood's latest windfall. Arriving soon at the police precinct, we rejoined our partner anxiously awaiting us at the station door.

Looking back toward the ghetto, already in deep shadow under the slanting sun, we could see, walking up the rise out of the dark mouth of the tunnel, escorted by a police officer, our shiny-headed youth. Holding him tightly by the hand was the lady of the balcony of the Via Porta di Castro.

The dénouement took place in the atrium of the station, in the cool and dimly lit green of the courtyard and its garden, roofed over with glass. Small disjointed groups stood talking, to be joined now and then by officers emerging from one or another of the offices surrounding the courtyard. There were benches at the perimeter of the garden, and on one of them sat the prodigy and with him, now and again, the self-declared guardian of "this motherless child." The three outsiders stood with the friendly officer, discussing sporadically the day's episodes, while at the center of another slightly less amicable group stood the matron, repeating to a series of official inquisitors the story of the lad's miraculous find and his equally auspicious impulse to honesty. Her embellishments varied imaginatively, but the central theme of her account held steady, confirmed always by her charge when she prodded him sufficiently.

The financial loss on which our concerns had first come to focus were dissipating in favor of a broader malaise that seemed to have a life of its own. Increasingly, the conviction of isolation and removal came upon us, transactions in process involving us as incidental objects. For the most part unconsciously, we were being used to reaffirm bonds that, perhaps at times precariously, held together a community of disparate and even desperate parts. Reflecting on these proceedings later on, the conviction hardened that the terms of settlement between the separate interests had been established long since, and on this occasion, the nature of the crime permitting, it was a matter of locating and confirming the particular terms applicable to the case. In the nature of the proceedings, then, it was only a matter of time before our contribution should become redundant. In bringing the charge to its close, the typist had noted, "No more to be added." Anything we might add could only be superflous, if not an impediment to, the preferred resolution.

So we stood to one side in the courtyard while, one after another, a series of questioners fenced with the fiery matron who, as nearly as we could determine, was deftly juggling the facts of recent history in accordance with a very perceptive assessment of the vulnerabilities confronting her. She was succeeding in conveying consistently the impression of a tale all-of-a-piece, and she led her interrogators each in turn into ever-tightening spirals of recessive reasoning out of which they successively plummeted to earth. Yet the performance cost her an enormous effort, and the strain became visible in her frequent demanding of the boy's confirmation of her assertion that he had "found it in the street." In a lull in her dexterous apologies she left the youngster seated on the bench. Approaching us, her face became as contorted as the masks in her chorus. She hissed at us, sotto voce: "The next time, no documents!"

While this penultimate confrontation was developing, a young teenager entered the courtyard from the outside. Dressed in satiny athletic clothes and running shoes—a jogger from the square in the early morning?—he averted his face as he bounced to the stone bench. Sitting next to the boy, he put a supporting arm around his shoulders and whispered to him at some length. Then, as inconspicuously as he had appeared, he vanished. It was only some hours afterward when, reviewing the day's films, one could place him in a different attire and occupation. He was sitting on the rear of a motorcycle, a winner holding aloft a trophy as from a high-school match, a plastic shoulderbag whose contents were our prospective financing of a tour of Sicily.

The afternoon was waning and with it much of our fury and all of our hope. The chubby and friendly policeman sought to dispel our depression and, although we talked seriously of thieves and the Mafia, it was all very much in the abstract. We came to see what we had known previously—that the streets were the schools and playgrounds on which the recruits to the fraternity were raised up or cast down. It became unmistakably clear that the social ladder is indeed a very narrow one up which many seek to climb. And those who progress step firmly on the hands of those below them. The ladder touching down on the back streets of Palermo and in the other Southern cities is made of the same stuff as in other famous cities of the East and West. At the top it debauches in Rome, New York, Buenos Aires, Hong Kong. There the "fit" emerge whose physical and spiritual qualities prove useful in so many contexts.

By the end of the afternoon the matron had won another day. Our hands were "tied to the tree" though we were safe enough. The inquisition wound down, and by common if unspoken consent we prepared to disperse to our different destinations. Realizing she had won, and with a magnanimity common among sportsmen, she came up to her victims for the last time. In an impenetrable ambience of ambiguity, she held out her hand. The ceremony had come suddenly to its climax, and an instant approval livened the countenance of our officer-therapist.

I stared at the hand in disbelief. Looking into those cold blue eyes, it was impossible to plumb the meaning of the gesture, just as it was impossible to believe that she was oblivious of the price she was exacting by her eccentric dedication to survival. The "motherless" little boy had no choice but to succumb to the relentless pressures making for a reflexively vicious life. The law and the outlaw were intimately bound in a whole from which the individual could escape only at the risk of a separate destruction. They were held inextricably by the conventions of centuries, even of milennia. The experiences of the day had heightened our awareness of the profundity of the instincts that had culminated in the relations we were witnessing. But nothing had given the clue to how one had to respond to the hand so unexpectedly offered.

I found that I could not raise up my arm. At the time, I did not understand why it could not be done. There came then a strangely awkward and tense silence, broken at last by an apologetic comment from the friendly policeman. "In his country," he informed the matron, "they have a different custom." Even then, this was frustrating and infuriating and I knew not why. It seemed as though what he had said was true. Its falsity was far from obvious.

Long after all of us had gone our separate ways, the day's events on the Via began to come all of a piece with those of the outside world from which, on that day, they had seemed so very far removed. In "his" country, as in many another, fumes of sulphur spew now and again from the crevices in social relations. What causes the schisms that frighten us we are everywhere discouraged from inquiring into too closely, and, as a result, the real bases of our fears continue to elude us. We come still to the dreaded and sacred sites in the manner of the primitives approaching the caverns of Sciaca.

As fears intensify, rites of placation are renewed. The need to sacrifice grows with each shock. The canvasing of possible offering develops in an atmosphere of ceremonial incantation. Within affected communities, a cloak of chauvinistic superstition conceals the real futility of the proceedings, reassuring congregations that something effective is in the way of being undertaken.

The forearms to be offered up may be those of the tourist, the reformer, the foreigner, "the enemy"—in any case those outside the fraternity whose blood and bones the gods may for this reason be expected to enjoy. Amidst the clash of global interests litanies of patriotism pour forth while the leaders of the nations shepherd their wolves on the lookout for lambs. So barbarism reasserts itself in the grander arenas, issuing its invitations to join in prayer and sacrifice to the unknown gods. Sounding the tocsins of the ancient religions, the priests and priestesses reach out to embrace us. All of us who value civilization must learn to resist.

Notes

1. A photo of a similar work is contained in E.J. Hobsbawm's *Bandits* (London, 1969), p. 56ff. He credits this version of the theme to F. Bonnano.
2. Margaret Guido, *Sicily: An Archaeological Guide* (New York, 1967), p. 100.

4

A Fulbrighter Joins a German Fencing Fraternity

Alfred Maurice de Zayas

Unus pro omnibus et omnes pro uno
Motto of Corps Rhenania zu Tübingen

Tübingen in the autumn of 1971: red and yellow leaf on beech, chestnut and birch all along the Neckar River, lush green hills flanking the Suevian stream alive with trout, languid punts and students leisurely floating toward Hölderlin tower, young voices laughing and singing out of tune, colored sashes and fraternity caps. . . . Memories of a Fulbright Fellow just matriculated in the law and history faculties of the Württemberg University, founded in 1477 and renowned for its theologians and philosophers.

Fencing was probably the furthest thing from my mind when I arrived in this idyllic town tucked away in the hills of the Schwäbische Alb in southwestern Germany, far from autobahns and tourists. My Fulbright project was not pro forma: I did genuinely intend to write my book *Nemesis at Potsdam*[1] during that year. But—and this is a big but—I also wanted to immerse myself in German student life so that I could return to the United States with the feeling of having seen more than just books and lecture halls. I was not interested in being just a foreign guest; my intention was to become a German student, to be one of them.

This was not my first trip to Germany. I had already spent the summer of 1969 in Westphalia, working at a firm specializing in tax law. At that time I was a law student at Harvard and eager to learn the art of making money so that I could afford to pursue my historical avocation. Little did I know of German universities and even less about German fraternities, being myself of Spanish-French descent and unable to claim any ancestor between the Rhine and the Oder. But, like any other American, I too knew Sigmund

Romberg's sentimental musical *Student Prince* and the touching lyrics by Dorothy Donnelly:

> *Down where the Neckar flows swiftly along,*
> *nestles a town that is famous in song:*
> *Laughing lads roam through its streets so quaint,*
> *no one's a sinner, much less a saint . . .*
> *Golden days in the sunshine of our happy youth,*
> *golden days full of innocence and full of truth . . .*
> *Drink, drink, drink to eyes that are bright*
> *as stars when they're shining on me . . .*

Well, that was the story of Prince Karl Franz's student days in Heidelberg, 100 miles downstream from Tübingen, of his love for Kathie, the blonde waitress of the *Inn of the Three Golden Apples*, his fencing and drinking bouts with boisterous fraternity brothers from Corps Saxo-Borussia. I would not necessarily recommend to other Fulbrighters that they read the original play by Wilhelm Meyer-Förster entitled *Alt-Heidelberg*, even if it inspired Romberg's 1924 Broadway success, made so famous by Jan Peerce and Mario Lanza. But I would suggest that they catch a revival of this American operetta whenever it comes their way again.

In any event, it so happened that my employer in the summer of 1969, Friederich-Wilhelm Schlenkhoff, was not only the head of the tax firm but also a very active *Alter Herr* (alumnus) of a fencing fraternity in Tübingen, Corps Rhenania. Thus it was no surprise when he invited me down to the annual meeting of the fraternity, the *Stiftungsfest,* a four-day bash to celebrate its founding on 7 July 1827. As a foreign guest I was very well received, and was able to participate in all sorts of festivities including the formal ball with a first-rate band and the grill party with Dixieland music. I had a colossal time and remembered that German word they used to describe the atmosphere of the event: *getmütlich.*

Two years later, in the fall of 1971, I had finished law school, passed the New York and Florida bar examinations, worked over a year as a corporate lawyer at a Wall Street firm and—at twenty-four—decided to take a leave of absence from the firm to continue my historical studies. Upon arrival on the *Europa* (Hapag Lloyd) at Bremerhaven, I was greeted by a fraternity brother I had met in Tübingen in 1969. He also made sure that I was invited to the house of Corps Rhenania as soon as I arrived in Tübingen. Without my knowledge, I had already been "recruited" as a *Spefuchs* or "prospective fox" (pledge), and barely two weeks later I was admitted as a *Krassfuchs* (young fox) and received the traditional sash and blue cap. A rather adventurous proposition!

I still did not know much about *Schlagende Verbindungen* (fencing fraternities), besides the fact that a *Corpsstudent* was expected to fence five matches *(Mensur)*. Surely this did not appear more dangerous than riding a motorcycle on the autobahn, and, after all, the other fraternity brothers seemed to survive it pretty well. Every now and then someone received a *Schmiss* on the cheek, but nothing unduly spectacular. As far as I was concerned, every fraternity was entitled to its own rules of initiation, and fencing seemed more fun than swallowing goldfish, eating raw liver, or being "paddled." On the other hand, what did turn out to be somewhat of a problem was the intensity of the *Activitas* expected from each fraternity brother. Corps life consisted of daily fencing with a fencing instructor, daily lectures by the *Fuchsmajor* (tutor of young pledges) on the history and rules of the fraternity, weekly excursions, organization of monthly *Vörtrage* (speeches) at the fraternity house with speakers from industry (members of the boards of leading German enterprises like BASF and Mannesmann), politics (across the spectrum from Franz Josef Strauss [CSU], to Graf Lambsdorff [FDP], to Hasenklever [Grüne]), and education (university rector Theodor Eschenburg and other eminent professors), programming at least one musical event per semester (most members of the fraternity play an instrument), planning the fall, Christmas, *Fasching* (Carnival), spring, and summer balls, playing billiards on an impeccably kept table, and last but certainly not least: drinking enormous quantities of beer. How convenient indeed that one of our *Alte Herren* happened to own the Dortmunder Kronen brewery.

Parallel to all this we were expected to attend the university and take our exams. Perhaps the amazing thing is that we all did. It was a feat of organization and discipline, and a sine qua non for membership; in fact, the fraternity suspends members who do not take their studies seriously. This reminded me to a certain extent of the Harvard atmosphere, where most of us tried to engage in extracurricular activities, look and act cool, while squeezing in a lot of concentrated study in-between. And as at Harvard, the ideal is to revel conspicuously and work with decent nonchalance. Thus, among the younger members of the fraternity many have gone to the United States with DAAD or other scholarships; among the older members are the former chairman of the board of Mercedes, the president of the Düsseldorf Stock Exchange, members of the Bonn Parliament, and several distinguished professors including the Roman law expert Franz Wieacker (awarded the Pour le Mérite). So, you may ask, how in the world was I ever admitted by this fraternity? Well, I guess they gave me the benefit of the doubt. As it happens, I am the first—and thus far only—American admitted to membership. And as a Catholic I am also in the minority—only 10 percent of the members are Catholics, probably owing to the general prohibition by the Catholic Church during the nineteenth century, when saber dueling was far more dangerous than the fencing practiced today, which although it is not quite like sport fencing, it has not caused any serious injury for 100 years. This is partly so because no one is allowed to a *Mensur* until he has attained a high degree of proficiency with the *Schläger* (the special sword used in the fraternity matches), and also because the fencing rules and the role of the *Sekundant* have evolved.

Prejudice and intolerance stem in part from lack of information, or may be attributable to generalizations based, for instance, on literary caricatures like that in Heinrich Mann's *Der Untertan*. Thus it would be appropriate here to briefly survey the history of these fraternities, which have existed for over two hundred years. German university fraternities arose during the European Enlightenment, influenced by the liberal ideas of the French Encyclopedians and later by German classical and early romantic poets and philosophers. There are five basic groupings: the *Burschenschaften* (still highly political, counting among their members Karl Marx, Ferdinand Lasalle, Carl Schurz and the Weimar Republic Chancellor Gustav Stresemann), the *Landsmannschaften* (poet Hermann Löns), *Turnershaften* (anti-Hitler leader Carl Goerdeler), *Sängerschaften* (composer Franz Liszt, conductor Wilhelm Furtwängler) and the *Corps* (composer Robert Schumann, industrialists Gottlieb Daimler and Otto Mannesmann, Reichschancellor Otto v. Bismarck). All these groupings exist today and the differences are less pronounced than in the nineteenth century. What distinguishes the Corps from the other fencing fraternities is that their Constitutions rest on the principle of tolerance and stipulate that party-politics and religious conviction shall not obstruct the overall goal of the Corps to promote the education of an intellectual and social elite and to further lasting friendships among their members. Obviously this does not mean that Corps members must be apolitical; on the contrary, the Corps welcomes a variety of political opinions and encourages debate on current issues, but—as an organization—it does not make political statements and internally opposes any pressures to induce among members a uniform political view. This is one reason the Corps and other fraternities had to close down during the Nazi years, some of them having openly protested against interference by the government to induce the exclusion of Jewish members. This partly explains why prominent Corps members joined the conservative anti-Hitler forces and some of them, like Ulrich von Hassell (executed 1944) paid for their opposition with their lives. Incidentally, when Brandenburgia Berlin was forced to suspend, it reopened in 1937 in Cleveland, Ohio, remaining one of the two fencing Corps in the United States today. There are also nonfencing German fraternities, whose members also wear sash and cap and share many of the customs of the Corps (prominent among them the "cv" or Catholic League).

Probably the most important distinction between German Corps and American college fraternities is that active association with the Corps is not limited to student days. For instance, after three to four semesters of activity and residence at Corps Rhenania, the young fraternity brother is *inaktiviert*, but as iaCB (*inaktiver Corpsbursch*) he is expected to pursue his relationship with the fraternity on a different level. If he remains in Tübingen, he advises the younger members and assists in the organization of fraternity activities. If he goes to another university, he represents the fraternity there and frequently joins a related fraternity as a VG (*Verkehrsgast*); there are upward of 100 Corps at some twenty-five German universities, but surely not all of them as good as *my* Rhenania. The iaCB is also expected to seek out other iaCBs and to meet the *Alte Herren* (old fellows), who usually get together at least once a month privately or at a regular *Stammtisch* (reserved table in a local restaurant). This continued contact is possible not only in the Federal Republic of Germany but also in other countries where such fraternities exist, e.g., in Austria (Saxonia/ Vienna), in Switzerland (Germania/Lausanne), and in the United States (Brandenburgia and Teuto-Rugia/Cleveland). Moreover, anywhere that fraternity brothers settle, they usually organize a *Stammtisch* or meeting place, e.g., in London, Paris, New York, Mexico City, São Paulo, Sydney.

The fraternity brother retains his status as iaCB for as long as he is a student, but upon graduation as lawyer, doctor, or economist (the three professions most frequently represented in the fraternity membership), he is *philistriert* and enters the new status of *Alter Herr* with the attending financial obligations to pay annual dues to defray the manifold expenditures of the fraternity. Luckily, since Corps Rhenania has 350 *Alte Herren,* the dues can be kept down to an acceptable level. There are, however, significant expenses. The beautiful premises, perched up on the Österberg, overlooking the Neckar River and the old town, consist of some three acres of yard and gardens and a castle-like residence built expressly for the fraternity in 1885. Even though the house has been declared a monument by the Province of Baden-Württemberg (which entails tax advantages), the cost of heating the huge building, repairing the old roof and tower, etc., constitutes a burden, as any house owner knows from experience. The house, however, is the heart of the fraternity. Not only does it provide comfortable quarters for as many as twenty active members, but attracts iaCB and *Alte Herren* year round, who may also spend the night there. Moreover, festivities are celebrated on the premises, including big *Stiftungsfeste* attended by 200 or more members with their respective wives. It has also become a tradition for many Corps brothers to hold their wedding receptions at the fraternity. The house, in fact, is so impressive that tourists sometimes come to the gate and ask when they can visit the "castle." And during the Allied Occupation after World War II, the house became the residence of the French military governor. It was not until 1956 that the house was returned to the *Alte Herren* of Rhenania.

There are many moments of fraternity life that I particularly cherish—memories of philosophizing (and drinking) through four in the morning and then going to the grand piano with ten other *Corpsbrüder* to blast out a slightly amended chorus from the glorious Ninth:

> *Freude, schöner Götterfunken,*
> *Tochter aus Elysium*
> *Wir betreten* ganz be*trunken,*
> *Himmlische, dein Heiligtum!*

Memories too of the summer ball, waltzing to Johann Strauss, followed by the Beatles and disco, watching the sunrise from the fraternity tower, and then taking a champagne breakfast with my *Couleur-Dame* while punting down the Neckar River. If this is decadent—Vive la décadence! Punters at Oxford and Cambridge will no doubt agree with me. It's jolly good fun! And those who would criticize the Corps as a strictly "men's club" ought to know that girls are very much integrated into fraternity life, even if they are not members. Their frequent presence enriches and completes the fraternity experience.

Other recollections are decidedly of a different character, like getting two stitches on my forehead after a fencing match—without anaesthesia—or going horseback riding with a hangover and pounding temples.

Many of the comments I have heard from American friends about German "frats" have to do with the prodigious amounts of beer that some of our members are said to consume. Indeed, I know of certain beer-drinking feats that deserve an entry in the Guinness book of records. But by and large, the drinking habits of my *Corpsbrüder* are surely no worse than what I already knew from my membership in college glee club, where we certainly drank too much whiskey and gin after (and sometimes before) concerts. Yet, what amazes me of German drinking is the organization, the Bacchanalian ritual, the so-called drinking code or *Trinkkomment*. Fraternity brothers of Rhenania don a blue uniform (*Kneipjacke*) and sit at the candlelit *Kneipe* to celebrate a *Kommers*, which is officially opened by the *Senior* of the fraternity with a *donnernden Schoppensalamander* (ritual toast), listen to formal words of welcome, followed by well-prepared speeches (sometimes humorous, sometimes eloquent, sometimes pedantic—depending on the *Senior*) and accompanied by no less than a dozen traditional student songs like "Gaudeamus igitur," "O alte Burschenherrlichkeit," "Krambambuli," "Dort Saaleck Hier die Rudelsburg," "Im Schwarzen Walfisch zu Ascalon," and "Student Sein." The formal or official part of the *Kommers* closes with the singing of the fraternity song (a kind of alma mater). By this time each *Corpsbrüder* has consumed at least one liter of beer—especially the *Füchse,* inspired by the *Fuchsmajor* and goaded by the iaCBs, who may have absorbed two liters. To paraphrase Coleridge: Beer, beer everywhere and every drop to drink! During the second and third stages of the *Kommers* more songs are sung and the *Corpsbrüder* move about to chat with other members. Beer mugs may get knocked over and spill across the table. No problem. The song books are all equipped with hobnails on both sides, so that beer can always flow under them without getting the pages wet—an altogether ingenious touch. The real discussions on "fundamental issues" begin after midnight, and then an avid hunter gets hold of his horn and starts blowing signals or playing the Halali. About half of our members are also hunters, so that at times two or three horns play in unison. And on with the singing, like in Carl Orff's *Carmina Burana:*

Bibit velox, bibit piger,	*(The quick man drinks, the sluggard drinks,*
bibit albus, bibit niger,	*the White man and the Black man drink,*
bibit constans, bibit vagus,	*the steady man drinks, the wanderer drinks,*
bibit rudis, bibit magus!	*the simpleton drinks, the wiseman drinks.)*

Á propos of another popular preconception, to wit, that Corps are generally elitist, I must concede that there is some truth to this. But, is not the Fulbright Program also elitist? Any organization that has to choose its members tends to be labeled thus. But, like the Fulbright Program, the Corps does not strive for homogeneity but rather looks for individualists. Still, not everybody in the Corps is a "good bloke." As in every human enterprise, there are some chaps who are more reliable than others, some who are honest fellows and others less so. The crucial thing is that the association or fraternity tries to live up to certain standards and that a spirit of openness prevails. Needless to say, there are *Corpsbrüder* whom I do not particularly like (and vice versa); but we are cordial and helpful to each other. Happily, I met enough good fellows to feel at home in the fraternity and to consider it worth my while to pursue the relationship. It is much more than just a club. In spite of the brevity of my activity during the Fulbright year, the experience was so intense that I have returned to the fraternity almost every year since then and count myself among the more enthusiastic alumni.

Still another criticism is that dueling is an anachronism. I agree. Certainly there has been no fraternity duel with pistols for 100 years. But dueling has never been confined to German fraternities. One need only think of the untimely deaths of Alexander Hamilton in 1804 in New Jersey and of the eminent Russian poet Aleksandr Pushkin in 1837 in Petersburg. Nor are there many saber duels today—or for that matter genuine duels for the purpose of satisfaction or honor. What we have today is a tradition of fencing according to very specific rules, which may appear bizarre to the olympic fencer, but which nonetheless are intended to test the technical prowess, concentration, and courage of the young fraternity brother. The mask used for practice is not worn during the *Mensur,* but only a small metal grill to protect the eyes and nose. The purpose of the match is certainly not to obtain a scar on the face (I have none), nor to "win" or to defeat one's opponent, but to show solidarity with the other members by enduring this test of nerves and self-discipline. Moreover, the *Mensur* is closely followed by the other fraternity brothers, who judge it according to moral and technical criteria. In this sense, all members participate in the *Mensur* by subsequently analyzing the match and thereby contributing to the pedagogical function of the fraternity. If by chance one of the fencers is hurt, there are always two doctors (fraternity members) to sew them up after the match is ended. We practice among ourselves but fence the *Mensur* only with members of other fraternities, e.g., Corps Franconia or Corps Borussia in Tübingen. Critics may caricature such fencing as slugging away with long knives and call it "a residue of the medieval tradition of monastic self-laceration," as a Harvard friend once put it in jest,[2] but I assure all Fulbrighters that it is safer than joining the Jets or the Sharks of *West Side Story.*

Contrary to what outsiders may think, the fencing requirement does not constitute a serious deterrent to membership in a Corps. In fact, fencing fraternities have enjoyed a remarkable renaissance after World War II and are very much a part of student life in Germany, even though their members only make up perhaps 2 percent of the student body. In view of the danger of becoming only a number and feeling isolated and lost in the Tübingen student population of 20,000, the fencing fraternities provide an alternative, since members have an opportunity to learn camaraderie by living, eating, drinking, feasting, fencing, punting, and making music together. Moreover, the corpsbrothers learn to assume responsibility by exercising specific tasks within the fraternity and also practice the arts of rhetoric and public speaking in formal fraternity events. Corps entails a commitment for life, not only for three or four semesters. And the friendships endure—a phenomenon I have yet to observe in the United States, where frat members disperse and lose contact with their buddies forever.

The reader of this essay should ask himself how many friends he still has from high school, college, or graduate school—more pertinently, how many friendships have endured from the Fulbright experience?

I am, in any case, enormously thankful to the Fulbright Program for the opportunity of becoming a student in Tübingen and indirectly for facilitating my membership in Corps Rhenania, which now awaits with pleasure the next Fulbrighter and prospective "fox." It is true that I did not finish my book *Nemesis at Potsdam* during the Fulbright year, but I collected much of the material and did many of the interviews for it that year, and when I finally wrote it, I had the benefit of enhanced perspective. Looking back at my Fulbright year, I know that because I practiced the "Gaudeamus igitur," I learned to understand and respect many German institutions, and while retaining my own identity, I was accepted as *Rhenane*. Thus, the Fulbright goal to promote mutual understanding was pretty well served, and I dare say that my German fraternity brothers enjoyed our "experiment in international living" as much as I did. Today, being an alumnus, I share with the other *Alte Herren* a sense of continuity and retain an active link to the university, whose development we follow more or less as insiders, since the new student generation that welcomes us at the fraternity house is like us *Rhenane* and reflects the *Zeitgeist* tempered by and in the light of our traditions. And thus year after year Corps alumni return to Tübingen to see old friends and young "foxes" and to sing Goethe's words with them:

> *Hier sind wir versammelt zu löblichem Tun,*
> *drum Brüderchen: ergo bibamus!*
> *Die Gläser, sie klingen, Gespräche, sie ruhn,*
> *beherziget: ergo bibamus!*
> *(Gather we here in laudable deed,*
> *so drink, brothers dear: let us drink!*
> *When glasses ring out, give discourse no heed,*
> *With spirit, sing out: let us drink!)*[3]

Notes

1. Published in 1977 by Routledge & Kegan Paul (Boston, 2nd rev. ed. 1979) with a foreword by the late ambassador Robert Murphy.
2. I am grateful to David Mednicoff for coining the phrase.
3. Author's free translation.

5

Bengal Land

Marshall W. Fishwick

My Bengal of gold, I love you.
—Bangladesh National Anthem

To most Americans the Bengal Tigers are one of the beefier teams in the NFL. If you choose Exxon, you can "Put a tiger in your tank," or stare at Tony the Tiger on your morning cereal box. Some get to know Tigger in A.A. Milne's *Winnie the Pooh.* Occasionally we see real ones—sinewy, stealthy, pacing silently in zoos and circuses—the Bengal tiger. But what do we know of Bengal? In most cases, little or nothing.

Few can even tell you where Bengal (Bangladesh) is, or why it is so crucial to planners and politicians. If asked to locate it on an older map or globe, they may conclude there is no such place. (Until 1971 it was known as East Pakistan.) Indeed there is a Bangladesh—eighth most populated nation on earth: one of the oldest cultures and newest countries. For centuries it was known as Golden Bengal, where elephants and tigers abounded.

There is nothing golden as we land in the monsoon rains as we approach from the Indian mainland; Dacca's main runway is awash; beyond is the country, much of it under water after days of rain. And there are countless scholars and experts, from all over the world, "studying" this "basket case of the Third World." To the outsider, one village looks just like another; rice fields and water buffalo are monotonously one. Not so to those who live there. Peasant societies everywhere have exceedingly complex social, ritual, and expressive ways of life. Matters embedded deep in the cultural and social matrix are never apparent to the casual observer. There are worlds within worlds, wheels within wheels. Somehow these people have endured. Is that the miracle of Bangladesh?

To leave the airport is always a traumatic moment in Asia. Wall-to-wall people, grabbing, clawing, begging; the sight, sound, and smell of humanity *en masse*. A sense of panic sets in. How can I get through? What if these people suddenly become a mob? How can I pass a maimed beggar, or a child swarming with flies, and not give them money? But if I do, will I be overwhelmed by all the others.

Over such a city hovers a great and dreadful expectation. Everybody is waiting for everybody else to die. Today's dead are mourned; yesterday's dead are burned; last week's dead are picked clean by vultures and vermin.

We go to Foundation House, where "our" people dwell in Third World countries, with all the comforts of home. The walls are white, the water is boiled, and everyone speaks English. My room has a pleasant veranda overlooking a grass lawn that could double for a golf green at any club in the world. On the wall is a picture of a Bengal tiger. He seems right out of William Blake:

> *Tiger! Tiger! burning bright*
> *In the forests of the night*
> *What immortal hand or eye*
> *Could frame thy fearful symmetry?*

Why has that "fearful symmetry" deserted the very land in which the tiger once reigned? If areas as crowded as Singapore, Taiwan, and Hong Kong can move into the twentieth century—why not Bangladesh? If neighboring countries like Thailand and Sri Lanka can feed their people, and find export markets—why not Bangladesh? Why, on the Bay of Bengal, is the tiger at bay?

> *What the hammer? what the chain*
> *In what furnace was thy brain?*
> *What the anvil? what dread grasp*
> *dare its deadly terrors clasp?*

How could I have known Blake's "deadly terrors" were as close as the knock on my door? One of the Foundation house boys (they never mature into "men") is there. His voice trembles and terror fills his eyes. "Sir, my young boy is very, very sick. You come and help? You come with me to hospital?" He is Ali, assigned to me, now dependent on me. I am as afraid as Ali, but I know he needs me. "Yes," I say. "How do we get there?" "In rickshaw, Sir. One is waiting." I had seen them—literally thousands of them—coming from the airport: three-wheeled bicycles, built to allow one or two passengers to sit behind the porter who pumps the vehicle. There are no gears, so pumping is extremely strenuous. Many are thin teenagers who make only a few pennies for each long haul.

Ali and I get in. He gives directions and we bounce over rough litter-strewn roads in one of the poorer overcrowded parts of the city. I cannot believe the dingy ramshackle building in front of which we stop is a hospital. Nothing in Dickens could equal the squalor, darkness, and despair. In a single room lie several dozen people, some moaning and crying, others too sick to utter a sound. There is no ventilation, almost no light, swarms of gnats and flies. On most beds sit parents or relatives of the ill. A single nurse moves back and forth, pouring water into dirty glasses next to the beds.

Ali moves quickly to the bed where his son lies: a small shriveled lad whose stomach is so extended that he looks as if he's swallowed a soccer ball. "How long has he been here?" I ask. "Three days," Ali says. "Every day, he gets worse, stomach gets bigger. Can you get your White Doctor?" "Stay here. Tell the rickshaw driver to take me back to Foundation House, and I'll try."

After what seems forever I track down an American doctor through the embassy, explain the situation, and have him take me back to Ali in his car. Now the local doctor is with Ali's boy; the two doctors talk, the local doctor leaves. "He gave me permission to examine him," the American doctor says. Five minutes later: "Just as I thought: misdiagnosed. This is a very sick child. He should have been put on antibiotics a week ago. All I can do is give him some tetracycline and hope for the best. I'll leave enough for three days."

Back to Foundation House—Ali stays on with his son. "Places like that shouldn't be called hospitals," our doctor says. "They're death cells. Few are equipped to treat a serious ailment. The place is so dirty that infection gets passed back and forth. Even if you're fairly well when you go in, you're lucky to come out alive. The government ought to close them down." "But where would the sick people go?" He shrugged his shoulders. "I don't have the answers. But today's Tuesday—if I hadn't seen that kid, he would have been dead by Wednesday morning."

The drug helped. Ali's son was alive but in great pain on Wednesday morning. On Friday morning he died. I hardly know Ali—I only saw the poor child once. Yet the bell is tolling for me. Could I have done anything more? Or did I, unintentionally, contribute to his death? From the inner recesses of my mind, two lines from Walt Whitman emerge:

> *Come sweet death, be persuaded O death*
> *In mercy come quickly. . . .*

Sitting on my cool, clean veranda, I think of Ali, his son, the human predicament. Where is the mercy, the justice? Even as I ask I notice, just beyond my immaculately-kept garden, where two female sweepers listlessly pursue a fallen leaf, a dark young woman squatting atop a huge pile of bricks. With a heavy hammer she smashes them into small pieces against a large stone—hour by hour, day after day, endlessly. Even on Friday (the Muslims' day of rest) and on holidays she works. Close by, her three already old children, midget-sized, torpid, play on the bricks. Their eyes stare out of deep sockets, their noses drip, flies swarm around them. The mother never stops, even when they cry. Her hammer comes down like the hand of fate, until finally the small pieces form a large mound. Then other skin-and-bone women come, put the pieces in straw baskets, carry them off on their heads.

The Brick Woman is my symbol for Bangladesh. Seasons, policies, programs, projections change—but she is as constant as the Northern Star. What does she think about, all day? Where does she go, at night? Has she ever dreamed of leaving the brick pile? What does she expect of life? How long will she live—is she *living* (in the humane sense) at all? I have no answers. I suspect she has no questions.

Meanwhile, I type this in my clean, white, air-conditioned room. Soon the bearer will come (in his clean white coat) with my tea (in a clean white cup). If I am tired, I can nap (on clean white sheets). Then the bearer will come, saying "Your car has come, Sab." He will hold open the door of the oversized air-conditioned car, which will whisk me to a palatial (air-conditioned) villa. There, after the appropriate number of properly-iced drinks, we will sit down (white tablecloths, white linen napkins) to a sumptuous six-course dinner, prepared and served by a small army of "kitchen staff."

During the conversation, someone laments the sad state of the economy. All our aid is going down the drain. "The British were right to get out," a flabby official with a bulging paunch says, his tongue freed by a fifth gin and tonic. "Lazy beggars, these Bengalis. They don't know the meaning of an honest day's work." Outside, the Brick Woman keeps pounding. How long, O Lord, how long?

Many Bangladeshi are not fortunate enough to break bricks. Estimates of what the government calls "underemployment" vary widely, some over 30 percent. So there are always people standing, looking, talking. There is no night in Third World cities. People are everywhere whatever the hour. Those who are lucky enough to sleep during the intense heat of the day enjoy the night. Those who have no place to sleep seek the night's dark corners.

Even if you were blind and deaf, you could make your way through many cities by smell. No words can convey those odors to people who put lemon Pledge on their furniture and deodorants on their body. Only the nose knows. Man, media, nose, and nature interact in countless directions, some obvious, some subtle. Man plus nature is one of history's basic equations. What does it equal, so far as the media is concerned? How is nature portrayed, for example, on Bangladeshi televisison?

Individuals write with pencils; culture marks with plows and trowels. The basic human story is written on the face of the land. The appearance of pastures, gullies, furrows, city blocks, rice paddies, slums, junk heaps— pieced together and interpreted—furnishes a commentary more profound than all the histories. This is the *real* Bangladesh.

"Landscape" means many things. On a hillside the poet sees an intimation of immortality; the engineer, the place for a new irrigation line. A farmer translates an acre into so many bushels of rice; a soldier into so many places for cannon; an oil driller into so many drill sites. The architect sees it as a place for a jute factory. What they all see is "true."

We see what we are prepared to see—the mind trains the eye. No two people perceive the same things. Landscape is the state of being of a place, derived from the inhabitant's inner mind. What, I wonder, does Bangladesh "look like" to Ali or the Brick Woman? What do Americans "look like" in the Third World?

I can never know. The Brick Woman keeps pounding. What I see beyond the hand-preened green is the ruthless ritualistic world which Spinoza summed up in a famous line: The big fish eats the little fish by supreme natural right.

I will show you all of life in a grain of sand, a mustard seed, a garbage dump in Dhaka. Whatever is thrown away is first picked over and devoured by people. Then come the dogs, who can handle bones people cannot digest. After the dogs come the cats; then the rats; finally the roaches and the ants. By the next morning, everything will be gone, and the cycle begins again. Darwin spent years on the *Beagle*, verifying his theory about the survival of the fittest. Might he not have seen it at work, in a single day, on the streets of Dhaka?

Thoreau said Americans lead lives of quiet desperation. In Bangladesh the desperation is noisy. Day and night, winter and summer, streets teem with love, hate, death. Men and women everywhere portray how they feel inside by what they make and use outside. The one thing the visitor to Dhaka can never forget (or escape) are bicycle-rickshaws. No one is sure how many there are—perhaps 90,000. They are a way of life and a way of art.

If rickshaws had voices they would sing. Instead, they parade. Each one is a moving art galley which displays collage, cartoon, painting, and cut-outs. On this one, the lion, king of beasts, delivers a speech to a guitar-playing monkey. The lion wears red and carries a microphone. There are three-faced winged snakes blowing fire. Even the poor rickshaw repairmen and technicians are getting attention. Lions, tigers, peacocks, monkeys, jackals, horses, crocodiles, storks, and eagles are there too. Many have musical instruments. Sometimes the animals fight with guns, smoke cigarettes, and encourage others to fight.

Rickshaw artists are untrained but undaunted. If they run out of paint, they do not hesitate to finish a white figure with red paint. Suddenly, a blue sky becomes half red. A blue ocean becomes half yellow. He has no time to wait; the wheels must roll. Plump First World cows are sometimes found grazing on Third World farmland. A mosque stands beside a skyscraper. Roads pass through lakes. Planes fly in the sky and trains zoom along railway tracks. Things never seen in three dimensions live instead in two. Folk artists are always at home in the realms of gold.

Meanwhile most Bangladeshis live, eat, work, and die in the dirt. They seem part of the dirt, and it of them. Where everyone is "dirty," no one is dirty. There is no shame connected with the earth. "From dust we come, to dust we return"; why should we fear it while we are moving briefly through life? Is this feeling for the soil in which we grow not only food, but folklore, earthlore, art, not material for the Odyssey of the human spirit? Is it not the glue of culture? Alfred North Whitehead says (in *Science and the Modern World*): "Men require of their neighbors something sufficiently akin to be understood, something sufficiently different to provoke attention, and something great enough to command admiration." These are riches in the poorest nation on earth.

Folklore, legends, stories, and folk art abound. So do mythology, music, drama, and dancing. Where they flourish, there will be no proleteriat. As Arnold Toynbee points out, the true hallmark of the proleteriat is neither poverty nor humble birth, "but a consciousness of being disinherited from his ancestral place in society and being unwanted in a community which is his rightful home."

Tradition dominates life. Is it desirable to preserve tradition at all costs? What happens when history grinds up old traditions like hamburger, and turns out something quite unlike the original meat? Might not unquestioned preservation, stunt or block economic, social, political, and scientific progress, and damage the community which traditionalists want to preserve and protect? Nowhere is the question more pressing than in South Asia.

And no question is more pressing to Fulbright scholars, whoever and wherever they may be. For forty years we have been girdling the globe, sponsoring major scholarship, helping to shape a new era of understanding. The high tone set for the program by Senator J. William Fulbright has served as a guiding star, in good days and bad. Let us follow our star.

6

The Finnish Experience

Chad Walsh

My wife and I, accompanied by three of our four children, watched the city slowly come alive with sunrise colors. Soon we descended from the train and headed for the dormitory where we were temporarily staying. Once these practicalities were taken care of, we were ready to marvel at our being in Finland for the next nine months on a Fulbright lectureship.

The first thing that struck us as we strolled along the streets of the city were the shop signs that could have been written by a visiting Martian. Nothing looked familiar. Among a hundred words there would perhaps be two or three international ones such as *radio*. Beyond that, a breakdown of communication! Before we sailed for Finland, I had done some homework and I knew that Finnish belonged to a different language family—closely related to Estonian, less closely to Hungarian, and distantly indeed to certain dialects of northern Siberia and central China. A truly international language, I thought to myself, even if only Finns can read it. How isolated these people must be! Only later did I learn how mistaken I was.

The language looked like a psychedelic experiment with its endless little dots on *a* and *o*. But daily events soon assured us that we were in a world not completely different from our own. The Finns themselves, ever eager to bestow honorary citizenship on visiting foreigners, communicate as best they can—increasingly in English—and do whatever they can to make tourists feel at ease. I remember one time when a foreign friend and I were walking down the street and noticed some workmen laying a roof. "Paivaa!" (hello) my friend called out. One of the men yelled to his companion, "These men aren't foreigners. They speak Finnish."

I have gone into some detail about the Finnish language, partly because its status has frequently been a matter of controversy. Briefly, Finnish came into Finland perhaps around the time of Christ. Swedish was much later, but the Swedes brought with them a highly developed culture. Gradually they converted most of the Finnish people to Christianity. They also be-

75

came the upper class, a situation that prevailed until the early twentieth century when nationalism swept through Finland and the Finnish tongue became a point of pride. It took close to a century to evolve a workable accommodation—aided by the fact that Swedish speakers were a small minority, less than 10 percent. In the 1930s, there were student riots over the language question. Gradually a system of bilingual education was worked out and has proved reasonably satisfactory.

In a way, the language question is being bypassed. The slow spread of English is everywhere. Moreover, a social revolution has taken place in the past century. Finnish speakers are now statesmen, doctors, and professors: Swedish speakers have learned to love what was once considered a barbarian tongue. Not many of them would agree with the lady who defended keeping Finnish at a distance by asking us, "Why don't you learn Navajo?"

The Finns are determined to be open to the great world. One of the ways they do this is by developing a corps of gifted translators. The day that a new book by some Nobel prize winner is due to be published, on that same day a Finnish version will be available. Finns are also great travelers, especially in the academic world. Any academic congress will bring together a very high percentage of top Finnish scholars, and the common language is, of course, English.

In addition to the language I began to learn how different the Finnish educational system is. I lectured both at the University of Turku (Finnish-speaking) and Abo Akademi (Swedish-speaking). They were both more ceremonious than their American counterparts. Doubtless my status as a professor made it easy for me to make contact with other faculty. As for the students, they did not seek me out, but were frightened and honored at the same time if I spoke to them. I remember one of my students who happened to go to the public sauna the same day I did. We were both stark naked as we solemnly bowed to each other.

But there were other deeper differences. I soon learned that university education in Finland is free, even books. So any student who can qualify is assured an education—he need never worry about scraping up $12,000 or saddling himself with an enormous debt. I was beginning to understand the Finnish value system, or part of it—education is important, not only to the individual but to the well-being of the nation.

In the university system itself there was plenty more to startle an American. They seem to get along amazingly well with no administrative superstructure, so there is no dichotomy between faculty and administration because members of the faculty are elected usually for three years, though they may be reelected, to serve as administrative officers. Some of those elected like the job, while others serve out a sense of duty and are eager to return to the classroom. Another great difference is that in Finland professorships are scarce. Only the chairman of a department has that title and he wins it by an arduous process. The position is advertised in academic circles and anyone is eligible to declare his candidacy. But the victor is always someone with a scholarly publishing record, usually an international status, and teaching experience. The victor gives a weighty lecture at his inauguration followed by a feast with much to drink. Visiting Americans profit from the fact that the term *professor* entitles them to the same elaborate respect accorded a Finnish professor. It is a bit heady to find oneself so high up on the social ladder, for professors command great respect in Finland.

Finland and its universities have changed much since my first time there. When I returned in the spring of 1982 to spend a month lecturing on contemporary American poetry, the great storms of unrest had blown in from Sweden in the late 1960s. Life had calmed down, but not until a partial democratization had been carried out. No longer did students rise to attention and bow as the professor entered the lecture hall. There are now all sorts of informal contacts and students have a much stronger voice in academic affairs.

The real academic tories insist that educational standards have fallen. I question this. My students wrote better papers than they did twenty-five years ago. No longer did they beg off from my literary questions by insisting that only a Ph.D. had the right to express opinions.

Not only did we confront a strange language and a different educational system, but we were impressed by the number of women who had professional status. Remember that this was the late 1950s, before the women's movement had gathered steam in the United States. It was startling to see a woman hod carrier on construction sites, to know that women doctors were commonplace, that 80 percent of the dentists were women, and that there were a number of women engineers as well. Women certainly functioned in the academic world, though not many held professorships. There seemed to be no battle of the sexes and it was taken for granted than an educated woman should have a career. If this seemed surprising, we also learned that Finland took the pioneer step of granting women the right to vote about 1900. With this weapon, the women of Finland could make themselves heard.

But what impressed us most of all was the relationship between Finland and Russia. As Americans we were still caught up in the paranoia of the McCarthy era—yet here was a small country which had dared to confront the giant, had lost territory, to be sure, in that confrontation, but had not been swallowed up as the Baltic states had been. We need to backtrack a bit. Finland has a vulnerable location, especially between Russia and Sweden. It has been ruled by both countries. During the nineteenth century, it was not ruled by the czar as such, but in his role as grandduke. This compromise continued until the end of World War I when Finland broke away. The country then fell into a bloody civil war until the conservative faction won. Around the time of World War II the Soviet Union began putting pressure on Finland and the Baltic states to make various concessions so the area could be better defended. The Baltic states were absorbed by the USSR, but Finland fought back in both the Winter and the Continuation wars. Losses were enormous; Finland lost a tenth of its territory, but it kept its sovereignty. We were told that Soviets offered citizenship to the Finns in the captured area and only thirteen accepted. So Finland had a tremendous job of resettling the refugees. All large landowners had to give up some of their property, but by the time we arrived this had been accomplished and the country was really beginning to recover from the wars. Food was more plentiful, though its variety was limited, and housing was not so tight.

The Finno-Soviet drama has taken an amazing turn in recent years. Both sides have discovered that they need each other. The Finns are avid tourists and find in the Soviet Union a convenient and inexpensive spot for a weekend drunk. The Russians need the hard currency that trade and tourism bring. There is another angle also. Many of the big tourist hotels are designed and built by Finnish companies. To be sure, the government of Finland is careful to maintain neutrality, to refrain from openly criticizing Russia, for much of its economic health depends on Russian trade. But it was an eye-opener to an American to see how Finland handled its relations with its giant neighbor—what steady nerves they seemed to have, how realistic they were.

As I write this account of experiences in Finland I realize that what I was most looking for was Finland's value system. I recognize it in their educational system, in their social services, in the mystique of the sauna, their love of nature, their architecture. They seemed to have an organic view of things—for instance, an architect will take advantage of nature in planning a building rather than stripping it of rocks and trees. He seems to be more concerned in saving nature from exploitation than being the exploiter. The Finns seemed less obsessed with time, less terrified of age and death. Instead of hiding it, when a Finn reaches fifty there is an announcement in the paper and he invites his friends to a party to celebrate with him. But what about religion in Finland? It seemed to play a minimal role in the lives of our friends. About 98 percent of the population nominally belongs to the Lutheran Church—they are married, baptized, and buried in the church, but a Finn's relation to nature, art, even the sauna have, if I am not mistaken, strong elements of the religious. The usual routine of prayer and sacraments may be less real to many Finns than the sight of a frozen lake or a smoking sauna, though I understand that in the 1980s the church seems to be enjoying something of a revival of commitment.

The Finns take no pleasure in setting two values in contradiction. Their unconscious seems to seek harmony. They have a deep aesthetic sense and music plays a large role in Finland. A book of poetry by a fairly well-known poet may sell as many as 20,000 copies. Every Finn who can possibly afford it has his place in the country where he can be close to nature. The whole feeling of the country was one where the emphasis was on improving the quality of human life in both its material and spiritual aspects.

There are, of course, darker features to life in Finland. There is heavy and often swinish drinking. The very isolation of the country with its long winters, the darkness, are conducive to gloom, brooding, and suicide. There is still occasional tension between the two language groups, and the shadow of Russia is always there. But the list of undesirable features seems to end up relatively short. If I could not live in America, I would choose to live in Finland in spite of the climate.

A few years later I had a six-month Fulbright in Rome. For lack of space I shall be brief. If being plunged into Finnish life was an invitation to do some soul searching, the Italian experience was an invitation to enter one of the world's most beautiful museums. But the two experiences were very different. In Italy I remained a witness and reporter of all the manmade beauty about me; in Finland I was a participant in a special way of life. Italy encouraged me to be a spectator, while Finland summoned me up onto the stage.

During our stay in Italy my wife and I were frequently invited into Italian homes, but in only one case was this the beginning of a lasting friendship, whereas, after a quarter of a century, a score of Finns are life-long friends. But why should I complain? Italy is so full of Americans they are taken for granted.

I returned to America from Rome and did not feel transformed, though my aesthetic sense was deepened. Italy deepened what I know and was. But Finland changed me on a deep level. It sounds pretentious, but in many ways Finland left me a changed and different man, and that is the permanent gift of Finland to me.

7

A Personal Memoir

David L. Paletz

I have never met a Fulbright scholar who failed to discourse gleefully on the bountiful personal benefits of being abroad. Of course there is often no lack of complaints: inconveniences and isolation are bemoaned, adjustment difficulties adumbrated, financial burdens itemized; but these pale before the gains.

I am no exception. My personal life and values were affected in at least three ways by my Fulbright to Denmark: through individual incidents, encounters with a different set of character traits, and exposure to social attitudes in action. The key was comparison.

Individual incidents abounded. I briefly offer three to illustrate the personal joys of my life in Denmark. I remember my son embraced by his soccer teammates as he scored his first goal for them in what turned out to be a monumental victory. I recall my daughter (the child with the darkest hair) surrounded by her Danish friends at a birthday party for one of her classmates. And I treasure a copy of my wife's photograph in the local Odense newspaper illustrating a story about how winter was coming early that year and Danish women were taking expeditiously to their woolly lamb coats. My wife is an unlikely looking Dane.

Character traits were equally challenging. My family and I attended a dinner to celebrate the successful completion of the harvest. We sat with some 200 Danes on either side of a long table. At the end of each course all plates were passed down to the end of the table. The only plates with any food left were from my family. We learned quickly; after the first course our plates were clean and empty too.

Danes do not waste food. Nor energy: The houses are smaller and better insulated than those in the United States. They taught me about the paramount importance of energy conservation and how to achieve it. In the process, my children taught themselves how to ride bicycles just like their Danish schoolmates—no more chauffeuring for their parents.

Danes are less litigious than Americans. One day my wife accidentally hit a car. The other driver stopped immediately, assured himself that my wife was uninjured, and departed. He repaired his own car. No police, no insurance claims, no litigation.

Character traits shade over into social attitudes. Even during the relatively brief period of the Fulbright award many of these attitudes could be understood and assessed. For example, Danes differ quite dramatically from Americans in their views about the importance of competition in daily life; they downplay it in schooling, business, even sports. They have a much more generous attitude about the role of the state in providing for the social welfare of its citizens: Most are appalled at America's lack of a national health system. And they are far more willing (albeit with increasing reluctance) to pay for such social services.

No need, then, further to expound the personal benefits of being a Fulbright scholar. Clearly, living in a different country facilitates illuminating comparisons between assumptions and reality. It encourages self-examination. Self-examination is good for the soul. But the American scholar wondering whether to apply for a Fulbright rightly poses serious and sober questions that transcend personal pleasures. In what ways can a Fulbright award be of professional significance to a scholar whose research interest is the United States? How might it stimulate research? Could it possibly improve one's teaching?

The question of research is the easier of the two to answer. Again, comparison is the spur. But it is sustained by immobility. Shortly after my arrival in Denmark I participated in the founding of the Dansk Fulbright (an organization of Danes who had received Fulbrights). The evening was greeted by Jerome Bruner's lecture on the delights of being a wandering scholar. Wandering has its place. And certainly I occasionally journeyed to conferences throughout Europe giving papers, discussing issues with scholars from all nations. But otherwise, I could be found in my house in the small farming village of Kertinge overlooking the end of a fjord. Wandering was brought to a halt by teaching obligations, the Fulbright Program's lack of funds for intercountry travel, the price of gas, and the snow. Our visitors came by sled. I was told it was the worst winter in fifty years. But every year every Fulbrighter in Denmark is told the same: The argument is losing credibility.

Then there was the food, which increased my girth and dulled my wanderlust. "There will be no revolution in Denmark," wrote one of my students in her exam, "because all the Danes are hurrying home to get out of the rain and eat dinner." And the beer, the glorious beer, which reinforced the effects of the food. When the snow lay on the ground, deep, crisp, and uneven, the roads were impassable and impossible, not a human figure or mode of locomotion could be seen, and the beer trucks sped through the streets and countryside on their merry ways.

Thus, I was not much of a wandering scholar. "Boredom is the enemy of scholarship," Professor Bromer had said. But boredom can be an inspiration for scholarship by eliminating all obstacles to thought and work. In this sense, diversion is the real enemy of scholarship. Diversion by committee meetings, social activities, tennis (from December until May the few courts were snow-covered). The lack of graspable diversions forces the scholar to put something down on that pristinely, obscenely white paper in the typewriter. In other words, to think.

So I became a wondering scholar. I had the time to explore and reflect upon, in Bruner's words, "the boundary between the natural and the conventional." Danish people, events, and institutions forced me to think and wonder about their American counterparts. And as a scholar who specializes in the relations between politics and the media, who reviews films, who is fascinated by the effects of technology on people's lives, my thoughts ineluctably turned to the television set, with its pictures in black and white, loaned to us by our good and generous friend Ebba Pedersen. Why, I wondered, were I and my family watching less television than in the United States, and enjoying it more?

Most of what people know about government—its institutions and members, their activities, decisions, defects, strengths, capabilities—comes from the mass media in general and television in particular. The media have the power to decide which issues will be brought before the public, the terms in which they will be presented, who will participate, and under what conditions. By dint of the subjects they cover and the way they structure them, the mass media tells Americans and Danes what to think about and how to think about it; sometimes, even *what* to think. By and through the mass media come the facts, arguments, and ideas with which most people make some sense or nonsense of their lives. Two million of the 4 million Danes over thirteen watch the 7:30 evening news.

My first encounter with Danish television was bemusing. Saturday night, prime time, when sponsors in America spend hundreds of thousands of dollars to buy a precious minute to show a commercial for laxative, mouthwash, or underarm deodorant. There were no commercials on Danish television. What did I see when I tuned in? A man adjusting a microphone for two minutes. An American television executive would have had apoplexy.

The first impression was not misleading. Subsequently, we watched one show on prime time devoted exclusively to the potato. It had its effect: The next time we went out to dinner our Danish friends served potatoes cooked two different ways. Then there was the clock with a bird attached which ticked the time away whenever there was a period between programs. The only American expression for such television is "laid back."

A second difference: American television programs are at once more puritanical and more sexually enticing than those on Danish television (except for those imported from the United States). Puritanical: limitations on obscene language, broadly defined, and on the amount of women's cleavage that can be exposed. Enticing: Sexual innuendo and attraction are everywhere on American television: in commercials, virtually irrespective of product, and on the shows. And there is so much more American television: more channels, more programs, more time. One of my Danish students took a trip to New York and spent most of his time there watching old movies all through the night.

But then my reflections took me past the relatively obvious differences to the more intriguing issues of sexism and violence. Their relative absence from Danish television is striking. How to explain it? Not by audience imperatives, as I discovered when my investigations took me to the research section of Danish Radio (as the state organization controlling broadcasting in Denmark is titled). Here I learned that around 50 percent of the Danish population is able to receive Swedish and German television programs; and that around half of them watch these shows each day. And what they watch are entertainment programs and sports. As for the Danes who are technologically confined to viewing their sole national channel, when asked what programs they wanted more of, they, too, sought entertainment: Westerns, thrillers, dramas. In other words, in both the United States and Denmark "people . . . just want to look at television and forget their troubles" (in the immortal words of National Broadcasting Company president Fred Silverman).

One may wonder about modern industrial societies (and other societies, too). Why are their members so alienated that they crave such mind-numbing, mildly titillating entertainment? The corollary question is: What is done about the craving? In the United States the financial incentive is determinative and entertainment predominates. Not quite so in Denmark. Danes may want more entertainment programs, but their desire is not entirely gratified. The reason: social policy, in part embodied in legislation.

The issue can be defined as freedom versus control. Despite some social, political, and economic restraints, American television is relatively free. Free to spend millions of dollars producing formula television programs of mutual significance. Free for its owners to gather as much profit as they can. Free to spread sexism and violence across the land. And free to make programs like *King, Roots,* and *Holocaust* which, no matter how limited by need to appeal to the mass audience, are risky and brave ventures.

In contrast is the Danish system, consciously designed to educate, making far fewer concessions to commercial and entertainment considerations than its American counterpart, yet constrained by inadequate funding and periodic political pressures. It is a state-administered monopoly system, assertedly run in the public interest but controlled nonetheless. And who decides on the public interest? Is it in the public interest to criticize or praise the society, or both? Is it in the public interest to urge children to stand up for their "rights" against their parents, as one program did? Control is open to abuse.

Much more, as it transpired. During my Fulbright, the American television program *Holocaust* was shown in many countries throughout the world, including Denmark. The program was provocative, reactions were widespread in Europe and particularly in West Germany. Sadly, the producers and distributors had made no efforts to undertake or even encourage the kind of comprehensive, comparative international study of *Holocaust's* effects that the subject warranted. Nonetheless, individual researchers and research organizations did conduct their own effects studies. Because I was in Europe at the time, I was able to track down and collect much of this data. I then worked with Willem Langeveld of the University of Amsterdam, editor of the *International Journal of Political Education,* to produce the special (March 1981) issue of that prestigious journal devoted to some of the best and most thought-provoking of the research on the effects of the television series.

Nor was that the limit of the professional work I was able to accomplish during my stay in Denmark. Free from the routines of daily life, time-consuming committees and other university administrative duties; happily without a telephone (and with a farmer landlord whose lack of English ensured that every message we received was gratifyingly, hopelessly inaccurate), I was at last able to synthesize my ideas on authority, political behavior, and the mass media into a coherent whole. Writing was never so easy (it was still hard, writing is never easy), as during those snowbound days when our only company consisted of the infrequently switched-on television set; the radio, which brought us the civilized overseas service of the BBC; fluttering pheasants; and a fox limping menacingly and sadly through the snow. Thus I wrote the first draft of my book *Media Power Politics,* the final version of which was published during the spring of 1981.

Fulbright awards bring personal pleasures; they fructify research interest, possibilities, and accomplishments. But what of teaching? My initial impression was that the rewards of teaching about America to Danish students would be problematic. I would simply have to simplify my American material for less knowledgeable foreign students. But the problems turned out to be more complicated, the challenges more demanding, and the results far more gratifying than I had anticipated.

My assignment was the first difficulty. I was asked to teach two different kinds of courses: my specialty and a general introduction to American society and government. The area of my expertise posed no problem; the students would be of graduate caliber. But how to convey the broad subject of U.S. society and government? What is the essence of America's culture? Of its economic system and social relations? Of its political institutions and processes? I had never been compelled to face these questions as determinants of Americans' behavior. For America is a contradictory country; its people cooperate, yet are competitive, are pragmatic yet idealistic, egalitarian yet elitist, materialistic yet spiritual. America is a nation of small hamlets and massive cities, of flagrant wealth and dire poverty, of racism and pluralism, of corruption and incorruptible integrity, of selfishness and self-abnegation.

I had to decide how to teach topics that were essentially alien to Danish students, such as constitutional law, judicial review, our elongated electoral process, political parties in transition, race relations, ethnic groups, single-issue movements, and the principle of "self-interest rightly understood," so brilliantly defined by de Tocqueville.

I was tempted to employ a textbook. But I rarely use textbooks in teaching: They homogenize complexity, denigrate the language, bore the best students. Such books could never communicate the diversity that is America to my Danish students. I found myself returning time and again to originals: philosophers and scholars who have tried to explain America to themselves and their readers. I asked my students to familiarize themselves with the U.S. Constitution; to read parts of *The Federalist Papers* and excerpts from de Tocqueville's *Democracy in America*; to consider Turner's frontier thesis. I had them read a set of interviews with three quite different Americans whose one common denominator was that they operated motion picture theaters; one ran drive-ins, another art houses, the third was becoming wealthy by showing "nudie cutie" movies. And I gave them the latest issue of *Daedalus*, which was devoted to exploring various aspects of American life and politics in the 1980s.

I lectured occasionally but taught mainly through discussion. This was a risk. Danish students, I had been told, were unenthusiastic about attending class, did not talk much when they appeared, and were generally reticent and shy. My initial experience seemed to reinforce the stereotype. I arrived promptly at 11:00 a.m. at my first class to find the classroom empty. Only later was I informed that class sessions formally begin fifteen minutes after the bulletin listing. Subsequently, I found my students articulate, argumentative, and droll. The discussions were invariably lively. We sought to discern what our authors were trying to say, if it had made sense in the past and whether it still did. We asked whether the United States had changed over the years and if so, why. We compared the United States with Denmark, the Soviet Union, and the United Kingdom, and tried to explain the differences.

Teaching was not confined to formal class sessions. The American Embassy supplied us with videotapes of *Meet the Press* and other television interview shows (sadly with the commercials deleted). Thus I was able to show the students, to their incredulity, how American politics could contain politicians so disparate in looks, language, demeanor, and conception of politics as Governor Jerry Brown of California and speaker of the U.S. House of Representatives "Tip" O'Neill.

We went to the movies, those artifacts of American culture which so influence foreign opinions of the United States. We saw *Saturday Night Fever, The Deer Hunter, Girlfriends,* Jane Fonda in a western, Jerry Lewis in *The Nutty Professor.* And we discussed what we saw. But we did not depend solely upon the Odense theaters. My wife proposed a program of classic American films to be shown in 16mm on campus, the first such innovation there. Her proposal was approved, modest funding for her and the films provided. The series was successful, attracting students during even the most horrendous weather. Among the films shown were *Citizen Kane, The Treasure of Sierra Madre, Little Caesar, Top Hat,* and the original *Invasion of the Body Snatchers.*

As part of the program, my wife prepared introductory lectures. More education for us both. Were the films representative of their genres? Of American society in general? What did they tell us about the United States when they were made? About the aspirations, expectations, and hopes of the people? Fortunately the university's library contained a useful selection of relevant literature; and the ever-helpful librarians expeditiously obtained whatever else we requested.

In summary, I discovered that it is very useful to view one's society and its institutions from afar. It is illuminating and challenging to teach about one's country to students who have their distinctive, sometimes peculiar, view of it—or no view at all.

These, then, are the personal and professional rewards that variously accrue, usually in profusion, to Fulbright recipients. They are rewards that live in one's daily teaching and research, and in the memory. And when all else fails they have their political uses: It is always possible to silence colleagues at a department meeting with the phrase: "Well, when I was a Fulbright Scholar . . ."

8

Fulbright Fandango

Peter I. Rose

"At'll be two bob 'n' thrup'ny, luv." Those words, spoken by a 15-year-old clerk in a chemist shop in Leicester, England, still resonate in my head. I heard them on the first day of my first trip abroad, the start of a year in the United Kingdom as a Fulbright Lecturer at the University of Leicester. I had gone into the shop to ask for some tissues (they called them "tis-sues") for two sniffly children who were beset by the flu the minute we touched land in merry old England. Asked how much I owed her, the lass behind the counter muttered the unintelligible phrase at a rapid-fire clip: "Atllbe-twobobnthrupnyluv." Even when I was able to separate the words I still didn't understand her. It was an inauspicious beginning. Yet, in a curious way she, and the many others I met in the next few months, changed my life.

That was twenty years ago. Since then I have become not only quite adept at deciphering the strange tongue of working-class Midlanders and students from the cities and shires of Britain, and those who claim to speak the same language in Australia, New Zealand, Kenya, India, Malawi, and Hong Kong, but, with considerable help from able interpreters, to get a sense of what is going on in countries where they speak "foreign" languages. In fact, I have spent time in over forty countries where I have gone to visit, teach, lecture, or to conduct research since 1964. Some of the research has been on the Fulbright Program itself.

To me, and to many of the several hundred individuals whose opinions and experiences I recorded in a study of officials and alumni of the Senior Fulbright Program in East Asia and the Pacific in the early 1970s, few instruments of American foreign policy have better served their specified goals. Time after time, those interviewed in Australia, Indonesia, Japan, Korea, Malaysia, New Zealand, The Philippines, Singapore, Taiwan, and Thailand told me how great had been their educational sojourns under Fulbright auspices. Their enthusiasm was echoed by hundreds of Americans who had crossed the Pacific to teach or conduct research as guests of one or another binational commission.

In many ways, my own experiences as a Fulbrighter in England in 1964–65, and in Japan and Australia six years later, were not entirely unique. Others reported feeling much of what I had felt, gaining what I had gained, and having had to confront many similar problems. Still, like each of them, I had many personal encounters that were very special. One of the first occurred during my year in the United Kingdom.

Being particularly concerned with racial and ethnic relations, I was most eager to get a sense of what was going on in Britain in the early 1960s, a time when the number of non-White Commonwealth immigrants was increasing at a rapid rate. (In the decade of 1952–62 the country had seen a rise from roughly 50,000 to over 1 million persons of West Indian, African, and East Asian background.) The invitation to teach at Leicester—and the supporting Fulbright award—made it possible to begin to carry out some comparative research.

In addition to duties in the Department of Sociology, I spent time observing the activities of various groups in the area and took part in numerous discussions with members of two newly formed civil rights organizations. I also got involved in a sit-in in a local pub where a Black friend had been denied service. While risking the danger of moving from being a nonparticipant observer to a nonobserving participant and of losing my passport, I was able to get a firsthand sense of the mounting tensions in a nation that, unlike the United States, was not even paying lip service to the notion of cultural pluralism. Nor, it seemed, was it taking its own professed egalitarian ethos too seriously either. (The United Kingdom is one of those places where everybody, not just the sociologists, is preoccupied with social stratification—and talks about it constantly.)

Owing to my "speciality" (as the British called it) or perhaps my notoriety after my protest at the pub had made the local headlines, I began to be asked for my professional assessment of the local racial situation. I demurred for several months but finally agreed to offer some offhand impressions and comparisons of their situation and our own at a special conference on minorities in Britain. A statement about how ill-prepared I felt the British were for dealing with what anyone could see was a mounting threat of serious racial conflict appeared, more or less verbatim, in many of the national newspapers the following day. But the way the various columns were headed made a world of difference.

Some of the papers played it straight. Some seemed to approve ("American Professor Tells What We Don't Want to Hear"). Some were outraged that I was "meddling" in their affairs. Some, including the pseudonymous columnist Peter Simple, headed their pieces with phrases like "Malcolm X and Peter Rose Should Go Back to Where They Came From." (Malcolm had spoken at Oxford a few days before my appearance at the conference.)

Several weeks later I was invited to be interviewed on the BBC's nightly news regarding the disruption of Martin Luther King's Selma March which had just occurred. I agreed and went to a Nottingham studio to be interviewed, remote, from London. Five minutes into our part of the program, Magnus Magnuson, the extraordinarily skilled and canny interviewer, shifted the subject and asked me about what I had actually said at the race relations symposium. I was dumbfounded but replied as accurately as I could, expanding on my thoughts as he continued to probe. These remarks generated letters of support, additional calls for me to go home, and further involvement in the problem there. It also led to a number of meetings with social scientists and community leaders, connections which were to prove invaluable in the years ahead when I would come back to monitor the racial situation as it did, indeed, grow more ugly and complex.

Perhaps as much as opening a new, if related, area of research interest, that first long stint abroad whetted my appetite for more foreign adventures, more foreign involvements, and more comparative work. In the late 1960s I spent brief periods in Israel, Greece, and Italy, as a guest of the Hebrew University, Pierce College, and the University of Naples' Department of Agricultural Economics and Rural Sociology, respectively.

Sometime in the early winter of 1970 I received an invitation to go to Australia as a Distinguished Fulbright Visitor to attend and speak at the Australia–New Zealand American Studies Association meetings in Melbourne and to stay on to deliver a series of lectures at the Flinders University of South Australia in Adelaide on the occasion of the inauguration of the first American Studies Department in the Southern Hemisphere. I was delighted to accept and agreed to stay on for their winter term, offering a seminar in comparative race relations (in which I would deal with both the United States and the United Kingdom and would try to get students to tell me something of the problems in their country, notorious for its "White Australia" policy).

Shortly after signing on to go "Down Under," another invitation arrived from the CIES. I was asked whether I could leave for Australia six weeks earlier to go first to Japan to become a lecturer at the American Studies Summer Seminar in Kyoto, a program in which the U.S. Educational Commission for Japan (Fulbright) had long been and was still involved. Needless to say, I was pleased when I found it could be arranged. In July 1970, my wife, children, and I left on our first trans-Pacific odyssey. The Japanese part of what turned out to be a six-nation tour was especially interesting for many reasons. Two stand out most vividly in my mind.

Not only did we have a chance to see another culture and work with an extremely lively group of colleagues and students (who were also college teachers themselves), but I was able to get their views on many areas of particular concern to me, not least on the nature of "dominant-minority" relations in Japan. That year the seminar offered four courses simultaneously: one on American literature; one on Southern history; one on econometrics; and my own, on ethnicity in America. My subject proved to be interesting to many, especially since they were quite familiar with the fact that the United States was a "Nation of Nations" (they had all read *Leaves of Grass*) and rife with racial tensions as well (they were avid readers of the daily press). Ethnicity itself, however, was a concept that was difficult for most to grasp, or "feel." Their society was entirely homogeneous, or so they claimed, even when pressed about their own minorities—the Ainu, the Koreans, and the "Eta" or Buraku-min.

The last group, an occupational caste that is neither racially nor culturally distinctive but is treated as if it were both, was particularly fascinating to me and I decided to learn more about it. With the assistance of a student, who in his regular work was an assistant professor of English in Nagasaki and who had taken the unprecedented step of marrying a Buraku woman, I met and interviewed several of the leaders of one of the three protest groups in the area, the Kyoto Branch of the Buraku Emancipation Movement. Intrigued by what I learned from these individuals and others with whom they put me in touch, I made plans to study the rhetoric of their civil rights struggle compared to our own.

A year after returning from the Asian-Pacific trip I applied for Fulbright support to do this on my next leave. I got through the American screening but did not make it past the Japanese members of the binational board in Tokyo. I was told it was simply too sensitive a subject. I was very disappointed but pleased that at least I had made contact with an important segment of what George De Vos once called "Japan's invisible race." (Incidentally, the little I did manage to learn about their political rhetoric was strikingly similar to that which we knew in the American civil rights movement. Over and over, in response to my query about the most important thing leaders must say to their people, I heard the echo of Martin Luther King's own words. "Hold your head up," they would say. "That's what we tell them, hold your head up.")

In addition to the rare opportunity to obtain some firsthand knowledge of the Buraku-min and to make some important and lasting acquaintances through the intervention of my student, there was another serendipitous encounter. Along with those of us on the teaching staff of the Kyoto seminar, several special guests were in attendance. One of these was a man much admired as the "dean" of American studies in Europe, the Norwegian scholar and poet Sigmund Skard. One evening with him and I could see why. He was (and remains) a most knowledgeable and perceptive student of American society as well as his own.

Within a few days we became fast friends. We spent many free hours sightseeing together, visiting the shrines of Kyoto and Nara, attending the Expo in Osaka, comparing impressions, and getting into lengthy discussions on topics quite far removed from either of our immediate concerns. Skard, who had spent the war years in exile working for the OSS in Washington, was especially intrigued by my wife's experiences in Holland during the same period. Years later he would publish several poems about her, relating how she had lived the life of Anne Frank and survived to see her children grow up in a very different environment. One of his poems describes an incident on a southern beach in Australia where, it turned out, Skard was also heading to attend the ANZASA conference.

In a move to truly internationalize my lecture series at Flinders, he was invited to fly from Melbourne to Adelaide to introduce me. He stayed on with us for several days. When I took him to the airport and said I hoped to see him sometime soon, he smiled and said, "You will. Next summer." (True to his word, I soon received an official invitation to give a short course at the Nordic Association for American Studies meetings in Sweden in July 1971 and a personal invitation to spend time in Norway beforehand. We spent six weeks there that summer where close ties were established with social scientists and those in "Americanistics" at the universities in Oslo and Bergen, places to which I have returned on numerous occasions.)

The Australian "winter" (August-October) proved to be another turning point. Not only did I thoroughly enjoy meeting many Australians interested in the study of American society, but a number who were helpful in introducing me to their own and to its social problems, including those relating to the aboriginal population and the new immigrants from Greece and Italy. Moreover, a meeting in Canberra with the American cultural attaché, Leonard Robuck, eventually led to a series of lecture tours of Asia and the Pacific over the next few years. They proved to be fortunate in more ways than one.

Many of those I first met on visits to countries in the area—when I went out as a Fulbrighter and later as a "STAG" (Short-term American Grantee)—were extremely helpful in the evaluation research I was soon to do for the Board of Foreign Scholars in the Cultural Section of the Department of State. Some of those who were my hosts at various universities where I went to lecture in various Asian countries and in New Zealand as well as Australia turned up in the samples of former Fulbrighters selected to be interviewed for the study.

I have been back to Australia five times since my term at Flinders and have maintained close ties with many of those I met on that first trip. Most recently, I have been in touch with colleagues there who are conducting research somewhat parallel to my own current work on the resettlement and acculturation of Indo-Chinese refugees. (While the United States has received far more refugees from Southeast Asia than any other nation by a factor of ten, Canada and Australia have taken in a larger percentage on a per capita basis.)

The Fulbright study itself was quite different from anything I had done before. Field work on the other side of the Pacific took place not in the field but mostly in offices that looked strikingly like my own, regardless of the site of the interview. But then, most of those spoken or, better stated, listened to were university professors or administrators. While most were quite eager to describe their experiences as Fulbrighters in America, to help me tell *their* stories, their willingness to criticize even when prodded was, in the lingo of the sociologist, "culturally specific." The Japanese alumni were generally most reluctant to say anything negative; the Australians had no such inhibitions.

Fortunately, these proclivities were detected during a reconnaissance trip to the area to set up the project, meet the executive directors and various members of their boards, and conduct some pilot interviews. When I returned again I had modified the approach somewhat. Those interviewed were not asked to tell me what was good about the program and what they did not like but how, if *they* were asked to serve on a commission of evaluation, they would improve the program. The shift in emphasis seemed to work and even the Japanese were quite forthcoming. A number had very pointed suggestions—particularly related to helping overcome language problems and the implicit loss of status "when no longer seen as professors"—which neatly veiled the criticisms I was after. The views of the alumni interviewed in Asia, Australia, and New Zealand together with those of Americans who had spent time as Fulbrighters in their parts of the world were reported in *Academic Sojourners* and in a summary published in the journal *Exchange* in the Fall of 1976.

Among the recommendations passed on to the CIES and the Board of Foreign Scholars were suggestions that more use be made of former grantees in preparing those going abroad and as hosts for those coming to their countries; that recent alumni in particular be used as advisory members of committees at all levels of Fulbright operations, from the selection committees to the binational boards; that the roles and expectations of the various "agents of exchange" be clarified and common orientations adopted; that all programs should maintain a flexible, relatively open system, one in which the humanitites, social sciences, and sciences be balanced with a certain percentage (20-40) of budget grants set aside for special fields; that all Senior Fulbrighters from abroad should be provided with air tickets from their homebase to the farthest coast of the continental United States regardless of their institution of affiliation; and that a new category of short-term Academic Consultant be added to those of Senior Researcher and University Lecturer for grantees going abroad or coming to the United States. The report concluded with this statement:

> Whatever suggestions have been made are based on the conclusive evidence that this program, at least that aspect of it that concerns binational activities for senior scholars in East Asia and the Pacific, has satisfied the original objectives of helping to create mutual understanding and enhance the exchange of educational information. It has long been a model of bilateral programming. Whatever policy changes are made should serve to adapt the program to changing academic needs and to expand its function as an important instrument of cultural diplomacy.

All told, the Fulbright Program has been a critical vehicle for expanding personal horizons and furthering professional goals, and, at least for me, a significant catalyst for the kind of peripatetic existence I have been living since 1963.

In recent years my research on refugee relief and resettlement has afforded the opportunity to combine continuing concerns with problems of discrimination and international relations. I am "on the road" as much as ever, though there are differences in the way I have been operating. While I do spend some more time interviewing in offices—places like Washington, Geneva, Vienna, Jerusalem, and Bangkok—I also am often in the far less attractive environs of overcrowded camps and processing centers abroad and housing projects and welfare offices here. In such places I find many who have done a hitch or two in the Peace Corps or were VISTA volunteers, and some who were IIE students or Senior Scholars, who, through the support of the Fulbright Program, have come to know and appreciate the ways of those who drink from other cups of life which they, like me, have had the opportunity to savor.

PART III
ON PERSONAL GROWTH

Introduction

While some of the Fulbright experience can be seen in terms of developing understanding across cultural boundaries, such understandings are often translated into personal and professional growth. Andrew Gordon tells of his attempts to teach American literature to students in Spain and Portugal and the adaptations he had to make. He includes a record, in letter form, of the results.

Marga Rose-Hancock and John Hancock focus on communication and their growing abilities at a particularly crucial period of their lives to look beyond words as the primary conveyer of meaning. Their Fulbright experience in Japan provided discontinuity which allowed them to explore new ways of comprehending their lives.

In a different vein, Otto Larsen reflects on his Fulbright experience in the development of his own sense of ethnic identity. Taken from a larger discussion presented first at the Pacific Northwest Danish Cultural Conference in 1979, Larsen starts with his childhood in Junction City, Oregon, and his struggle to find out "how much of me was Danish and how much American."

In the next two selections in this section, Albert Wilhelm points out that one of the important by-products of his Fulbright in Poland was to begin to know his own country better and the significance of the writings of William Faulkner in communicating the American experience around the world. Ray Marshall, who served as U.S. secretary of labor from 1977-81, relates how his experience in Finland provided him with access to segments of decision makers that would have been impossible in the United States. However, he was also educated about the works of William Faulkner, as self-defense against the questioning of interested Finns. So the Fulbright experience provides many opportunities for learning, many opportunistic, but some to protect our self-images.

Personal growth can be both liberating and threatening. As Mary Lee Field suggests, learning a new language and a new culture gives you double vision. And her initial Fulbright experience has pushed her to extend that experience in learning Greek, on to French, Japanese, and Chinese, underscoring her learning to be open to change. Jay and Julia Gurian found that Turkey pushed their understandings of the requirements for a democratic society and the potential role of the military in moving toward a stable society. No longer would they make glib assumptions about how democratic goals might best be achieved and no longer would they assume there is only one way to jump to a conclusion.

9

‛Let a Thousand Fulbrights Bloom

Andrew Gordon

In the spring of 1974, while I was serving as a Fulbright Junior Lecturer in American Literature at the universities of Barcelona and Valencia, I went on a lecture tour and spoke one afternoon at a provincial Spanish university on the subject of the absurd in recent American novels. After I had finished talking for forty-five minutes about Ken Kesey, John Barth, Joseph Heller, Kurt Vonnegut, Thomas Pynchon, Philip Roth, and Norman Mailer, I asked if there were questions from the audience. There were. The Spanish students in the large auditorium were eager to learn more about *Love Story, Jonathan Livingston Seagull,* and the latest Harold Robbins. It was suddenly brought home to me with great clarity that, for most of the world, such works constitute American literature. And it occurred to me that it might take ten thousand Fulbright lecturers laboring around the globe to undo the damage caused by one Harold Robbins novel. But I was young and undaunted. Why not, I thought in my missionary zeal, let a thousand Fulbrights bloom? I am older now and more easily daunted, yet the proposal still strikes me as a not immodest one.

Through the Fulbright Program we try to disseminate the best of American culture, helping to a certain degree to correct partial or distorted images of America abroad fostered by our exported mass culture (music, movies, television programs, and best-selling fiction). But more than any specific subject matter we teach, it is our living presence in the classroom which conveys real images of America to students around the world. Let me relate an anecdote about what happened to me in June 1979 as a Junior Lecturer in American Literature at the Universidade do Porto in Portugal.

The American Studies Program within the Department of English and German was begun at Porto by Professor Carlos Azevedo after the Portuguese revolution of April 25, 1974, so that when I was there it was only a few years old and the library and other facilities still small. For the more than a hundred students jammed into an overcrowded classroom, I was the first American teacher they had ever had; for some, the first American they had ever met. It was certainly the first time they had had a teacher who demanded they speak only English in the class and write all exams and papers in English.

So we started slowly, and over five months I nursed them through Ralph Ellison's *Invisible Man,* Saul Bellow's *The Victim,* Jack Kerouac's *On the Road,* Ken Kesey's *One Flew Over the Cuckoo's Nest*, and a batch of contemporary American short stories. We studied the works chapter by chapter, and I prepared lengthy glossaries explaining all the slang. In the process, as they learned about twentieth-century American history, politics, culture, and literature, I learned more of their language and culture, and of the ways in which America and Portugal are distinct and different and the ways in which we are surprisingly alike.

I came to class the last day, my bags already packed into the car, prepared to give the usual final lecture summing everything up. To my delight, I found that the students had prepared a farewell surprise party, complete with a cake, an inscribed plaque, and a letter. I was touched by this gesture of warm hospitality of a kind rarely encountered in an American university setting.

But most of all, the letter the whole class signed provided the true summing up of the course, for it proved that they had absorbed contemporary American literature and made it a part of them. Here is that letter; the parts that may seem at first a bit obscure are all paraphrases or parodies of the novels we read:

One Flew Over the Faculty

He was the spirit of the U.S.A. sitting right in front of us. He was simply a youth tremendously excited with the books, and we began to learn with him as much as he probably learned from us. This man discovered something to make the classes live forever, and we want to say that we owe him something.

Andrew is a calm man with a face that sometimes makes you think you've seen him in the faculty, like it is a face too intelligent to be just another American in Portugal. It was drizzling and mysterious at the beginning of classes, but we were all delighted, we all realized we were leaving confusion and nonsense behind and performing our one and noble function of the time: literature. And we "literatured" . . . We flashed past *Invisible Man.* It burned in our brains, all the way to the short stories, then *The Victim,* later *On the Road,* and finally landing in a *Cuckoo's Nest.* But why? Why? The students' good, of course. Everything done here is for the students' good.

We suppose sometimes a man has to plunge outside Portugal. In this way he becomes invisible to us. But in Portugal, when the sun goes down and we sit on the Old Douro river pier, we think of Dr. Andrew Gordon, we even think of old Andy, the American teacher we found once.

And who knows but that on the lower frequencies, we'll meet you again?

Porto 7-6-79

10

Zen Berlitz

Marga Rose-Hancock and *John Hancock*

Communication across cultural borders is a specialized activity. Its practice requires particular skills and sensitivities of all who would or must engage in it, and its accomplishment brings unique rewards. However, cross-cultural communication is by no means restricted to specialists, despite Edward T. Hall. In fact, everyone does it all the time, and its benefits may be widely shared and applied. It takes many forms, not all of them recognizable to linguists. The Fulbright experience is all tied up with these facts, and the success or failure of the experience can best be measured by the extent to which the grantee, the grantee family, and individuals in the host country register the communication between themselves: the true value of exchange.

Most of our communication in Japan had the feature that it was as rich in meaning as it was poor in its linguistic form and received exactness. That is to say that our speaking and listening skills in the language of our host country were rudimentary, to say the least. Although we would not wish to defend or encourage such ignorance, it is true that it gave the opportunity to appreciate and practice the art of extraverbal communication.

Not to know the language is a particular blessing, only at first perhaps disguised, for people whose usual work—teaching, writing, and academic administration in our cases—is so connected with and dependent on exactness and quantity in reading, speaking, and writing. In fact, since we were almost immediately comfortable with Tokyo as a city, wandering where we could not understand the language was not only not threatening but actively pleasurable, and we experienced a kind of relief at not having to overhear the concern of others.

It soon became clear, however, that we would need some means for acquiring and transmitting more complex concepts than directions to the department stores, as we thirsted for experience and explanation and companionship. Of course many Japanese people speak English, and colleagues were oftentimes as fluent as we or more so. However, sometimes no amount of simultaneous translation or encyclopedic explanation conveys the situation adequately. Other means take over then.

An extraordinary experience for us, beginning early in our stay, was our relationship with the nearly octagenarian landlady of our Tokyo house. We were guided through the rental arrangements by the extremely competent staff of the U.S. Educational Commission/Japan, but from then on we were on our own with this lady and her husband, a retired chemistry professor. Since the rented house was but a few feet from their residence, and since she took an active interest in our affairs, the relation was close.

From the first day, she spoke to us in rapid-fire Japanese, effectively unmoderated for our untutored ears. We in turn at first made vain motions with our dictionaries and our language-tape pleasantries, trying hard to be fastidious in our understanding; but this proved impossible. Somehow she persisted undismayed, so that finally in hysterical desperation, we began talking back to her in English, of which she knew not a word, mixing it only moderately with pantomime and with our mispronounced and grammatically poor Japanese. This sounds like Babel—and yet, and yet: that was the mode we struck on and stayed with, enjoying each other for hours on end, getting to know each other via this most odd means. During our months in Japan we had hundreds of cups of tea in each other's houses and in museums and shops, many meals, frequent shopping and other trips around town, and even a two-day trip to Kyoto, with this—yes—close friend, ostensibly without a common language.

This is not "The Miracle of Kita-Shinagawa," but rather a demonstration that there is much relation that has nothing to do with words, and that major sensory, intellectual, and emotional as well as factual content is transmitted nonverbally. The phenomenon may often be observed in long-married couples or close family members, but it is also potentially present—and perhaps even more accessible—in those of greatly dissimilar backgrounds, as this vignette illustrates.

In some ways, communication which takes place across language and culture may more readily transcend expectations and the defensive aspects of routine than those in which there is an apparently common background, or language in the extended sense. Over borders, the parties must locate, choose, and establish a common ground, since none is ready-made; and this they do via a mutual process, which prepares a cooperative background for what is to come. Although our purpose here is not to define the phenomenon or to write a primer for this special communication, we do know that the necessary conditions for its occurrence include foremost the mutual willingness to let it happen. Parties to the exchange must—at least initially—be willing to lower their thresholds, relaxing the requirement for objective accuracy; and, with grace, lower the expectation to display and be shown perfect "politeness" or conformance with culture-specific codes of conduct. These are marvelous freedoms to be given and to give in any human transaction, and their gift is basic to excellence in understanding.

There is, of course, much to be said for thorough prior study of the land, culture, and language to be partaken of as a visitor; and certainly industry and informed courtesy in observing local customs and taboos may be appreciated and will produce significant command of a cross-cultural experience. The "exchange value" of this approach is of a different quality, however, from that of the relatively unstudied but willingly exploratory and experiential participant. It is very much the advantage of the Fulbright Program that it facilitates both these approaches, and that intercultural communication on the large scale is enhanced by experiences along the full range of this spectrum, of grantee scholars, teachers, and families.

A mixture of formal cultural study with spontaneous experiential insight might enrich both. For example, this Fulbrighter taught American urban studies topics (in English) to undergraduate students at the University of Tokyo—truly excellent students, conscientious and thoughtful seminar participants at East Asia's foremost university. Learning together about the ways groups live and work together in society—Japanese or American— took a leap forward in one class session, taught jointly by the grantee and his wife, in which we focused on women's roles. Part of the presentation was the singing of a traditional American women's lament regarding the "hard fortunes of all womenkind." Somehow this had the effect of loosening up the students, who responded with unusual animation, and swiftly and in most un-Japanese fashion began to take strongly opposing viewpoints among themselves, lining up men versus women. They related their own intensely felt personal experiences and views, all listening carefully to one another and with each class member's making a contribution to the discussion. Several things were clear: that some of the men in the class were unaccustomedly considering some social and emotional phenomena as they might be seen from the perspective of women (in a sense, cross-gender phenomena may be cross-cultural in kind); that for these students to be speaking in a language other than their own permitted some relaxation of usual inhibitions; and that all of us were absorbing quantities of information about each other and the meaning of our institutions. The means for this was, at least in part, the unusual communicative device of song, which in Japan as in many cultures has tremendous socializing impact, and can transmit and evoke meaning in an inexact but direct and illuminating way.

In some ways, all transactions between humans have an intercultural quality. This fact "came home" to us in the Fulbright year in Tokyo, which also happened to be our honeymoon year. Although we had believed we knew each other well and were no strangers to each other's beliefs and principles, moods, and quirks, we found ourselves in constant discovery of the "cultural" differences between us, over daily features of a newly-joined life: the manner in which we were to treat each other and others; the assignment and performance of various domestic duties; the time, status, and priorities accorded specific items and activities—as each of us might be certain that this thing or that is *always* to be done by families in this way or that. These differences were not necessarily arguments, just previously unrecognized prejudices in ourselves and in each other that were now thrown into relief as we began to formulate and form a new set of common values to serve as the basis of our life together.

So too in Japan it was the quotidian experience, the dealing with the routine minutiae of shelter, food, getting around town and country and so on, that most confronted—and fortunately, also most delighted—us with the illustration of the Japanese way and its differences from what is done in the United States. To give a homely example: At the grocer's, all meats were prepared for sale without bones—frustrating for cooks used to stock-making, baking, and slow simmering. It was quickly apparent that bonelessness in meat is not merely a commercial quirk but is part of a larger philosophy of food preparation and consumption favoring simplicity and naturalness in food as it is seen and eaten, and demanding absolute freshness unconcealed by heavy spicing or the chemical changes of lengthy cooking. This in turn was part of a national reverence for natural phenomena in all forms, a preference for that which most simply expresses connection to the earth. A growing appreciation for the "meaning" of boneless meat did much to offset the occasional homesick longing for all-day chili or roast stuffed turkey.

Our adjustment to Japan and to our life together was assisted by the very lack of the familiar. The pressure was off to assert or simulate previous patterns, so that we had more degrees of freedom to develop new ones. At the same time, the prospect of the rewards to be won from managing to gain a view across the borders between us two and also into the culture around us was enticing. In both instances, the effort to loosen preconception in favor of immediate experience, to lower the threshold of habit in favor of new choices, and to learn and teach from whatever and by whatever means we could, produced excellent results.

The permeating value of these experiences has been renewed attentiveness and sensitivity to, patience with, and respect for the differing "customs" and languages of those with whom we come into contact. We may be more careful not to assume commonality in approach from those we meet. This may come out in as simple a way as giving a person who comes to the office a longer time to visit—or to express by other means the purpose and meaning of the visit, instead of hurrying in with comments and conclusions before the situation is well laid out. At home, it may mean delaying reactions to each other's "odd ideas" and expectations, prolonging and relishing some increased sensitivity to cultural resonances of human interactions.

Perhaps most valuable is having evidence from this Fulbright experience that there are many languages for communication, of which only a fraction are learned in school or are even rational or conscious. Transmission and comprehension via these modes are active in all of us at all times, and can transcend momentary frustrations with apparently meager formal tools. The potential for using this range of communication skills can be enhanced by awareness of its existence, knowing that all of us are in constant communication with each other about ourselves and our customs, at home and abroad.

11

The Evolution of an Ethnic Identity

Otto N. Larsen

I left Oregon at the age of eighteen to attend Grand View College in Des Moines, Iowa. In my mental baggage was the concept of "Danishness." Grand View did not alter this conception, but it did reinforce and enrich its structure and implication.

It could hardly have been otherwise. Most students of 1940-42 came from Danish immigrant enclaves. Many of their parents, as was the case for me, had attended Grand View a generation earlier. Some of the great teachers knew both generations. Lasting positive sentiments emerge from such bonds. And the bonds extended even further when students married other Grand View students of Danish heritage—as was the happy case for me as well as for two of my brothers. A picture of a perpetual ethnic inbreeding machine somehow arises from such facts.

At Grand View it was not long before we recognized that there were at least two kinds of Danish-Americans with quite different emphases from their heritage: (1) We were happy, folk-dancing Danes who could smoke and drink beer and frolic with songs and games while (2) our cousins at Dana College in Blair, Nebraska, were the somber, pietistic Danes whose lifestyle was guided by other traditions and values. Both these schools were founded by Danish-American immigrants, but the cultural stream divided before the turn of the century over differences in interpreting church doctrine.

The "Danishness" of the little world of Grand View was not shattered by such revelations. Nor did it falter as inquiry revealed a rich Danish-American experience for non-Lutherans, such as the Mormons, and for a considerable body of Danish-Americans who were outside the orbit of church life altogether.

Denmark and the Question of a Changing Heritage

After Grand View, a couple of other colleges, and World War II, I came to the University of Washington to shape my career as a sociologist. That institution is very hospitable to things Scandinavian. Indeed, the only subject matter specifically mandated for its curriculum by the state constitution is Scandinavian Studies.

From the very start of my long association with the university, I was not permitted to overlook that fact. In 1946, when I first appeared as a student, an advisor named O'Brien took one look at my name and sent me to the Scandinavian Department to study Danish literature. Although I was fascinated by the works of Holberg, Drachman, Georg Brandes, and others, social science became my major interest and my career.

Sociologists study organizations; they rarely join them. This inclination was reinforced by my commitment to Marxism. Let me hasten to add that I am a lifelong follower of Groucho, not Karl. It was Groucho Marx who said, "I refuse to join any organization that allows people like me to become a member."

For a long time I used that philosophy to avoid becoming a member of almost everything, including the Danish church in Seattle and the Danish Brotherhood. Despite this tactic, I could not mask my ethnic identity or my joy in associating with our own kind. As a result, two good things happened: (1) I was married to Greta Petersen and (2) we went to Denmark for a year in 1960.

This was Greta's third trip to Denmark, but it was my first. Now at last, at age thirty-eight, I was "going home," ethnically speaking. The circumstances involved conditions of privilege that contrasted markedly with those that had attended my parents when they came the other way more than a half century earlier. I was to be a Fulbright Professor at the University of Copenhagen.

This was a momentous experience, a jarring confrontation with the question of ethnic identity. I was Danish, wasn't I? After all, I knew some songs and dances, and even some literary phrases, most of which I discovered that the real Danes had not heard or seen for years. For them, my "Danishness" had the fascination of an occasional trip to an anthropological museum.

Thus, as a Danish-American seeks a heritage, two questions loom large at the outset: Are we relating primarily to a romantic past or does a heritage change as the culture changes? Further, what do we do if we find that we do not treasure the values of contemporary Denmark as much as those from an earlier era?

I did like the Denmark of 1960 very much, at least for the first six months. Many of the things I had thought of as Danish (including how well they spoke the language) were happily confirmed. There was order, wit and humor, and fastidious neatness. There was coziness, trust, and pride in workmanship. And there certainly was meticulous attention to food, not to mention drink.

We thoroughly enjoyed the generosity of our university hosts and my wife's relatives. We were also impressed by the courtesy and helpfulness of public officials from mailmen to cabinet ministers. However, the aloofness of neighbors was not in accord with the expectations of hospitality generated by the Danish-American experience. In the two towns north of Copenhagen where we lived, neighbors guarded their privacy intently.

Gradually, other gaps between expectations and experience began to appear. These afforded personal reflections that were novel at the time. I was visiting Denmark but I was also discovering America. Maybe I was more American than I thought. When Danes attacked things in America, even those persons and conditions that I had often criticized, I became defensive and even tried to turn the argument around. I began to judge Danish society from the perspective of American values and standards. Ethnocentrism of the American variety had invaded the evolution of my ethnic identity.

Ethnicity versus Ethnocentrism

Ethnocentrism finds expression in many ways in every society, even in ways that are deemed minor and may be benign. When a Dane says that salads are for rabbits or Americans and that the only decent vegetable is a potato, he is exhibiting an ethnocentric attitude. So, too, is an American when he says that Danish is not a language, but an impediment of speech; or when he says that any currency other than the dollar is "play money."

Ethnocentrism does not encourage mutual understanding or tolerance. It tends to foster a feeling of superiority on the part of members of a group as they judge nonmembers. Since every culture encourages ethnocentrism, this raises a critical question about the pursuit of a heritage: Can we be ethnic without being ethnocentric?

I am uncertain about the answer. I think we can if we allow others the legitimacy we accord ourselves in the pursuit and promotion of a heritage. But it will probably take more than that if we are going to have a world that is safe for diversity. To combat ethnocentrism and yet hold on to our ethnicity, we may have to develop an appreciation of ethnicities beyond our own. However, it is not easy to be a cultural relativist, as any of us senses as we begin moving about the world.

In the second half of our year in Denmark, the American in me became alternately bored and impatient with much of the Danish scene. Variety seemed lacking. Towns looked alike, and every bakery had the same set of items and flavors. Everything was so *hyggelig* and appeared so homogeneous and bland.

In 1960, there did not seem to be any issues in Denmark, except for the price of beer and the choice of a vacation site. The church was neutralized, the radical parties were conservative, and other institutions bearing on change seemed cautious and content. The spirit of moderation prevailed. Had the Danes not read their own Søren Kierkegaard? He spent his life assailing the spirit of moderation. For him, mediation and compromise were abhorrent. We should make choices, not seek syntheses. Existence was a matter of either/or, not a matter of both/and.

Like an American bulldozer, my thoughts pushed across the quiet Danish scene. I was restless because Danish society did not seem to be moving and leading and because I was addicted to the American style of competition and its politics of confrontation. I was irritated by the constant reference to Denmark's small size when it came to its voice in large policies on the world scene. With initiative, I felt that Denmark could provide new models for human relations as they had in the past with cooperatives and folk schools. I was appalled at the waste of their major national resource. Less than 1 percent of the young people of the relevant age categories were pursuing higher education (a situation markedly changed since 1960).

At this point, then, the American part of me led me to perceive Denmark as bland if not dull, content if not listless, apologetic if not apathetic, and all to the point where I wished the king would decree a day a week to encourage the open expression of something bold, new, diverse, and dynamic.

Denmark, the Subtle Society

Was Denmark really as I had perceived it, or were such views simply naive, wrong, and arrogant? A chance event led me to redefine the situation. It rocked me out of my American ethnocentrism, and once again posted a positive prospect for ethnicity without ethnocentrism. The event sensitized me to the necessity of looking at Danish society and culture through Danish, not American, or even Danish-American, eyes. This meant a shift in scale and in quality of concern of an order implied in a move to a Danish nightingale from an American bulldozer.

In fact, the nightingale was involved in this transformation of perspective. There was a party, with much food and drink. It grew very late. Finally, the Danish host said, "Shouldn't we go out for a walk in the woods and listen to the nightingale?" At first, I thought that the aquavit had affected him. But the Danes were serious. The dark woods beckoned. And, lo, we heard the wondrous sounds of the nightingale.

Thereafter, I sensed that the Danes were masters of perceiving, creating, and appreciating delicate but discernible differences. It is expressed in their humor, their art, their homes, crafts, engineering, flower arrangements, food, and in every facet of their lives. Efficiency and utility, yes, but delicacy and beauty in style and design even more so.

I was startled by how much variety there was in the society. It was not bland at all. I had just been looking at it from an American scale. From then on, I began to experience Denmark as something other than a homogeneous welfare state. I began to see it as the subtle society where just noticeable differences made all the difference in the quality of life. My ethnocentric blinders had been removed. Seeing Denmark through Danish eyes produced many new revelations. Let me conclude with a summary one.

An American might be disposed to look for large redeeming social values or blunt moral lessons in the stories of Isak Dinesen (Karen Blixen). If so, there would be disappointment. Her stories might even be deemed frivolous, or perverse propaganda in favor of the aristocracy. But take a Danish look at her book entitled *Carnival: Entertainments and Posthumous Tales*, released by the University of Chicago Press in 1977. Read the story "The Ghost Horses." It is really not a ghost story but a story of substituted values, an exercise in the subtle expression of aesthetics. For the two children in the story, a cache of jewelry has value not in economic terms, but because the different pieces are stand-ins for the horses and carriages in a coronation procession. The assembly of this procession makes a dazzling and charming picture, but the story as a whole, slight as it is, also serves as an example of Dinesen's special Danish treatment of values.

Not only are esthetic considerations, as here, more important than monetary ones; in general, aesthetic considerations take precedence over moral ones. For this great Danish writer, and I think for Denmark generally, aesthetics are a moral consideration. That helped me to sense and appreciate many just noticeable differences. The centrality of aesthetic considerations says more about Denmark, and perhaps our heritage, than any other single observation. But given my questioning stance, I will keep looking at Denmark, and our heritage, through Danish eyes, Danish-American eyes, and through American eyes. I invite you to do the same. The triangular vision from three cultural vistas will surely yield a heritage worthy of preservation and promotion.

12

Reminiscences about Finland

Ray Marshall

My first exposure to a Finn was Professor Bruno Suviranta, who was a visiting professor at the University of Mississippi in 1954-55, where I was an assistant professor fresh from graduate school at the University of California at Berkeley. Until then, about the only thing I knew about Finland was that they paid their debts. However, Professor Suviranta himself and his discussions of Finnish economic problems made me want to know more about that fascinating country with democratic institutions and a long border with the Soviet Union. I also wanted to broaden my educational experience by spending some time in another country.

My next exposure to Finns was on the six-day trip aboard the *Kungsholm* in August 1955, after being selected as a Fulbright research professor. This was a relaxing and delightful experience because there were a number of Finnish passengers who were willing to help me learn Finnish and tell me more about Finnish institutions. I had some Finnish grammar books and an English-Finnish dictionary, but the closest I could come to finding a Finnish-speaking person at the University of Mississippi was a Latvian, which I later learned is not very close. Most of these Finnish passengers had spent some years in the United States, so they could help me contrast Finnish and American institutions. It is too bad that air travel has largely replaced ocean voyages, since the latter do a lot to help people learn about each other in an informal and relaxed atmosphere. After arriving in Helsinki, my pace became much more hectic as I tried to learn as much Finnish as possible through an organized class at the University of Helsinki (and constantly pestering Finnish friends, who helped me all they could— probably to overcome my abuse of their language). I eventually got comfortable with Finnish, although it would be inaccurate to say I had learned it. However, on my first trip back to Finland in 1977, I was surprised at how fast the language came back, especially understanding people when they talked. Although not much Finnish is spoken in Mississippi, Louisiana, and Texas, where I lived most of the time after returning from Finland, I never regretted the hard work to learn as much of the language as I did. Understanding something of the language made it possible for me to have a better understanding of Sibelius. In addition, my relationships with Finns seemed to be strengthened because I made the effort to try to learn the language.

My greatest recollections of Finland came from my efforts to understand their political and economic institutions. As a labor economist concerned with human resource development, Finland strengthened my faith in democratic institutions, as well as my conviction that the real source of national prosperity, stability, and viability is in the character, knowledge, and skills of a country's people. I also developed a strong appreciation for the value of international comparisons as a way to isolate principles applicable to many countries from those unique causal relationships based on the history, culture, and institutions of particular countries.

Because it is a relatively small and isolated country, Finland provided an exciting and unique opportunity for an economist to study problems in microcosm. I was particularly interested in how a democratic society with few natural economic resources had nevertheless maintained its national autonomy and character despite conflicting influences from a predominantly West European culture and close proximity to the Soviet Union. Moreover, despite few resources, the Finns had managed to achieve a higher standard of living than its physical resource base would suggest. My conclusion was that Finland's strength was in the education and training of its people and in democratic institutions like cooperatives, trade unions, private enterprises, as well as in a political system that protected the interests of different groups while maintaining national unity. I was sufficiently impressed with the value of cooperatives as a way to simultaneously develop physical and human resources that I later helped develop a cooperative movement for low-income people—mainly Blacks—in the rural South.

My Finnish experience not only provided insights into the value of democratic institutions, but also demonstrated the importance of a country's culture and history as a source of national pride, identification, and unity. This unity is not automatic nor is it always harmonious—it requires leadership by various factions to remind people that the things they have in common are more important than those that divide them.

Finland provided a young American professor access to a higher level of decision makers—past and present—than would have been possible in the United States. In part this was because of the high status of professors in Finland. As one of my Finnish colleagues once put it, as compared with their American counterparts, Finnish professors had half the income and twice the prestige. For whatever reason, the level and continuity of access with decision makers and scholars provided a rare insight into Finland's political, social, and economic institutions and processes. I was particularly interested in how Finland attempted to maintain price stability and relatively full employment through a mix of free market forces and public-private and cooperative mechanisms. How to maintain price stability, full employment, and free institutions continues to be the key domestic economic problem of democratic societies. We still have not solved the problem, but my study of Finnish institutions strengthened my understanding of the uses and limitations of various approaches to conflict resolution, consensus building, and economic policy. Moreover, the subsequent experience of other countries shows the value of investing in human resources. Indeed, there is almost an inverse relationship between the economic performance of countries and their natural resources, as the Japanese experience in the 1960s and 1970s illustrates.

I also learned a lot about the United States in Finland. In part, this is because studying foreign institutions naturally forces comparisons with those in one's own country. But my understanding of the United States was also strengthened by the need to explain our institutions to the Finns, who were full of questions about America, where many Finns had relatives. I therefore was asked many questions and invited to lecture on a variety of subjects besides economics. Since I was from Oxford, Mississippi, the home of William Faulkner, I often was asked to discuss Faulkner's works. Since I knew William Faulkner better than I did his writing, I read many of Faulkner's works for the first time in Finland—mainly to avoid being embarrassed by Finns who knew more about his writing than I did.

I also learned to appreciate the unique quality of Finnish humor. For example, in my effort to immerse myself in Finnish customs, I learned to ski a little and tried to become an expert on the sauna, neither of which had much meaning for a Mississippian. However, I approached both undertakings with considerable determination and apprehension, a fact that was probably very clear to my Finnish friends and tutors. When I asked the Finn who was trying to teach me to ski if it hurt to fall, he said, "No, it doesn't hurt to fall, but it does hurt when you hit the ground." My greatest apprehension was over the sauna, to which my wife and I ultimately became addicted. But on my first experience in a very hot sauna, on the top shelf and with no cold water or birch leaves, it became clear to me after about fifteen minutes that I probably could not walk if I tried. I asked my Finnish host, with what undoubtedly was at least a touch of panic in my voice, "Say, has anyone ever died in the sauna?" He responded gravely and calmly, "No, not for the record. They always have made it to the door!"

Like most Americans who have spent much time in Finland, I formed an identification with Finns and follow events in that country with great interest. I was therefore very pleased that when I was secretary of labor, the Finnish ambassador, Jaakko Iloniemi, frequently included me in his activities in Washington, and Finns would tell people that I was the first Finnish-speaking cabinet officer in U.S. history. While it is an exaggeration to say that I speak Finnish, I nevertheless am proud to be identified with Finland. I even bristle when Americans who know very little about Finland speak of Finlandization in a pejorative manner. From my perspective, the world could benefit from more Finlands—though my experience assures me that there will never be another country like it.

13

The Shortest Way Home

Albert E. Wilhelm

From its genesis in 1946 the Fulbright Program has attempted to extend national horizons—to increase mutual understanding by allowing American scholars to study and teach abroad and scholars from other countries to pursue similar activities in the United States. Now, forty years and over 150,000 awards later, no one could seriously question the value of such an ideal or the efficacy of the Fulbright grants in promoting it. If my experience has been typical, Fulbright grants also produce an important by-product. While serving in Poland as a Fulbright lecturer on American literature, I learned much about Poland, Slavic culture, and about Eastern Europe in general. Equally important, I began to know my own country better. As the Fulbright experience broadened my awareness of another culture, it also intensified my understanding of my own.

Even though I went to Poland as an "expert" on American literature, I soon discovered that the experience of teaching familiar texts in a foreign culture could frequently provide new insights into my own specialty. Repeatedly, my understanding of American literature was greatly enriched by observing how various works were perceived by my Polish students and colleagues. At times, I even felt like the naked emperor in the fairy tale when my students pointed out striking truths previously obscured by my own ethnocentrism.

In one class I was laboring to clarify the differences between New England or Yankee humor and Southwestern or Frontier humor. I had emphasized the quiet, understated craftiness of the Yankee comic type as opposed to the flamboyant physical exploits of the backwoodsman. Unfortunately, the examples I offered to clarify these generalizations fell flat. My class knew little of Davy Crockett or Mike Fink and even less about such Yankee prototypes as Jack Downing. At this point, one helpful student offered as an alternative example a comic character who had become well known in Poland because of the importation of a popular television series from the

119

United States. This student aptly suggested that the detective Columbo with his bedraggled raincoat, sad basset hound, and dilapidated automobile had much in common with the traditional Yankee comic figure. By hiding his investigative brilliance behind a façade of bumbling ineptitude, Columbo could prevail over his foes through guile if not through brute strength. Picking up on this analogy, other students proposed additional contemporary examples of the two basic comic types. One student saw in the cartoon character Road Runner (again a television import) the same persistence and craftiness displayed by the traditional Yankee, while another argued that Popeye was a latter-day embodiment of the frontier superhero. Perceptions such as these are in themselves hardly earthshaking, and perhaps they might have been made by a comparable class of American students. My point, though, is that my Polish students helped me to see much more acutely the continuity of American comic traditions and provided me with some examples that I continue to use effectively in American classrooms.

One major American writer whose works my Polish students and colleagues taught me to appreciate more fully was William Faulkner. Although none of Faulkner's works were published in Poland before 1957, he became immensely popular there during the next two decades. By 1979 Polish publishers had issued almost 1,500,000 copies of his books—far more than for any other American writer during that period.[1] As a Fulbright lecturer I was at first surprised by this intense interest in such a difficult foreign writer. Given the complexity of Faulkner's language and narrative style, I wondered also why so many of my students had chosen his works as the subjects of their M.A. theses. I knew, of course, something about Faulkner's "Polish connection"—his acknowledgement that the Polish novelist Henryk Sienkiewicz was the source of much of his youthful inspiration to be a writer. During my early weeks in Poland, however, this knowledge was little more than an isolated bit of information from a remote graduate school lecture; instead of providing an answer to the riddle, it merely increased my bewilderment. As I continued to talk with my students and gradually learned more about Polish history, I began to understand better both Faulkner's debt to Sienkiewicz and the widespread Polish affinity for Faulkner. In short, I began to see obvious parallels between the history and culture of Poland and those of the American South. Later, when I came across a perceptive comment by Malcolm Cowley, I was much better equipped to understand its significance. Cowley wrote: "The life of the Polish gentry—with their habit of command, their fierce pride, their chivalric illusions, and their estates on the edge of a wilderness—bore an inescapable resemblance to the life of Mississippi planters before the Civil War. Among Sienkiewicz's heroes, it would be Pan Michael, 'the little knight' who was the bravest swordsman in Poland, with whom Faulkner could most easily identify himself." Thus, through teaching Faulkner in an intensely proud but frequently defeated European country, I gained new perspectives on his treatment of a proud but defeated region of the United States. After a year as a Fulbrighter in Poland, my rereading of Faulkner is inevitably filled with echoes. Now when I read such works as *Light in August* and *Absalom, Absalom!* I seem to hear their powerful themes resonate across the plains of Central Europe through the tragic centuries of Polish history.

These brief examples of relearning American literature through teaching it in Poland can clarify to some extent the nature of my Fulbright experience, but they can reveal little about its scope. To be sure, incidental insights like the ones described here were a tiny segment of the total experience—an experience whose diversity this short essay cannot begin to describe. The important point is that my education as a Fulbrighter was both extensive and intensive. As my knowledge of another culture expanded, my perceptions of my own became more concentrated. Perhaps a brief remark by Stephen Dedalus near the end of Joyce's *A Portrait of the Artist as a Young Man* might serve as an appropriate commentary on my experience. When asked why he was going away from Ireland, Stephen responded tersely that "the shortest way to Tara was *via* Holyhead." In other words, one must frequently leave his own country so that he may truly find his way home again.

Note

1. For this data I am indebted to Dr. Franciszek Lyra, professor in the Institute of English Philology at Marie Curie Sklodowska University, Lublin, Poland, and author of several works on Faulkner.

14

The Importance of Context: Turkey

Jay Gurian and *Julia Gurian*

As American studies (Jay) and public health (Julia) specialists, we learned invaluable lessons during our Fulbright year in Turkey (1982-83) about the need to examine worldview and historical and institutional contexts before judging national cultures outside our own frame of reference. Like most Americans, we pictured Turkey sprawling in the dark behind a backdrop curtain for Greece. A movie, *Midnight Express*, had dramatized brutality in Turkish prisons. We had heard about the ferocity of the Turkish soldier. We knew that intrigue-filled Istanbul was the terminus for the Orient Express. In terms of national interest, we also knew that Turkey, with its long Soviet border and sovereignty over the Bosphorus, was a strategically important NATO bastion.

But our careers had often centered on human rights and civil liberties concerns. How could we cope with the other "facts" that we began to learn about Turkey after the Fulbright offer arrived? (1) Martial law had been in effect since a coup on September 12, 1980 in which the military had overthrown the elected civilian government. (2) Gun-wielding extremists on both Left and Right had been killing up to thirty-five persons a day. (3) The military had admitted to Amnesty International that political prisoners were being tortured in Turkish jails. (Incidentally and typically, the military later reported back to AI that offending officers were being prosecuted.) (4) The media were censored. (5) All political parties had been banned. (6) All trade unions had been dissolved. (7) After trial, several hundred political prisoners had been executed while others still awaited their fate.

We accepted the lectureship with some very judgemental and biased attitudes toward both the military government and the political process. Shortly after arrival, we began to learn that the artistic establishment was heavily monitored and that university faculty were subject to summary dismissal without benefits for pre-1980 "political activism" as defined by the ruling National Security Council, and were subject to involuntary removal from home campus to outlying, less developed sites on the basis of a lottery.

The details of Turkish political life *seemed* to fit neatly into our preconceptions of totalitarian dictatorship. Yet as anthropologist Clifford Geertz warns us in *The Politics of Meaning,* "the main temptation to be resisted [in making political judgements] is jumping to conclusions and the main defense against it is explicitly to trace out the sociological links between cultural themes and political developments" (from *The Interpretation of Cultures*). The political structure of a society is created by the interaction of its cultural content with its historical past. We must explore the variables shaping a *relevant* context against which to measure our preconceptions. In the case of Turkey, the four most important of these appeared to us to be worldview, Ottoman history, the idea of the military, and Ataturk himself. These were so totally interwoven that they would have to be understood as one.

Mustafa Kemal, later known as Ataturk, was surely among the most dedicated and gifted of world leaders in this century. He rose through the military to become a general in the Ottoman armies, defeated the Allied invaders at Gallipoli, rebelled against the dismemberment of Ottoman Turkey after defeat in World War I, declared a maverick republic on pure guts, set up a countergovernment in Ankara (then a village in central Anatolia), defeated the Allies and Greeks on Turkish soil with a ragtag loyalist army, then proceeded both to Westernize *and* ethnically to Turkify politics, culture, the economy, the language, the educational system, and agriculture. Through devotion, energy, brilliant tactics, and sheer charisma he hauled the remnants of a decayed order into the twentieth century. He always used his power for the people, was studiously *not* corrupt, and today is nearly deified—with just cause—by a grateful posterity. His likenesses and aphorisms are everywhere. Though ruthless when he felt the good of the republic was at stake, he venerated Western liberal traditions, among them human rights. His insistence up till the day he died (in 1938) on human rights met with a great deal of reactionary opposition.

Our sociopolitical worldview is firmly grounded in those same human rights. Ever since Ataturk had declared the republic in 1919, there had been a series of democratic constitutions guaranteeing extensive freedoms along Western lines. For example, Article 14 of the Constitution of 1961 banned state torture; Article 19 called for freedom of conscience and religious choice; Article 22 guaranteed freedom of the press; Article 47 provided for collective bargaining and the right to strike, and so on. Within a year of the 1960 military takeover, while this very constitution was being written, the ban against political parties was lifted. Eleven parties were formed. But as earlier and in the years to follow, the proliferation of parties was accompanied by a tendency for the tactics of those on the Left and Right to become increasingly extreme: Arms would be used for what should have been electoral goals.

In American society, political movement tends to be centripetal; yesterday's radical goal is often embodied in tomorrow's Capitol Hill legislation. In Turkey, politics tend to be centrifugal so that, ironically, the democratic process exaggerates differences among factions. For one thing, profound ethnic rivalries often express themselves violently, as an extension of honor. Despite Ataturk's revolutionary aims and the earnest attempts of most of his followers to live up to them, Turkey cannot escape the influence of a 600-year history of intrigues and corruption that characterized the Ottoman Empire, long known as "the sick man of Europe." Not only was Istanbul (then Constantinople) the capital of that far-flung empire, but as the seat of the Sultanate-Caliphate it was also the secular-political and spiritual-political center of Islam. As "The Defender of the Faith" the caliphate was hereditary, political though not spiritual successor to Mohammed. Sacred to Islam is the doctrine of *jihad*, or holy war, which honors violence in the name of Islamic goals. Deeply embedded in the worldview of the people, this kind of political-religious "call" therefore has carried over into the arena of daily politics.

In 1924, Ataturk forced a bill through the National Assembly officially abolishing the caliphate as, previously, the sultanate. He was determined to secularize the republic. But traditions such as *jihad* die slowly, whether they are formally practiced as in today's Iran or only provide a value and behavior tendency, as with rightist Turkish parties pushing Islamic fundamentalism, or parties on the Left pushing radical collectivism.

Given all this, we were not surprised to learn that during the middle and late 1970s, cadres of lesser educated unemployed youths combined with some students were taking over university classes and forcing other students to swear party allegiance at gunpoint; that party groups were dividing neighborhoods in the cities into "camps" with no-man's-land areas into which civilians moved at risk of life and limb. By September 1980, Parliament was at a total standstill, for eight months unable to form a coalition that could elect a president. The government was paralyzed. Earlier, inflation had peaked at 135 percent; essential goods were scarce. The streets were unsafe at all hours. Both Turkish and foreign commentators generally agreed that the country was on the verge of an all-out civil war.

Given the anarchic effects of this centrifugal tendency, we had to ask ourselves a serious question *in the Turkish context*: Can it be morally correct in any society to suspend freedoms when the survival object is the nation itself?

We soon began to realize that the key to answering this question was the military. It was the only force able to stop the centrifugal process and was regarded with respect, not with fear. Almost everyone at all levels trusts its intentions even while they may criticize specific tactics. From villages to campuses, the people we knew were amused and disturbed by the Western tendency to assume that the Turkish military was corrupt, power-mad, and dangerous.

As we explored these new contexts, we were able to understand the thrust of the National Security Council's strategy during the time we were there for returning Turkey to democracy. First, Kenan Evren, chairman of the NSC, was elected president on a secret ballot by 90 percent of the people—as the only candidate. From the American perspective, this had to be paternalism and authoritarianism of the most blatant kind. But from inside Turkey's worldview and historical reality, honoring a figurative extension of the family nationwide was an exercise in rational social politics.

Working with a rump assembly, Kenan Pasha and the NSC put together a plan for the establishment of new political parties, banning all previous parties and all previous party politicians. Relations with NATO, the Council of Europe, and the governments of Western Europe have been strained because of such "undemocratic practices." As parties declared themselves, the NSC scrutinized them, banning all but three that were basically centrist.

No doubt there were injustices in this process. Some of the NSC's decisions baffled and angered people we knew. But again, the context: By approving only three fairly middle-of-the-road parties, the NSC was trying to reverse the centrifugal tendencies of the past. When elections took place late in 1983, a fine was ordered against any eligible voter who failed to show up at the polls. Again, from our perspective, this was a violation of the democratic ethos. But Turkey is mainly rural; has a gradually rising literacy rate. There is a tendency to think in terms of doctrinal extremes and a history of local feudalism and blood feud. Within this context, the penalty should be regarded as rational, even liberal, because its intent was to reform popular habits rooted in past anti-democratic traditions.

In terms of national character, we found Turks to be down-to-earth, very open, "real," practical, and patient. We were not surprised that when the people voted for their Parliament, they chose the party *not* supported by the National Security Council, whose choice came in third. Though not to his liking, Kenan Pasha honored the result. Having carefully guided the founding of parties, he could in good conscience allow the option he least desired. As he had said in dozens of speeches while we were there, *this* time the military was going more slowly so as to ensure that it would never have to intervene again.

Does our experience suggest that death squads, coups d'état, systematic political torture, and "disappearances" should be condoned or at least ignored because, after all, every country has its own context? Of course not. We continue to believe in irreducible human rights whose codification since the Renaissance has advanced the human condition. But the contexts of life in Turkey caused us to redefine our assumptions about the relationship of civil liberties to military rule. We realized that both in idea and action, a military was possible which bore little resemblance to those of Latin America.

Gradually, we also realized that we intellectually had rejected simplistic views defining social and political order as if every society should operate from a long-standing tradition of democratic practices in a politically stable environment. But that on some deeper level, we had completely "shut out" the possibility of a healthy relationship between a military government and a civilian population. Our Fulbright year in Turkey gave us an understanding of the complexities of the issue for other societies that we could not have comprehended without this *in vivo* experience.

15

"That Thing"

Mary Lee Field

She was young, about twenty-five, country-raised, and totally ignorant of other cultures. She spoke only English, with a Midwestern accent at that. Still, she applied for a Fulbright. It seemed challenging; it provided the opportunity to travel, to live in another culture, to teach in a new setting. She did not know what it would mean. In March she got the official notification that she had been selected as a Fulbright teacher in a special program which would place native speakers of English in high-school classrooms with Greek teachers of English. Ecstatic, she called home. Then she learned that the experience was more significant and threatening than she had anticipated—overhearing her mother turn away from the phone and call to her father—"It's Mary Lee. She got . . . that . . . that . . . she got that Thing."

What kind of "Thing" was it? Her first trip out of America, her first immersion in another language, her first chance to teach English to speakers of another language. It was a "Thing" which shaped her life, influenced her career, changed her way of thinking. Those results did not occur immediately, but elements from that experience continue to influence the stages of her life.

Learning the language was her first hurdle. With considerable foresight and planning, the Fulbright Commission in Greece had arranged for language training for the new crop of Fulbrighters that year. From the second day they were in Athens, all of them attended four hours of class in the morning, worked with the tape machines in the afternoon, and spent the rest of the day trying to find opportunities to speak Greek. The training went on for two full weeks, even longer for those who were staying in Athens. The group began to break up at that point, and the formal orientation was over. She was not particularly good at the language and felt awkward and shy about speaking so poorly. But the rewards for even simple exchanges with the people around her were stunning. Actually to communicate in another language gave her a thrill unlike anything else she had known. Still, most Greeks in Athens wanted to speak English with her, so she could not practice as much as she wanted.

She left Athens, flew to Thessaloniki, and began searching for an apartment. There the few sentences of Greek that she knew were much more useful, and she was away from the constant reassuring help of the Fulbright office. The staff of the USIS office was generous and kind, but they were busy with other problems. The manager of her apartment did not know one word of English, and somehow she had to communicate with him. It seemed that a cleaning woman was part of the apartment arrangement; a woman who had worked for years there with each tenant, and she would continue to work for this American tenant. But she did not know a word of English either. The pressure to learn Greek was greater, but so were the opportunities.

The adjustment to a new language went on for the whole year. Her coteacher coached her during their free hour at school every other day; on alternate days she helped the coteacher with English structures or specific problems. Greek newscasts on the radio were hard to understand, but there were no current English newspapers in Thessaloniki, so it was important to understand as much as possible. She traveled, alone, during the Christmas and New Year's vacation. Days went by when she did not speak English to anyone. During the Easter break she traveled again, daring to rent a car and drive through the Peloponnesus for more than a week. When she turned in the car in Patras and went to a restaurant, she realized that the people next to her were speaking English. Moreover, she realized that she had been able to cope with daily communication and simple conversations for some time in Greek.

Being finally able to communicate led to conversations with people, simple ones, but still disturbing. It was 1965-66. The colonels would bring off their successful coup just eight months later. The Greeks were upset by the violence and the force of the demonstrations which were occurring throughout the country. The day before she arrived in Athens there had been tear gas bombs thrown outside her own hotel windows. People said to her that the American CIA was involved in supporting the demonstrations. She was aghast and protested that the American CIA could *never* engage in such activities. She warmly defended her government, proclaimed the openness and fairness of the CIA, and assured everyone that the American system would never interfere with Greek political structures. During the late sixties and the seventies, as the role of the CIA became clearer to the public, she cringed and blushed remembering the conversations she had had with Greeks only a few years before. Those uninformed protests, perhaps more than anything else, caused her to reexamine her own country and to doubt the knowledge she had about it. The Fulbright experience had given her a new perspective on her own country because she had to look at it more closely, question it more carefully.

That double perspective, that ability to see from more than one side, was both liberating and threatening. It set her free from past notions and allowed new interpretations; it also challenged the political and moral truths which her Midwestern and rather conservative background had made real for her. And truths challenged in this situation could be challenged in others. Having once experienced that dual perception, she could never accept the singular without challenging it again.

The metaphors which had shaped her image of the world began to crumble. America as a gentle, moral, helpful giant became also America as a meddling, amoral, sometimes violent presence. The metaphors which shaped her language were also replaced. Like all languages, Greek has its own way of seeing the world, its own way of describing reality. In a subtle way, speaking Greek changed her identity. When she spoke and thought in Greek for long periods, she had a different personality. She thought in different images. She was not going crazy, but she was stunned by the things in Greek which were virtually untranslatable into English, and vice versa. There is no English equivalent of the terms *ya sou*. The use of the familiar was a vital part of her relationships with students and friends. Those differences revealed something about language and understanding which she had never before considered. These new processes began to reinforce each other—the dual vision of knowing two languages, the dual vision of seeing her own country from the inside and from the outside. And there was more.

Teaching English to students in the Girls' High School was also a formative experience. The girls were delighted to have an American for a teacher, but it was difficult to give them the thrill of communicating in a new language when they only met in English class for one or two hours a week. She was frustrated by the different processes involved in learning a language and teaching it, the different skills, focus, and talents each required. She tried to make the process as real and vital for her students as it was for her. There was a methodology to learn, completely different from teaching high-school English to students in America as she had done earlier. The methodology itself was still being shaped; theories still being argued. Acquisition of a second language was then even more an open topic for discussion, and the oral/aural method was at its peak.

These three encounters—learning a language, gaining a new perspective on her own country, and struggling to find the best methods to teach English as a foreign language—shaped her future. She continued her efforts to learn other languages because of the excitement of that first foreign-language learning experience. She repeated the attempt to lose her own identity in the process of learning French, then Japanese, and most recently Chinese. Each time her touchstone was the Fulbright year experience.

Living abroad to experience again the "outsider's" perspective on her own country repeated with variations the Fulbright experience. When her Chinese students asked her why Americans hated and distrusted the Chinese so much after Liberation in 1949, she formed another image of America, quite different from the one of her youth. When the Japanese asked her why the United States did not support the United Nations more vigorously, she questioned again. Each experience in a new culture gave her a new way of seeing, new metaphors, and the desire to continue the exploration of new perspectives.

Her mother's intuitive response to the Fulbright as a "Thing" which would have deep and lasting significance was prophetic. She continued to teach English as a foreign or second language—in Japan, China, and in the United States. Helping others master another language, any language, became vital work because of the possibilities it opened to them. Each teaching assignment, each seminar, each paper or conference since the Fulbright in Greece has been shaped by that experience. Now she uses the works of Lakoff and Johnson, of Ali Mazrui, of popular novelists like Maxine Hong Kingston to provide bridges to better cross-cultural understanding for American students. If there was an imperative in the Fulbright experience, it was to continue to change, to be open to change, to "pass it on."

PART IV
CREATING SOMETHING NEW

Introduction

While all Fulbrighters may hope to have a permanent impact, there are few markers of lasting impressions, except in the testimonies of those who have been affected. There are, however, some instances when Fulbrighters are at the right place at the right time to be of assistance in creating something new. Those instances often are created when a Fulbrighter is on location at a critical stage of development within his host country. Chester Hunt was one of the early Fulbrighters who arrived in the Philippines at a critical period of educational development and found himself an acting chair of a department with the tasks of building a curriculum and hiring faculty.

Few Fulbrighters, however, have had the opportunity to create the impact that the Asantes made in Zimbabwe. In that newly-independent country, this Fulbright couple were able to see clearly the results of their efforts. Kariamu Asante was asked to create the National Dance Company of Zimbabwe and bring it to its first international tour. Molefi Asante was able to work in the new Institute of Mass Communications to help produce journalists and information officers. He became involved in curriculum and in the development of guidelines for the future development of the media in Zimbabwe. Their enthusiasm for these exciting times is well communicated in their essay.

In Harold Allen's case, most of the overt results of his Fulbright experiences developed from his evangelistic concern for teaching English abroad as a second language in spite of cultural barriers and bureaucratic roadblocks. From Egypt, to Iran, to Hungary, to his American homeland, he led in the movement to organize TESOL, for Teachers of English to Speakers of Others Languages, and to disseminate its methods and materials worldwide. From his Egyptian experience, as happens sometimes along the way, he became passionately involved in Middle East politics—a zealous upholder of Arab positions and an anti-Zionist in that region's bitterly divisive discords.

Of course, former Fulbrighters do not restrict their ability to create new forms and structures to other places. Many returned Fulbrighters are deeply involved in those aspects of international life which are evident in most American communities, large and small.

135

16

A Cross-Cultural Saga between the Zambezi and Limpopo

Molefi Kete Asante and *Kariamu Welsh Asante*

Zimbabwe lies in the southern part of Africa, between the Zambezi River on the north and the Limpopo River on the south. After a protracted war for liberation of the territory from the settler government of Ian Smith and the Rhodesian Front, the liberation forces won control of the country in April 1980. After lengthy discussion at Lancaster House in London, elections were proposed for the country. The Zimbabwe African National Union won the majority of seats in parliament and elected Robert Mugabe as prime minister.

We seized the opportunity to seek Fulbrights to the newly-independent Zimbabwean nation because the elected prime minister, Robert Mugabe, Minister of Culture and Education Dr. Mutumbuka, Minister of Telecommunications and Information Dr. Shamuyarira, and Deputy Minister of Community Development and Women's Affairs Dr. Nhiwatiwa made an appeal to us to bring our skills to aid the young nation while we were in Zimbabwe on a personal visit in December 1980. At the time, we did not know precisely how we would return to Zimbabwe but we were convinced that we had to seek a way.

Both of us had achieved considerable recognition within our own respective fields and felt that we would have a chance at the Fulbright. Our plan was to return to Zimbabwe as soon as we could determine the best method of securing a livelihood while there. At first, we thought of sabbaticals. Molefi had already taken a sabbatical to Howard University in 1979-80 and could not possibly get another one so soon. Kariamu had one coming from the Center for Positive Thought where she was the resident artistic director and choreographer for the professional troupe, Kariamu and Company. But could the center afford to lose her for a year?

We both applied for Fulbrights: Molefi in communications and Kariamu in dance. Fortunately, we knew that our fields were in demand in Zimbabwe. Prime Minister Mugabe had told us in December 1980 that he needed someone to take the traditional dancers from the level of village performers to an international level of performance. Furthermore, he had said that the Zimbabwe Institute of Mass Communication would need teachers, advisers, and consultants until it was firmly established as a training institute. These statements were supported and underscored by the two ministers responsible for culture and communication.

The Council Says "Yes"

While we waited to hear from our applications we read all we could find on Zimbabwe. There was not much, but what there was, we consumed. Terry Ranger's history book on Rhodesia; Lawrence Vambe's *From Rhodesia to Zimbabwe*, Samkange's historical novels about the legendary kings of Zimbabwe, and all the materials we could find on the Great Zimbabwe and the Monomotapa kingdom. By the time we heard from the Fulbright applications, we were thoroughly convinced that service in Zimbabwe could be one of the most important things that we could do. The news was electric: We both had been granted Fulbrights! Somehow, we had expected that we would both get awards since we were equally good in our respective fields. Kariamu had been called the Black American choreographer in the direct lineage of Katherine Dunham and Pearl Primus. And Molefi had contributed more to African communication than any of his contemporaries, having produced sixteen African Ph.D.s, some of whom held high posts in their governments. Dr. Naomi Nhiwatiwa, deputy minister of community development and women's affairs, had received her doctorate with him in 1979. We celebrated our selection for the fabled Fulbright Program with dinner at one of Buffalo's famous restaurants. The conversation turned to the things we wanted to teach and the things we wanted to learn in Zimbabwe.

Introduction to USICA-USIA

The director of USICA, which returned to its former name USIA under the Reagan administration, was John Burns, a highly competent and helpful officer. John Burns did not leave a stone unturned or a phone uncalled in an effort to secure for us the most satisfactory situations. His wide knowledge of Zimbabwean culture and politics was useful in our orientation to the exigencies of living in a new society. Kariamu enrolled in Shona classes, the major language, since she would be working directly with people from the villages and rural areas whose English was not fluent. John Burns and his staff put at our disposal all their expertise in getting adjusted, finding a bank, enrolling our son in school, renting an apartment, and learning to drive on the left side of the street. Fortunately for us, we knew Dr. Nhiwatiwa personally and she was always willing to have her driver or staff assist us with practical matters. In little time, we were well situated with an apartment in the Avenues within walking distance of the Ministry of Education and Culture, and with a little more effort, the Zimbabwe Institute of Mass Communication. The price of automobiles was outrageously high; we decided to rent instead.

The Work Begins

The mechanism for the development of a national dance company had not been set up prior to Kariamu's arrival; consequently, there was much work to be done. Most of it she had to do herself since there was no one in the country with the type of choreographic and arts administrative abilities needed to organize a professional company. Rules had to be drawn up for various local competitions of dancers. Contracts had to be written and approval sought from the ministry. A schedule of classes with course descriptions had to be developed. Certificates had to be prepared for those who would eventually take the classes in the *mfundalai* technique of dance. Salary and status of the chosen dancers had to be negotiated with the ministry. Costumes, shoes, shirts, T-shirts, and musical equipment had to be purchased. Kariamu's workdays were cut out for her by powers greater than herself, the power of origin. But there was also passion and joy, excitement and intensity, in the challenge.

In Molefi's case, he entered the Institute of Mass Communication with an office already set up by Mr. Ezekiel Makunike, the director of the institute. Makunike had worked exceptionally hard to establish the guidelines of the institute prior to the arrival of Molefi. Yet much work remained to be done. Immediately, Molefi gave a seminar on theories of communication and then got down to the task of teaching young journalists how to write for the media. He did not have to busy himself with the details of the operation. Kariamu, on the other hand, was burdened from the day she started with the task of outfitting the dancers, choosing the ones to be in the national company, and rehearsing them—all without an office!

Not a Dull Moment

Both of our areas of interest generated lots of intellectual and cultural stimulation; we were inundated with excitement from our students and colleagues. Molefi taught students who planned careers in the media, electronic and print, as well as students who wanted to secure jobs in the foreign service. Most of the students had positions already lined up for them with the civil service or foreign service. There was an enthusiastic effort on the part of the government to obtain positions for the trained communicationists. Since many Whites had left for South Africa or Australia or elsewhere during the transition to African rule, the media institutions needed people.

The Zimbabwe Institute of Mass Communication officially opened on August 14, 1981, although it had been functioning a few months prior to that time with seminars and workshops. As the major training center for journalists and information workers in Zimbabwe, it was highly lauded by the government and places in the classes were extremely competitive. For example, of 2,000 applicants for one class of students, we were only able to accommodate 60. It goes without saying that the country would not have been able to absorb all of those who wanted to be trained as journalists. Yet since the government had announced a progressive policy to place information officers, essentially news gatherers, in each one of the fifty-six districts of the nation, the need was considered significant and urgent by many young people.

Fortunately, Molefi's Fulbright coincided with the official opening of the institute and he was listed as a member of the initial staff. Because of his expertise in communication theories and research, he was asked to work directly with Mr. Makunike in the development of curricula and research plans. In addition, Molefi wrote the first brochure of the institute's services and capabilities. As the year progressed and the staff and director grew more comfortable with Molefi as a special consultant, he was given more responsibility and asked to create a journal of African communication to be housed at the institute. He initiated the writing of a research guide in mass communication which was published by the institute. The director approved the initiative and made it possible for the manual to be published.

The National Dance Company

The National Dance Company came into existence as a child of the Ministry of Education and Culture, but it was a mistreated child, misunderstood by the bureaucrats responsible for giving it life, and maligned by those who thought that a national dance company was frivolous. Kariamu almost single-handedly shaped the by-laws of the organization, set the salary scale, and negotiated for space to rehearse. Mr. S. Matiure, a music teacher, had been hired to assist her in the establishment of the company. He was a valuable aide because of his knowledge of the communities, the dances, and the language. Although Kariamu had studied Shona, she did not speak it fluently and Mr. Matiure would often have to interpret and translate. This was not considered a severe handicap; at any rate, when Kariamu danced the traditional dances, which she learned in two months' time, the dancers knew what she was saying. There is a universal language in movement.

Both Kariamu and Matiure worked directly under the ministry's representative, Mr. Mavengere, who was charged with looking after all institutional culture in the country. His was a large job and the fact that he had been a vernacular novelist did not necessarily mean that he knew anything about dance. Yet he held the purse strings for the company and always needed convincing that the company needed a certain costume or quality of printed program or additional space for rehearsal. During the early days of the competitive trials, Mr. Mavengere was not sure there would be a company. But Kariamu was determined to mold the dancers into a professional company that would be the envy of every other nation. The pace at which she worked was like the pace at which she had worked with her own group, Kariamu and Company, in Buffalo, New York. The Zimbabwean dancers were ready for her; they were used to dancing for three and four hours, sometimes all night long! Finally, the company of twenty-one dancers and seven master teachers was born.

Since it was the purpose of the National Dance Company of Zimbabwe to be a cultural representative of the nation, it had to master the technique of dancing within a certain time frame, entering and exiting the stage, and theatrics. Kariamu took the seven major dances in the repertoire and molded them to fit the proscenium stage. She taught them how to end a dance with a definite signature so that the audience would recognize the end of the dance. All this was achieved before the opening night. By the time the dancers had been outfitted with their various costumes for the different dances, Kariamu was exhausted. Part of her exhaustion came from the fact that she dreamed up the idea of having the National Ballet Company, an all-White company, on the same program. But it was necessary for her to put three dance pieces on the National Ballet Company.

The National Ballet Company had never had a ballet choreographed for it by an African or African-American artist. One or two dancers dropped out after the first two classes, giving excuses such as being sick or their parents' going on vacation. Nevertheless, Kariamu was able to choreograph three pieces for the National Ballet Company and the company danced on the same program with the National Dance Company. Each company demonstrated the versatility and creativity of Kariamu in both the African dance and European dance genre. The audiences loved it; Black and White together, in their different and varied styles, on stage. Kariamu had made history in Zimbabwe. It was the first time that there had been an integrated bow before an integrated audience in Zimbabwe. The success of the opening performance of the two dance companies, each working in the way that they had been trained by Kariamu, brought immediate recognition to her work in Zimbabwe. The government officials who attended the performance gave her and the director of USIA, John Burns, high marks for a job well done.

In the Archives

The days following the debut of the National Dance Company were spent in the National Archives. Molefi went to the archives to look for work on the early newspapers in Zimbabwe and South Africa; Kariamu wanted to find out all she could about the dance of Southern Africa. The archives proved to be richer for Kariamu than for Molefi. There was not much in the archives on the early press in Rhodesia, that is, there was not much information about the relationship of that press to the African population. However, Molefi did find that the characterization of the Africans by the press was derogatory. Crude cartoons appeared almost as soon as the Rhodesian *Herald* was started. They depicted the Africans as savages. None of the materials could help Molefi with his book on the history of the media in Africa as it was developed among Africans. Yet there was a certain color to the historical period that could be gained from reading the early White newspaper.

On the other hand, Kariamu found valuable articles on early dances, reports of cultural activities, and observations of dances by early White missionaries. In addition, she also found photographs of early Shona and Matabele dancers. Many of these dances she recognized from the photographs as early forms of contemporary dances of Zimbabwe.

Fortunately, Mrs. Kamba, the director of the archives, was known by us and she facilitated the work we had to do at the archives. She made accessible to us the various officers who knew where specific pieces of information, films, tapes, and other documents were kept. Since Africans had not been in charge of the archives long, it was necessary for Mrs. Kamba to rely on some of the Whites who had been working at the job for several years. They were helpful and showed no reluctance in helping us to secure the proper information we needed for our work.

As a senior advisor to the Institute of Mass Communication, Molefi was asked to perform two very important roles. The first was to chair the International Press Seminar at the Ranche House College. This seminar brought together a large number of journalists and media specialists from all over Southern Africa. As chair of the seminar and editor of the final proceedings, Molefi had an opportunity to hear the opinions of the leading journalists in that part of Africa. Coming as it did prior to the mid-point in the professorship, the seminar provided lots of information that could be processed in a positive way throughout the remaining portion of the professorship. The second role Molefi was asked to play was as representative of the Institute and Mass Media Trust on the research team that analyzed the role of the media in Zimbabwe. The report written by Molefi and a representative of the Friedrich Naumann Foundation of West Germany was presented to the Ministry of Information and Telecommunications. Mr. Gunther Noack of the Naumann Foundation served as coevaluator of the project, although Molefi was the chief evaluator for the Zimbabwean side.

The First Road Show

When the Commonwealth Games were being planned in Brisbane, a cultural program was also being organized to accompany the sports. Zimbabwe, as a new member of the Commonwealth of Nations, was asked to participate by sending a cultural delegation to demonstrate Zimbabwean culture. Kariamu, as artistic director and choreographer for the National Dance Company, was asked to prepare the dancers to travel to Brisbane, Australia. None of the dancers had ever been outside the country. Many of them were apprehensive about air travel, being away from home, flying over water, and the type of food they could eat in Australia. These were serious concerns that had to be talked through with the dancers. Kariamu immediately began organizing costumes, changes of clothing even for the dancers, shoes, and getting together a small hygiene bag for each dancer. When the day arrived for the dancers to board the plane for Australia, they were ready.

In Brisbane they won the hearts of the crowds for creativity, originality, and vitality. The dancers were superb; they did the famous Jerusarema dance like they had seldom done it at home in Zimbabwe. The audiences loved the dancers and they danced at many venues throughout Queensland.

There is still much more to tell but we hope that we have told enough for others to be inspired by the Fulbright Program. Our tour was exceptional in every way. The country we chose had a lot to offer in terms of human resources, natural beauty, and excitement. We found that we learned as much as we taught; that is the essence of the Fulbright Program anyway. When we returned, we had been enriched and that enrichment could be passed on to our American students. Professionally, we gained immensely by the experience and believe that the support of the Fulbright Program during our stay in the country was remarkable. In no way were we hampered in doing our jobs or in learning about the culture in which we lived for a time; we were aided with books and video tapes for our students.

Intercultural communication, an increasingly significant field of research, is at its most practical level in the give and take of a true intercultural interaction such as is made possible by the Fulbright Awards. We entered the country with limited knowledge of the two predominantly African cultures in the nation and left with a high degree of understanding and appreciation for cultural difference. We enjoyed our tour and look forward to another tour under the program in years to come.

17

Something New for the Philippines

Chester L. Hunt

My Philippine interests are exclusively due to my experience as a Fulbright lecturer, an experience which was largely accidental. Back in 1952, I was anxious to extend my horizon and the Fulbright Program seemed a likely vehicle. The Philippines was about the only place listed on the announcement which welcomed sociologists, hence the application. I was the only applicant, hence the most deserving. My own knowledge of the Philippines was extremely vague. I assumed that since the United States had acquired possession as a consequence of the Spanish-American War, the Philippine nation was probably located somewhere between Hawaii and Cuba. My first action after receiving the award was to call a friend who was a Spanish professor informing him that I was to go the Philippines and therefore must have a crash course to supplement my one semester of high-school Spanish. Fortunately, he was better versed in the world than I and told me to relax, since the early Americans had made English the language of education.

The trip to the Philippines was an adventure in itself since we were required to go by the American president liner, air travel in 1952 being too expensive. (In 1961 we had to travel by air as the ship was too expensive.) This required trip was a three-week voyage spent in complete and lavish luxury only slightly marred by the necessity to sculk off the boat at Manila ignoring the outstretched hands expecting tips I was unable to pay. The voyage itself was a type of orientation since it provided contact with a combination of State Department, military, business, and missionary types, all of whom had international concerns. Needless to say, something has gone out of the Fulbright experience now that we shuttle back and forth in a few hours.

Arriving in Manila, we were met by a contingent of graduate students who told us of their joy that they finally had a bona fide professor of sociology. The faculty who manned the sociology department before the war had disappeared and it had only been revived by a visiting American, John deYoung, who had returned to the United States shortly before my arrival. Consequently, I moved into a rather extraordinary position for a visiting Fulbrighter. I was appointed acting chairman of the combined departments of sociology and social work. The making of a curriculum and the hiring of faculty were very largely in my own hands. Sociologists were so scarce that it was a question of locating them rather than selecting the most competent from a considerable pool.

We were assigned a *sawali* house on the University of the Philippines campus, one of a number which had been built to house American air force officers and which were utilized by faculty after the war. The house was humble in appearance but open to the breeze and seemed to us an ideal adaptation to a tropical climate. Among its other advantages, it was located only two blocks away from the university golf course, which was a source of enjoyment and of Filipino-American contact.

I stayed two years on this Fulbright appointment, and the first year the Hunts were one of only two American families on the University of the Philippines campus. This gave us an extraordinary opportunity to become acquainted with Filipino faculty and students. We found Filipinos quite accepting and lavishly hospitable. This was partially because they labeled me as "a poor American." My Fulbright grant was probably twice the salary of a Filipino professor, but it was only about half the income of most resident Americans. Hence I had the best of both worlds as far as socioeconomic status was concerned.

The family accompanied me and was a major help in adjusting to the country. Mrs. Hunt found that housekeeping in the tropics was a challenge in which the availability of servants counteracted the shortage of modern conveniences. She kept a comfortable home and entertained Filipino friends frequently. My two daughters, aged two and six, formed friends on their own, and thereby brought to us some participation in the life of Filipino families. Since we were eight miles from downtown Manila and had no car, most of our social life took place on the campus with just enough contact with Manila to maintain a degree of balance. We were also there before the advent of television had ruined conversation. By the second year of our stay, the number of campus Americans had been swelled by participants in AID educational programs, but by that time our Filipino contacts had been firmly established.

The Diliman campus of the University of the Philippines was a quiet and comfortable place in which to live, while Manila offered the contrast and excitement of a metropolitan city. Although we had to travel either by bus or in the cars of friends, we did manage to develop a number of Manila acquaintances. Philippine upper-class society at the time was extremely small and academics were at least marginally included. Some of my students came from distinguished families and were anxious to show the American professor around. Their efforts were augmented by government officials and politicians, clergymen, and local Americans. All in all, our acquaintances covered a much wider social spectrum than would have been possible on an American campus.

Our stay in the Philippines was not only a type of tourist experience but also one of intellectual stimulation and activity. There seemed to be so much to be done, so many problems to be investigated, and so few scholars available. Opportunity was wide open. I traveled around the islands from Appari to Jolo, completely fascinated by the variety of scenes to be observed in a limited time. There were mountains and plains, jungles and cities. People included the Chinese, the Indians, and a variety of other resident aliens along with Igorots, Muslims, and sea gypsies. The Christian Filipinos seemed sufficiently like Americans that contact was easy and sufficiently different that their reactions were seldom predictable.

President Quirino illustrated the cosmopolitan nature of the country in a reception at Malacanan for the delegates to the Pacific Science Congress. At the time he was old, worn, in ill health, and undoubtedly aware of the electoral defeat which lay ahead of him, but he spoke with quiet dignity. He told the delegates that he had been reading *The Sea Around Us* by Rachel Carson. It seemed to him that even as the sea had brought to the shore all manner of life, so it had brought to the Philippines all manner of people. The Filipino therefore was a bit of the Malayan and the Chinese together with the Spanish and the American. True Filipino identity lay not in uniqueness of origin but in the manner in which these varied strains had been blended in a common heritage.

Filipinos hoped that sociology might help them to better understand the problems of a developing country and were supportive of efforts to expand instruction and research. I taught ten to twelve hours per semester, administered the department in an undoubtedly autocratic fashion, introduced new courses, hired faculty, selected students to go abroad for graduate training, and participated freely in the total university community. I worked to separate social work from sociology but enjoyed the contacts that our social work contingent made possible and for a while served as advisor to the Social Welfare Administration.

Researchwise, I had the summers free and managed to make a study of ethnic relations in Cotabato, social distance among Filipino students, employer-employee relations in a sugar central, and functional literacy in rural barrios. In addition, I participated in the establishment of the Philippine Sociological Society and the founding of the *Philippine Sociological Review*. I collaborated with department faculty in writing a basic text which is still widely used, in revised form, a third of a century later. I understand now that Filipinos are a sensitive people apt to be critical of meddling foreigners, but fortunately at the time, I was ignorant of this alleged cultural trait and found cordial cooperation as I tried to measure up to the exhausting potentialities of the job.

Finally, at the end of two years, we returned to the United States via another voyage on the president liner. We boarded the *President Cleveland,* kissed friends goodbye, the bands played, the streams of decorations binding the ship to the shore were severed, and we said farewell to the Pearl of the Orient. Since then, we have been at other universities, Silliman and Central Philippines, on subsequent Fulbrights. The first Fulbright was a marvelous experience. The others were even better.

18

My Fulbright Experience

Harold B. Allen

What has the Fulbright experience meant to me? Many of its components, I suspect, can be paralleled in the experience of others who have held
Fulbright grants; yet my particular combination must be unique. Certainly
it is a combination that has profoundly affected what I have done and what
I have come to believe over the past thirty years. First, the combination;
then the overt results; finally, the beliefs. Unable in 1918 to persuade a
recruiting officer that I had more than my obvious fifteen years and rejected as a 4F in 1942, I had not had even a military experience abroad.
Consequently, when in late 1953, the Linguistic Society of America asked
members to apply for a Fulbright lectureship for teaching English in Italy, I
drew for background upon my 1943 summer stint as a phonetician at the
Mills College English Language Institute, swallowed hard, and leaped at
the chance. But once the application was approved, the Fulbright office
called to report that the Italian government had determined not to allow
foreigners to teach in Italian universities. Would I be willing to go to Greece
instead? But of course! Then came a second call, advising that the Greeks
now wanted an American literature specialist, not a linguist. My family's
dream of a year abroad vanished. But then came a third call. Would I serve
with Freeman Twaddell as one of two senior linguists on a six-person team
in Egypt?

Ah, this was something else again. Egypt? What did I know about Egypt?
Joseph, Cleopatra, crocodiles, camels, hieroglyphics, pyramids . . . I asked
for a 24-hour delay before responding and hied myself to the university
library for some intensive reading about modern Egypt. Then I telephoned
Washington and said, "Yes." So in 1954-55, I taught in both the Higher
Institute of Education and the University of Cairo, besides directing the
practice teaching of some students in several secondary schools.

Four years later, in 1958, at the request of the Egyptian Ministry of
Education, I was given a Smith-Mundt grant (the Fulbright program in

149

Egypt was temporarily discontinued) to return for the purpose of working on textbook preparation. This time no culture shock. We felt at home within a few days. But unexpectedly, I found myself again teaching advanced students in the Higher Institute of Education and, in the evening once a week, preparatory-school teachers seeking to upgrade themselves in order to teach English. I also taught for one week in a workshop at the University of Damascus in Syria.

The next Fulbright grant came in 1972, to Hungary (between two assignments to Iran provided by the University of Illinois project, where my job was to set up a Master's program at the University of Tehran). The intervening Fulbright grant in 1972, one of the first awards in Hungary before the signing of the cultural agreement, was for a series of lectures on American English at the Kossuth Lajos University in Debrecen.

That is the sum total of my foreign teaching experience (except for three assignments at the University of Victoria in British Columbia). What were the overt results?

Most of the overt results of the Fulbright experience derived from my developing in Egypt almost a second career with its own evangelistic concern. Central in my academic life was—and is—a love for the English language, with the concomitant urge to do research in it and the desire to help others to appreciate its richness and beauty. I had not sought the first Fulbright grant solely as a diversion or as an opportunity to provide a foreign experience for my wife and two young daughters. I felt that the teaching of English abroad could be an important factor in the growth of understanding and agreement among nations, an instrument for peace. During that first year in Egypt, this feeling became what might almost be termed a missionary zeal.

But my work in the secondary schools in Cairo persuaded me that experimentation and improvement in Egypt was blocked by an inflexible bureaucracy, with its regimented inspectors who rigidly controlled the uniform classroom assignments, methods, and testing throughout the country. Twaddell and I discussed how this roadblock could be removed. Upon our return to the United States, he was able to obtain Rockefeller Foundation fellowships for ten inspectors to obtain the M.A. in linguistics at Brown University. (This should be mentioned as a Fulbright plus, since Twaddell is no longer with us to mention it himself.) A spinoff from that project was that through which nine top teachers came to get the Ph.D. in linguistics— three at Cornell, three at Michigan, and three at Texas. A tenth I brought over to teach for me in the Communication Program I was then directing at the University of Minnesota. He remained here after getting his doctorate and now heads the ESL program in a Western university.

Impressed by what I read and learned about the English-teaching methods of teachers in the British Council, upon my return I put together a collection of both British and American articles on teaching English to form the first anthology bringing together the best from both countries. The first edition, published by McGraw-Hill, was followed by a second, with the cooperation of Russell Campbell of the University of California at Los Angeles.

In the meantime, a more significant involvement with publication had begun when in November 1959 the U.S. Information Agency, prompted immediately by a need for adequate English textbooks for use in Francophone Africa, requested the National Council of Teachers of English to consider a contract for the preparation of series of ESL textbooks for USIA use abroad. It fell to me to join the executive secretary in negotiating a contract (later canceled when shifting political winds altered USIA policy) and choosing and contracting with the publisher, McGraw-Hill International Book Company. I then chaired NCTE's advisory committee in overseeing the preparation of both the first and second editions of the six-book series *English for Today.* As editor for the series, I obtained William R. Slager of the University of Utah, whose own Fulbright experience in Cairo in 1952–54 had led to the formation of the linguistics team in 1954 and with whom I had become acquainted when he was teaching at the American University in Cairo in 1958. More recently, changed circumstances dictated my becoming—with Edward Voeller in Japan—coauthor of what had been intended as a third edition but developed so differently that it is actually a new series, just published by McGraw-Hill as *Pathways to English.*

My Fulbright-engendered concern with English as a second language had a still different outcome because the only organization directly concerned with it was restricted, as a subsidiary group within the National Association of Foreign Student Advisers, to the teaching of English to foreign students. But two major classes of teachers lacked any affiliation, those teaching English abroad and those teaching speakers of other languages in the United States. From an unsuccessful attempt to form a relevant group for them within the National Council of Teachers of English, I went on to join others in setting up a series of national conferences on teaching English as a second language. The third conference, held in New York in 1966, adopted a constitution and transformed itself into a permanent organization, known usually by its acronym, TESOL, for Teachers of English to Speakers of Other Languages, of which I had the honor to become the first president.

But the result of my two sojourns in Iran, through temporarily successful, has now surely succumbed in that nation's tragic upheaval. The organizational framework, including curriculum and needed books, that I had devised for a graduate program to train students as English teachers in colleges and technical institutes was accepted and functioned well under the direction of an Iranian trained in Michigan's English Language Institute. I am afraid now to think of what has happened to her and to the administrative officials who supported the establishment of the program.

Yet another outcome resulted specifically from a trip that Professor Slager and I made from our workshop site in Damascus when we had the opportunity to ride with a diplomatic courier to Beirut. There we learned that the English-teaching personnel in Beirut, in an Agency for International Development project, had no knowledge of what was going on in Egypt or any other Middle Eastern country. Questions in Cairo revealed further that little there was known about English teaching in Jordan or in Iraq, to say nothing of Poland, to which I had been offered a lectureship.

Anticipating a meeting in Washington in March 1961 sponsored by the International Cooperation Administration for an open discussion of a plan for a worldwide program of English-teacher-preparation centers, I obtained the approval of the NCTE executive committee to present a pertinent resolution. The resolution called for the formation of a nongovernmental group to coordinate relevant information on a voluntary basis about the English-teaching activities of various governmental agencies. The resolution was approved and the Center for Applied Linguistics undertook to set up the group, which, known as the National Advisory Council on Teaching English as a Foreign Language, or NACTEFL, met regularly for more than a dozen years with representatives of the Department of State, the Peace Corps, the Department of Defense, the U.S. Office of Education, the Trust Territory, the Bureau of Indian Affairs, the Committee for the International Exchange of Persons (the Fulbright committee), and USIA.

More productive was the short Fulbright stay in Hungary. There I found that as yet there was no awareness of the status of teaching English as a second language as an independent professional discipline calling for special preparation. To help develop such awareness, I initiated with Kossuth Lajos University and the Hungarian Cultural Affairs Institute a project that, with the cooperation of the Department of State and the University of Minnesota, enabled four students to come to Minnesota for the master's degree in TESL. My continuing relationship with them and with other former students in Hungary, three of whom are now teaching at that university, underlay my return visit to Debrecen in September 1983, both to lecture and to help initiate an action that I hope will materialize as an exchange program between Kossuth University and the University of Minnesota at Duluth.

Although perhaps peripheral to this statement, two matters may well be included here. One is that when the Department of Linguistics was established at Minnesota, it was my familiarity with the work of Walter Lehn at the American University in Cairo while I was there that led to my successfully asking him to apply for the chairmanship. The second is that after years of administrative resistance, a new dean and a new vice-president enabled me to set up Minnesota's program in English as a Second Language, a program both for instruction of foreign students and also for preparing future teachers in the master's degree sequence.

It has been requisite, of course, to use the first personal pronoun almost *ad nauseam* in the preceding paragraphs, yet in using it, I hardly feel susceptible to criticism of being on an ego trip. True, I have been active in the creation and recognition of a new discipline in the field of education, with much activity directly resulting from my Fulbright experience. But I cannot help feeling that I have simply been part of an inevitable movement, a powerful development that in a single generation has provided professional purpose and professional goals for teachers who had lacked professional status and an organizational home. I have simply been an instrument for a force produced by the temper of the times.

Another, quite different, commitment resulted from my two grants to Egypt, a slow and painstakingly thorough conversion to a pro-Arab political position. We arrived in Cairo in September 1954, with a typical American ignorance of the Middle East. While on shipboard in the Atlantic we had heard of the arrest of General Naguib and the assumption of power by Abdul Gamal Nasser. We had no knowledge that would help in understanding events like that. We had long been sympathetic with the Jews who had suffered in Europe, but we had no information other than that of the headlines that would have given some insight into the background of the Jewish migration to Palestine and the events leading to the formation of Israel as a political entity. Zionism was something I was quite unaware of.

Gradually in Cairo, I found myself experiencing a sea change. I saw my wife working in a center where clothing was dispensed to Palestinian refugees. I saw a refugee camp near Damascus. I listened to the UN soldiers whom we entertained at dinner while they were in Cairo for R and R from the Gaza Strip. I talked with our neighbor, Commander Elmo Hutchinson, who related to me some of the incidents described in his book, *The Violent Truce,* written after his assignment as military observer with the UN truce supervision team. I learned from an Egyptian general the inside story of how the United States really brought about the Egyptian takeover of the Suez Canal. Upon my return, I became faculty adviser for the Arab-American Club and hence heard many reports of personal tragedies from Palestinian students whose families had suffered from Israeli persecution and from Israel's confiscation of their homes. I began to read all that I could get my hands on about the recent history of the Middle East and particularly of the Zionist movement. I became a full-fledged convert to the Arab cause and found myself sympathetic to the solid base of the PLO, a base ignored or deliberately misrepresented in the American press.

With this position adopted, I could not avoid supporting and joining organizations concerned with the rights of Arab-Americans and with the Arab-Israeli confrontation in Palestine. Nor could I avoid the next step of writing "letters to the editor" and going on to give lectures on the Middle East and to organize programs with speakers on Middle Eastern topics.

With respect to beliefs and attitudes that I hold because of the Fulbright experience, besides my pro-Palestinian position, it is clear that the most productive is that in the value of a professional basis for the need for teaching English as a second language in non-Anglophone countries. I believe, further, that such teaching must include a cultural component if international understanding is to be facilitated.

In Cairo I was frustrated in the writing of the textbook that came to be used throughout Egypt for several years. It was insisted that the setting be Egyptian and that the characters be Egyptian as well, with typical Arab names. Although occasional comparison with British and Irish children was acceptable, I had to write lessons in which, for example, the principal characters are Zeinab and Zuhdy, whose father works in an office in Cairo and goes home at two o'clock to eat and take a nap. Happily, in our just published six-book series *Pathways to English,* Ed Voeller and I were free to expand his focus on English as a medium of international communication and intercultural awareness. The characters are from many countries and cultural differences appear in the various situations.

But although this and other commercial series are now available to meet the insistent and increasing demand in other countries, our own government is correspondingly decreasing its concern with English teaching as a factor in promoting world peace. For a recent address at a TESOL convention, I undertook a study of the decline since the highpoint of concern during the Kennedy and Johnson administrations. While England, despite its financial stringency, has maintained its worldwide English teaching program through the British Council, our own government has relentlessly reduced the number of Fulbright grants for English as a second language and, even more significantly perhaps, has sharply reduced the numbers of ESL personnel in the U.S. Information Agency and the funds available for USIA libraries abroad. The English-teaching officer who arranged for my lecture in Bangkok two years ago lamented that he probably was the last ESL professional in the foreign field. This trend must be reversed. It is better to deploy books and teachers than ballistic missiles.

Another belief stemming from my Fulbright experience is that it is high time for us Americans to cease imposing our values and customs on peoples with differing cultural backgrounds. I was idealistically moved when, years ago, Woodrow Wilson told us to "make the world safe for democracy." I accepted the slogan of the Student Volunteer Movement in the 1920s, "The Evangelization of the World in This Generation." To provide exemplary conduct for voluntary imitation and adoption is one thing; to dictate such adoption and to judge according to the refusal to accept such dictation is quite another.

Surely like many other Fulbrighters, I have come to believe that Americans can no longer justify ignorance about international concern. If we are to elect a responsible Congress and provide our representatives with knowledgeable reactions to international affairs, we ourselves should continually keep abreast of international news. We should encourage the daily press to accord more emphasis to that news and we should also go to other sources than the local press and network television, especially when the press and television fail to offer an unbiased report.

Among other attitudes which, if not engendered by the Fulbright experience have been measurably strengthened by it, I would like to conclude with this: I believe that the first and only sound approach to preventing and removing international disagreement—with Grenada or the USSR—should be in negotiation, formal or informal or both, public or private or both, but certainly face-to-face. Military threats and weapons labeled deterrents are not the way to peace. When national leadership calls for bigger and better weapons, the wrong persons are on the saddle.

For what I have been able to do and for these beliefs, I am profoundly grateful to J. William Fulbright. Even now, I feel that gratitude renewed, as I take up my new assignment to reconstitute and chair the U.S.I.A. Advisory Panel for English Language Teaching.

PART V
TRANSFORMING CAREERS

Introduction

Of course, separating personal growth from the effects of Fulbrights on professional careers is difficult and perhaps unnecessary. For most Fulbrighters, careers and personal growth are part of one complex whole, not easily separable.

For John Blair, his first Fulbright experience at Strasbourg subsequently led to a rather profound change in career direction: a position as Professor of American Literature and Civilization at the University of Geneva in Switzerland. Thus the international perspective is continuously a part of his daily perspective.

James Thorson relates how the interests of Yugoslavs stimulated him to become aware of parts of American literature, on American Indians. In turn, his subsequent increased interest in science fiction led him later to discover a group of Yugoslav writers with few academic connections. So the Fulbright experience provides the base for future discoveries.

19

Directionality in Fulbright Transformations

John G. Blair

It may be rare that a single Fulbright experience totally transforms an entire career; if so, all the more reason that this story should be told. Brains may drain in more than one direction and the results may further international understanding in ways and to extents which no one could have foreseen at the moment of a Fulbright commitment.

My Fulbright Professorship of American Literature at the University of Strasbourg in 1967-68 was the first experience outside the United States for myself, my wife, and our daughter who was five at the time. The year 1968 proved an extraordinary time to be in France but more importantly, the introduction to what has become our life and work for the last sixteen years. Our initial motivations were not unusual: My wife wanted to turn her French major into exploration of the country and preparation for teaching language in the United States, our daughter could learn French taught as a foreign language to Alsatian children, and I set out to teach Emerson and company to university students. Little did I know that their entire intellectual formation would lead them to deny that such a writer deserved serious study. Like everyone who changes cultures for the first time, we were troubled with nostalgia and ambivalence, both of which were reinforced during the strange month of May 1968 when nothing whatsoever worked in France and we remained in contact with the rest of the world only by being close enough to cross into Germany for mail and to listen to armed forces radio, more informative than any other source at the time.

The negative experiences were more than counterbalanced by the riches brought us by France (and the Europe we toured in a VW camperbus): encounter with history as a palpable presence, an unending series of lessons in how to eat, trips tracing back our Western culture in space and time (as far as Crete), family time together in ways that could never have been available in the bustle we called home. Intellectually speaking, looking back on the United States, its life, and literature from the outside yielded an excitement of new insight, a perspective we wanted to reengage as soon as possible on sabbatical leave in 1969-70, which we centered in Paris. I projected a book involving English, French, and German as well as American literary texts. It was finally published in London as *The Confidence Man in Modern Fiction* ten years later, substantially delayed after our temporary residence in Europe became continuous as of September 1970 when I was named Professor of American Literature and Civilization at the University of Geneva in Switzerland.

I describe some of the circumstances for the curiosity of those who might seek out a similar opportunity because this appointment was extraordinary in every way: My new title was even Professeur Extraordinaire for the first two years, taken, alas, in its literal Latin meaning rather than the honorific English sense. Switzerland, unlike its neighbors in Latin Europe, does not require professors to be nationals. Instead, the international city of Geneva was seeking native speakers as professors of the major languages. My knowledge of the opening was by pure chance, emerging through tea in Austria with the subject of my first book, W.H. Auden, and correspondence with his collaborator in translations from Icelandic, Professor Paul Taylor, the first American ever to be named Professor of English in Switzerland. Only local newspapers carried summary announcements of the competition and the bureaucratic barriers were formidable: thirty copies of vita and list of publications, including double copies of major publications—not easy to assemble far from home. (As a measure of the increase in red tape since 1970, fifty copies are now required.) I sent off the necessary packet in December and heard not a word, not even an acknowledgement of receipt, until a sudden phone call in early May 1970 inviting me to lecture in Geneva the following *week* since I was "among the final candidates"! These details underline the chance quality of so many factors—it seems pointless to think of planning such a career just as it is impossible to know in advance how to respond if a genuine offer does finally emerge.

Our choice was essentially to return to a tenured post in the United States or accept an open-ended appointment in Geneva that would extend our Fulbright experience and perspective into a career in itself. One glaring cost would be long-term distance from the country which not only constituted our origins but which would also be the continued focus of professional energy itself. It proved impossible to decline the adventure and that has made all the difference.

For my wife, it meant years of shifting and uncertain activity as a teacher of English as a foreign language with the United Nations, Webster College in Geneva, and after a long credentials battle for partial recognition of her

American doctorate in psychology and women's studies, in the public high schools of Geneva. Coping with local culture, particularly the hierarchical bureaucracy, has not proved easy, though no one could deny that it has been "broadening." Had we not left the United States, she would not likely have written the two books she has published so far: *Meaning in "Star Trek,"* 1978, a psychological analysis of the science fiction series we first saw on sabbatical in 1976, and *Cubal Analysis: A Post-Sexist Model for the Psyche*, 1983, a reworking of her dissertation which extends her experiences in moving to another culture to consciousness-raising games which have emerged in her classroom to help students enter the foreign world of English. Even in the perspective of a second sabbatical leave stateside, there is still no easy way to sort out the negative grating against Genevese culture and the creativity which has stimulated two books and a variety of articles in the several fields of her interest.

For our daughter, the primary difference has been a traditional European education through the end of secondary school. Starting with that first year in Strasbourg, she always went to school "in French," to the extent that we had to work to make sure that she would retain enough English fluency to be genuinely bilingual. At the Collège Calvin in Geneva, the principal public high school, her major subjects were mathematics, French, German, Latin, and Greek, a background which has stood her in good stead through an undergraduate career at Harvard majoring in history and science. If she persists in her present plan of training as a historian of the Middle Ages and the Reformation, those same skills will serve her better than any American high-school program could. Culturally, however, she reports feeling more European than American in a variety of life's dimensions and she still looks forward to returning to Europe over the summers. As a token of her affection, she has qualified as an official tourist guide for Geneva and environs.

For the professor himself, this perpetual Fulbright exposure has generated a profound professional transformation. Hired above all to teach American literature, he discovered the impossibility of seriously carrying out such an assignment without engaging and disengaging the cultural stereotypes and prejudices that students from the host culture brought with them. Step by ineluctable step, that has shifted the emphasis of both his teaching and research in the direction of American studies, that is, the placing of literary and related texts in their total cultural context. And since the immediate audience is European students, the basic enterprise can hardly be other than comparative in approach.

The second audience is composed of European scholars concerned with American literature and civilization. Despite their differing languages and cultures of origin, these students of the United States are also engaged almost inescapably with comparative culture studies. And they are legion—about two thousand according to recent estimates of the European Association for American Studies. The rapid growth of the EAAS attests to its dramatically enhanced capacity for encouraging and organizing serious study of the United States. When the biannual convention was held in Geneva in 1972, less than one hundred scholars attended, whereas the Paris conference of 1982, under the Presidency of Professor Maurice Gonnaud of Lyon, brought together nearly six hundred. With their increasing contact and sophistication, European scholars have perspectives to offer which usefully complement American research or even correct some skewed perspectives that are almost inevitable for Americanists who stay home. A single example must suffice, drawn from a contribution to the Paris conference by Rob Kroes of the University of Amsterdam: Recent European studies of nineteenth-century American immigration see many workers as present-day *gästearbeiter*, namely expecting to return home after a period of time with the capital lacking in the place of origin. American research, out of an easy ethnocentrism, habitually presumed that those who came to the United States did so as converts to the American way of life, not as exiles or temporary workers but as immigrants eager for Americanization. Though the European perspective may also suffer from ethnocentrism, it serves as a useful corrective to native blindspots.

American specialists who have never left home in any serious way constitute an especially important if difficult audience for comparative American culture studies: External perspectives prove indispensable in so many contexts. Attempts to define what is American about America without reference to cultures and ways of life outside the United States are about as likely to succeed as other forms of lifting oneself by one's own bootstraps. The comparative perspective can and increasingly does offer American specialists insights into the larger contexts crucial to understanding American phenomena. While Europe and the United States define one set of comparative relations that is historically indispensable in showing where the United States came from, the logic of comparative culture studies does not stop there. The world of the twentieth-century is genuinely and irreversibly a *world*, so an American studies worthy of our time must broaden its perspective to take in the globe.

Indeed, the whole non-Western world sees as central to its present problems and future hopes that elusive process we call development or modernization, which began with European expansion whenever the Middle Ages can be said to have ended. Obviously, the United States itself comes into existence as part of this world-remolding process. Modernization is hardly a trouble-free concept, but its greatest difficulty as commonly conceived over recent years is that it is so often used in a hermetically Western or simply American perspective. The United States, if not the developed nations as a whole, seem to define the desirable end-point for the process. Developments along other tracks appear deviant, whether they concern economic or less tangible matters. Such ethnocentricity clearly will not do, any more than Buffon's Eurocentric biology could satisfy Thomas Jefferson. When other cultures are devalued by the very conceptual act through which we acknowledge their existence, interdependence as a ground for mutual comprehension and respect can neither be perceived nor affirmed.

De-self-centering the concept of modernization will hardly take the United States out of the core of disputes about this elusive process which proves so difficult to stop or control, let alone describe adequately. The United States will remain crucial and central to globalized American culture studies, but such a reorientation may prove our best chance to make a palpable contribution as academics to the survival potential of our world as well as our nation.

As an example of how Fulbright perspectives may become relevant to those who stay home, I want to dramatize this point by quoting from my remarks to the American Studies Association in Philadelphia in November 1983:

> I applaud the following statement from the Preamble to the 1982 Constitution of the People's Republic of China: "The future of China is closely linked with that of the whole world." Since I too do not believe that the twenty-first century is guaranteed to this planet and its life forms, I believe that mutual tolerance based on understanding and respect offers the best hope for an alternative to the multiplication of more and more destructive weapons all over the world. I think of this project, then, as future-oriented American Studies, or perhaps "futurist history." Since we as a discipline have our specificity in conceptualizing the United States in all its richness and particularity, I believe we can and should do something to further the continuing existence of the world without which our own national continuation is unthinkable.

Over the last sixteen years, the implications of our Fulbright adventure have transformed personal and professional concerns to the point where the international perspective is central in all senses. Thus the spirit of the Fulbright enterprise can result in transformations in all directions.

20

The Fulbright as Beginning

James L. Thorson

The impact of my Fulbright experience on my life is, quite simply, incalculable. When I went to Yugoslavia in the autumn of 1971 to take up a senior lectureship at the University Kiril i Metodij in Skopje, I did not know what to expect, but I did not expect the experience to change my career as radically as it did. While I may never fully understand all the ramifications of the changes, I can unequivocally say that they have been positive.

Despite a great deal of confusion upon arriving in Belgrade without any Serbo-Croatian, we were given an excellent orientation by the binational commission. My wife and I were impressed with the speakers and the other new Fulbrighters. The information we absorbed during the three days was added to the knowledge which we had put together in our own research before leaving the United States and gave us at least some background for living in this unique socialist state. Then it was on to Skopje to begin teaching. Though all the materials had said that we would probably not be entertained in homes much, the people could not have been warmer or more hospitable. We visited in dozens of homes. The warm-hearted welcome which lasted through the year and has persisted through three subsequent visits to Yugoslavia will undoubtedly keep me going back through the rest of my life.

Though it is those personal contacts that have given me part of the impetus to return, there is also a much more hard-headed and professional reason for my continuing interest. I discovered that there was important research to be done, that I was in the right position to do it, and that I could get recognition for doing it.

I enjoyed my teaching in Skopje very much, though I found very quickly that I had grossly overestimated the amount of reading that I could assign with any reasonable expectation that it might get done. I suspect that my experience along these lines has been replicated by hundreds, if not thousands, of Fulbrighters over the past forty years. Nevertheless, with every passing class, I came to realize more and more that my Yugoslav students and colleagues could teach me a great deal about my own country and its literature. Their enthusiasm for American culture, literature, institutions, and material goods was tempered in most cases by a very healthy skepticism about capitalism and the social problems in our country. Their own country shared a number of characteristics with ours, and they were able to see the similarities without chauvinistic distortion but with patriotism nevertheless. Like the United States, Yugoslavia is a federation of different states and contains a wide variety of ethnic groups. During the academic year that I was there, the old tension between the Croats and the Serbs flared into prominence again. Tito was able to bring it under control without much violence, though there were some large demonstrations in Zagreb. The question that everyone asked me when they learned of my Yugoslav experience for the next several years was—"What will happen after Tito?" My answer, then as now, was that the union would stand, that Tito had built into the complex governing mechanism the collective leadership that would continue to move toward his dream of a strong united Yugoslavia that would be in neither the Eastern nor the Western block, but would be a leader in the Third World. That dream may have lost some of its luster with the economic problems which seem to be plaguing the country recently, but it still lives on.

Yugoslavia also shares newness with the United States, and even outdoes us in this category. Though Serbia, Croatia, Slovenia, Macedonia, Bosnia-Herzegovina, and Montenegro boast of long histories, Yugoslavia is a creation of the twentieth century, and the socialist Yugoslavia which exists today only came into being during and after World War II. There was and still is the excitement of building a new system and trying to make it work everywhere in the country, even in some of its most backward areas. I grew up in South Dakota, and I empathized strongly with the pioneer spirit that pervaded the society which I saw developing and particularly with the excitement in the growing universities, with their young and ambitious faculties.

In many ways, I felt that my most important function during the Fulbright year was as a resource to my colleagues on the faculties, primarily at Skopje, where I spent most of my time, but also at Belgrade and Novi Sad, where I gave lectures. In the spring I was fortunate enough to be selected as one of the faculty members for a seminar for teachers of English at Brela on the Adriatic Coast which was sponsored by the Croatian office of foreign language instruction, the American Embassy, and the British Council. Working with those teachers and talking with them about Black literature by Americans was very instructive on both sides of the podium. I had taught James Baldwin's work at Cornell University while I was a graduate student there, and the change in perspective was very enlightening. Though there was little antagonism toward America, and in fact a surprising number of the teachers had visited our country, they were most anxious to learn about race relations in America, and especially about American Indians.

I have always had an interest in American Indians, in part because I grew up with Sioux friends in South Dakota, but had never considered it a field of study until one of my Yugoslav students came to New Mexico to obtain a master's degree and wanting to do her M.A. thesis on American Indian poetry. I studied it with her and found a great deal to admire, not only in the poetry, but also in the prose writers, one of whom, Leslie Silko, had been my student at New Mexico. The point here is that an interest by Yugoslavs stimulated me to study a part of American literature that I had not taken time for before.

During my year on the Fulbright in Skopje, I also took an interest in the criticism which some of my colleagues there were writing on American literature from their own perspective. Unfortunately, most of their contributions were written in Macedonian, and though I gained enough proficiency in that Slavic language to order in restaurants, obtain train tickets, and get the other necessities of life, I could only make the smallest dent in scholarly publications in the language. Fortunately, my colleagues were able to explain to me in English what they were doing, and it sounded interesting. Then, when I visited Novi Sad to give a lecture at the university there, my host, Aleksander Nejgebauer, gave me an article which he had published in English (in *The New Republic*, no less), and I can still recall sitting in a hotel room and thinking "this is really good, and really interesting." During my brief stay in Novi Sad, I was able to use one of the oldest libraries in the country, the Matice Srpska, founded early in the nineteenth century. There I discovered the names of many more of the critics whose work I was later to study and publish.

After my year in Yugoslavia, my wife and I had the good fortune to go on a tour of the Soviet Union with a Yugoslav group and to spend some time in Hungary and Bulgaria. We then realized more than before how free the Yugoslav society was in comparison with those countries. During the next year, when I was on sabbatical in Oxford, I continued to read more about Yugoslavia, though most of my research efforts were on Restoration and eighteenth-century English literature. While working in the Bodleian Library, I discovered more commentaries by Yugoslavs on American and English literary topics that were in English, and I was even more impressed. Oxford had just allowed students of English literature to select one question on American literature on their school examinations, and I was pressed into service as a visiting tutor to help satisfy the demand for tuition in American topics. This additional perspective added to my own understanding of my country's literature.

When I returned to the University of New Mexico in the summer of 1973, I was still excited by my Fulbright experience, and I wrote a paper on American literature in Yugoslavia which I presented at the seminar on American Literature Abroad at the meeting of the Modern Languages Association. I subsequently became cochairman of that seminar for 1974 and again in 1975. Those three seminars further opened my eyes to the widespread interest in the subject of how we could present our literature in a foreign setting.

By the academic year 1974-75, I believed I had done enough spade work to be able to profit from another visit to Yugoslavia, and the Research Allocations Committee of the University of New Mexico was impressed enough with my proposal to pick up the tab for most of a two-month trip to Europe. Most of that period was spent wandering from one Yugoslav university to another, talking to teachers of American literature and writers on American subjects, and gathering an enormous amount of printed material and notes on the various scholars, their interests, and publications.

In 1976-77, I was elected to a Visiting Senior Research Fellowship at Jesus College, Oxford, and spent most of the year working on English literary research, but I was also able to slip in a two-week lecture tour to five Yugoslav universities, where I picked up some new essays, renewed some old and made some new acquaintances, and generally saw the Yugoslav project gel. I was also able to interest Ardis Publishers in the project during that year. Returning again to New Mexico, I was finally able to get almost all of the essays I wanted to include translated into English, and the manuscript of *Yugoslav Perspectives on American Literature* (Ann Arbor, 1980) was completed in the autumn of 1977.

I was in Oxford again when *Perspectives* came out, and my interest in American Indian literature, which also had continued, allowed me to participate, with USICA sponsorship, in a seminar for Danish teachers of English on American Indian history, literature, art, and politics. I taught the literature part of the seminar, which was held on the estate of Karen Blixen (Isak Dinesen) outside of Copenhagen. I learned a great deal from the other parts of the program and a good deal about Blixen from some of her fans among the participants as well. My original Fulbright experience had enabled me to ride the gravy train again, and I also gained yet another perspective on the literature of my own country.

One of my other peripheral interests that became a teaching interest during my career at New Mexico has been science fiction. Before going on my Fulbright year, I had taught a couple of sophomore courses in science fiction, and during the Belgrade orientation I asked one of the lecturers on literature whether there was any science fiction in Yugoslavia—his answer was a fairly brusque "no." He went on to explain that most literature in Yugoslavia was "more serious" than science fiction and talked at some length about satiric fiction, novels, poetry, and all sorts of other "more serious" literature. As I grew to know more about Yugoslav literature, I found that there was a great deal of important work, and even quite a bit of it in translation into English. There is a streak of humor in many contemporary Yugoslav writers that is very appealing, though there is occasionally a tendency toward sentimentalism which puts me off, but this is beside the point. The point is that there was apparently no literary recognition of science fiction in the country at the time.

When I returned to Zagreb during the lecture tour in 1976, the assistant cultural affairs officer at the consulate there noticed my interest in science fiction and said that he wished he had known about it sooner, since there was a considerable group of fans in Zagreb, and he was sure that they would love to hear from me. In 1983, I was able to attend the Sixth World General Meeting of World S.F., and got to meet lots of Yugoslav science fiction fans, as well as writers, scholars, and fans from numerous other countries. The Yugoslav sponsors are even working toward hosting the World Science Fiction Convention in 1988. I was given copies of novels by several young science fiction writers and a copy of the periodical *Sirius*, which is a monthly and contains translations of American writers' works as well as original works by Yugoslavs. Without my original Fulbright experience, I probably never would have made contact with this fascinating group of writers and readers, only a very few of whom are involved in the academic study of literature or language.

On the swing through Yugoslavia in June 1983, my last stop was in Skopje, and it really was an emotional experience. The city and university which had welcomed a stranger a dozen years before treated me like a prodigal son on this return. Several of my former students are now on the faculty, and several of my faculty colleagues have gone on to complete more advanced work. The young woman who came to New Mexico to study is now married and the mother of two lovely children who are studying English. She is currently applying for a Fulbright Scholarship to return to the United States to continue her studies. The warm-heartedness of my Macedonian friends was overwhelming.

In short, the feeling of accomplishment in personal and emotional terms is virtually unmeasurable. There is a temptation to go on anecdotally to try to mention the numerous people who have made my experience so happy for me, but I will resist. I have been very fortunate in being able to find a good deal of professional satisfaction from studying areas related to American literature from a foreign perspective. My own understanding of American literature has been broadened and deepened, and my commitment to American traditions and institutions has been strengthened by the Fulbright experience. I unabashedly believe that I am a better teacher and scholar for the experience which was the beginning of an exciting part of my career.

PART VI
ON RETHINKING A
DISCIPLINE: PSYCHOLOGY

Introduction

Fulbrighters come to the exchange process, not just as a product of a particular type of cultural learning, but as representatives of a discipline—as psychologists, historians, or specialists in American literature. And they profess a body of knowledge which claims to constitute a version of truth. Graduate education in the United States is not, by intent, parochial. It strives to achieve the universal and the educational process emphasizes that goal, certainly as an ideal.

For many academics, that assurance of the universality of our knowledge is a key element in our personal motivations. We wish to know more and we wish to convey our knowledge to others. For many Fulbrighters, there is the opportunity to teach and think about our disciplinary assumptions. The results are often a decline in our confidence about the nature of our knowledge but paradoxically this process strengthens our knowledge since it raises new questions and problems as the previous answers become unsatisfactory.

Such was the experience of three psychologists whose experience in quite different locations provided challenges to their previous assumptions about behavior. Albert Gilgen records his discontent with the conceptual disunity of psychology, which was heightened by his year in Galway. He also chronicles his subsequent attempts to bring some unity to his conceptualizations. Jeffries McWhirter, with his training in counseling psychology, found that his experience in Turkey heightened his sensitivity to cultural factors in understanding behavior. That experience also raised questions about the feasibility of many goals commonly accepted by counselors in America. For Antonio Puente, the experience of dealing with Argentine colleagues in the days after the Falklands/Malvinas defeat, raised questions for him about the proper conditions for the development of a universal approach to their discipline. Their own thinking about the nature of their discipline had been profoundly altered by their Fulbright experience.

21

A Year in Galway

Albert R. Gilgen

Western Ireland is a wonderful place to think. While Irish psychology has been strongly influenced since World War II by American psychology with its emphasis on experimentation, statistical analysis, and data production, Ireland as a country inspires contemplation and an examination of basic assumptions. At least that was the case for me.

As a Fulbright-Hays exchange lecturer at University College Galway (1971-72), I naturally had teaching duties, which I shall discuss later. However, I easily found the time and inclination to write two papers and to make a presentation at the First Annual Congress of Psychology Students held in Dublin. Both papers were published in Ireland—one in *The Irish Journal of Psychology,* the other in the *Thornfield Journal.* They concerned, respectively, a model for integrating psychology based on systems theory, and the inquiry process itself from a psychological perspective. The Dublin lecture was a phenomenological analysis of the conceptual structure of psychology.

The paper on systems theory derived from a long-standing discontent with the conceptual disunity of psychology. The ideas developed in the article, however, were arrived at and worked out in Galway. The essay on the inquiry process and the lecture on the structure of psychology each involved issues I had never seriously explored before. I was, in fact, surprised when my thinking took me in the direction of such very general yet fundamental topics.

Although these scholarly efforts might have found an audience in the United States, they seemed more at home in Ireland in the early 1970s. Incidentally, *The Irish Journal of Psychology* had just been launched, and my article appeared in the second issue. It was fun to contribute to a new journal which has since become one of the leading publications of Irish psychological research and thought.

An experience abroad is easy to romanticize and even more so when it occurred over a decade ago. One cannot be sure whether it was the getting away from home territory with its attendant duties and routines or the going to a particular new place with more time to concentrate on specific academic projects that was responsible for whatever professional growth resulted. I am convinced, though, that the special ambience of western Ireland made my leave singularly fruitful professionally and personally. The peat fires and Guiness stout; the narrow streets, stone walls, and small intimate shops of medieval Galway; the rough beauty of the Connemara land- and seascapes; the distinctive smells of the waterfront; the misty rains and bright rainbows; the relaxed pace of the people; and the respect afforded academics—all helped create the kind of atmosphere wherein I could be the quiet scholar I had always wanted to be.

I very much enjoyed teaching at University College Galway. Quite frankly, I appreciated the respect afforded professors and found it rewarding to interact with academically mature, highly motivated students. I feel I was especially effective as an instructor in Ireland, not only on account of my warm reception but by reason of the different structure of the courses there. Because students were tested only at the end of the year, I was stimulated to focus more on truly important concepts, theoretical formulations, and findings, and to present the material more systematically.

The opportunity to lecture to medical students and nuns and priests, as well as the usual types of undergraduate and graduate students, also made me increasingly aware of the triviality and superficiality of much of mainstream North American psychology. It became even clearer to me than it had been in the United States that the fad-prone, fragmented discipline which I was representing to the Irish students was crying out for organization. I became convinced, too, that psychology would never be transformed into a fully developed field of study until psychologists were encouraged to work seriously at constructing a unified body of psychological knowledge.

In order to learn more about the general outlook of my students, I constructed and administered a short questionnaire. I primarily wanted to sample the views of the Irish concerning basic differences between men and women and their perception of the proper role of women in society. Interestingly, the group least likely to believe that men and women should have equal rights turned out to be nuns. Other women tended to agree with lay men and clerics in favoring equal rights. At the same time, a high percentage of all respondents believed that woman's primary role is to be a good homemaker, wife, and mother. Nevertheless, except for lay men, many of the respondents also thought that women should be more active in political and societal matters. Thus, it was priests and women other than nuns who were most apt to believe both in equal rights for men and women and in wider social participation for women beyond the home. When differentiating the respective traits of men and women, though, female students, including members of religious orders, tended to agree with each other in perceiving women as more compassionate, loving, caring, understanding, and conversely less selfish then men, as opposed to the males, lay and cleric, taking my courses. Moreover, women were seen by many students of both sexes as better than men at work characterized by routine and detail.

Did my year in Ireland have a long-range effect on me professionally? I think so, both because much of my work has continued to center on ways to reduce the conceptual disunity of the discipline and because I have become increasingly interested in psychological developments taking place in other countries.

22

A Counseling Psychologist in Turkey

J. Jeffries McWhirter

For most of us, one of the major benefits derived from our Fulbright grant is the increased sensitivity of cultural factors. While these are most evident in relation to our host countries, for many of us this heightened sensitivity extends to our own country as well. For many, the Fulbright experience became "a window into ourselves." For those of us in the social sciences and in education this has provided a particularly important contribution to our own development. As a counseling psychologist this increased sensitivity has been especially important.

In late August 1977, I arrived in Ankara, Turkey, with my wife and five children to take up my fellowship as a Fulbright-Hays Senior Lecturer in counseling at Hacettepe University. Thus began one of the most important, interesting, and thought-provoking professional and personal years of our lives. My professional assignment during the year was with the Department of Psychological Counseling and Guidance at Hacettepe University. My lecture assignment consisted of two courses each semester, one with a translator and the other in English. I also initiated several research projects: one to assess the effectiveness of three different parent-training programs; another to evaluate the effect of an encounter growth group on Turkish students. In addition to teaching and research, I conducted an encounter group (marathon format), counseled several students, participated in faculty meetings (held in Turkish which I do not speak), and did several workshops and colloquia at Hacettepe, Ankara University, and Bogazici University in Istanbul. I also was able to visit elementary and secondary schools, child guidance clinics, hospitals, and counseling centers.

Counselors and counseling psychologists in Turkey are employed in the public and private school systems and in universities. In most schools, a guidance counselor is designated to test students, provide career and educational information, and to counsel students. Generally the counselor is given a few hours of released time from teaching and is sometimes paid extra for the guidance function. Another source of employment is within one of the numerous federal ministries. Counselors in these settings deal with personnel matters including testing, career pathing, and employee assistance.

Earlier historical forces which created a need for counseling in the United States are currently active in Turkey. That is, the psychological testing movement, vocational/career choice, and mental health concerns are currently paramount in defining what counseling psychology is and what counselors do. Turkey, being a developing country, is subjected to the problems of urbanization and industrialization with the concurrent increase in career and educational options, the breakdown of family networks, and the modifications of traditional cultural patterns. These factors have created a real need for counseling psychology.

The development of counseling psychology as a distinct discipline in the social sciences rests on several factors. The mental health movement, the psychological assessment movement, and the career development movement are all considered antecedents to counseling psychology. The career development movement is the single influence that continues to make counseling psychology a unique subspeciality in psychology. Counseling psychologists are expected to know something about normal human development and of the world of work. Counseling psychologists have developed instruments and methodologies to aid in career exploration and decision making. While I was aware of these antecedents prior to the Fulbright experience, the year in Turkey provided an opportunity to live experientially in an environment in which career issues were paramount. Many of these evolved out of the dramatic urbanization and industrialization which is occurring in Turkey and other developing countries.

As Turkey had developed from an agrarian to an industrial economy, massive migrations began to take place. External migration has come about since the late 1950s. Many people from the lower brackets of society migrated to Western European countries in search of higher wages. They work there in factories and industrial plants for several years. They return to Turkey with new experiences, new points of view, and new ideologies. They also have new options. Migrations from rural to urban areas have been even more important. Large cities began to be encircled by shanty towns. Today 60 percent of the population of Ankara lives in these dwellings. Ankara was designed for 500,000 people. In 1977 it was estimated that the population was easily between 2.5 and 3 million.

Because of industrialization and urbanization the traditional career decision-making apparatus is rendered asunder. In village life the career options for the young Turk are dictated by history and tradition. A young man does what his father (and usually grandfather and great-grandfather) did. There is little need for career exploration because the youngster lives it. Indeed, there are few options for decision making anyway. With an expanding and industrialized economy, options become available. The young Turk tends to rely on father and older brother in decisions regarding occupation. If these are absent, the village elder (*muhtar*) is available to provide this function. With increased urbanization two things happen: First, the options are increased, and second, the support and decision-making apparatus are no longer available. The *muhtar* is back in the village and the family support system—father, brothers, even mother—are forced by economic necessity to work long hours to maintain subsistence for the family. The young man is thus limited in resources for information, support, and guidance. Enter the counseling psychologist. As an individual knowledgeable of normal needs, values, interests, and aptitudes, and knowing something of the world of work, the counseling psychologist becomes a key substitute in providing those functions that have traditionally been provided by family or village members. Counseling psychology developed in this country due to similar needs of the society. Career counseling continues to be one of the key components in counseling psychology and in counselor training.

The final area of importance is my own commitment to preventive strategies and to improved service delivery systems for counseling psychology. For some time I have been interested in small-group and family intervention methodologies which contain preventive emphasis in remediation and which increase the degree of influence and impact of the counseling psychologist. This commitment has expanded because of Turkey. It is impossible to train adequate numbers of people needed to provide improved mental health services. While this is a true statement for the United States, it is blatantly obvious in Turkey. Even though there are two counselor training programs, the lower class is so large and the mental health needs are so great that it is simply impossible to meet the demands. Again, this is true in this country but the obvious is masked under the illusion of affluence of the general society.

The Turkish Fulbright experience convinced me that if we continue to train people in traditional one-to-one approaches, we will never be able to meet the needs and demands. Alternatives to this include the notion that as counseling psychologists we must strive to give our skills away.

23

Argentina and the Malvinas Crisis

Antonio E. Puente

In his classic article "The Snark Was a Boojum" (1950), Frank Beach warned that the overwhelming interest shown by psychologists for white rats as a subject of psychological experimentation was seriously restricting the development of a truly representative psychology. After reviewing major psychological journals, Professional Beach discovered that psychologists had used white rats in over 70 percent of their studies and that most of these studies were related to conditioning and learning. By 1950, psychology was quickly becoming the study of the acquisition of behavior in one species of animal.

Perusal of today's major psychological journals suggests that psychologists have heeded Professor Beach's warning but only in a restricted sense. Species other than the white rats (including the "introduction to psychology college student") are currently being used in research. However, most of the species used tend to inhabit the temperate zones of the Northern Hemisphere. The overuse of specific species, for convenience or familiarity's sake, will eventually result in a continued restriction of psychological knowledge. In contrast, more latitude has been shown the topics of study. The problem is that it is rare for researchers from countries outside of North America and Europe to contribute (i.e., publish) to psychological knowledge. While one expects that American and European scientists are unbiased in their research efforts, one wonders whether such inbreeding may result in a limited view of the world (e.g., as in the interpretation of "unbiased" data).

The limited perspective of psychological reality may be playing an important role in what Epstein (1980) calls a crisis in psychology—a crisis due to the "extremely inefficient procedures for establishing replicable generalizations." The importance of replicating findings stems from the need to account and reliably predict overtly appearing, random fluctuations in behavior. According to Epstein, the most common technique for solving the problem of replication is to "exert careful controls in the laboratory." If enough variables are adequately controlled, the scientist can gauge reliably how one variable affects another. However, there are serious limitations to this methodological approach. If controlling the species used as subjects results in using species only from northern climates, one has probably increased the reliability of the findings. Nevertheless, the generalizability (or ability to extend these findings to, say, Southern Hemispheric species) is quite another story. If the origin of scientists conducting experiments and the locale of experimentation is additionally controlled, reliability should be increased but potential problems of generalizability arise. Psychology has mounted an effort to become a "true (i.e., replicable) science" at the expense of becoming a valid one. To increase the reliability of knowledge, we have inadvertently controlled the validity of our understanding of behavior.

The current exclusionary trend in modern psychology has been difficult for me to accept, especially since I emigrated from Cuba twenty-five years ago, and being excluded from activities was simply part of my life during my early years in the United States. During the process of acculturation, I became interested in trying to conceptualize psychological issues from a bicultural perspective, American and Cuban. Eventually, this interest was to be extended to the commonality of behavior across all cultures. The important questions in my life revolved around examining what behaviors (especially those which are disordered, as found in brain-damaged individuals) were culturally sensitive and alinguistic in origin. Nevertheless, formal education in the United States went far in squelching these questions. Indeed, my graduate training in psychology was a labor in adaptation to dogmatic, methodological empiricism. With hopes of relighting my interest in the questions of non–culturally biased psychological issues, I was delighted at the invitation to join the faculty at St. George's University Medical School in Grenada, West Indies. After a year of battling the elements, voodoo, and political unrest, the desire had been rekindled. However, it was not for several years and until my necessary return to the United States that I was able adequately to translate these questions into research paradigms. Unfortunately, by then I found myself surrounded once more by the limitations of North American psychology.

The opportunity finally arose in 1981 to initiate a research program which could begin to answer what, if anything, was common to individuals across cultures. As part of the American Psychological Association's Visiting Psychologist Program, several studies comparing patterns of conceptualization in Puerto Rican and American schizophrenics were initiated. It was not enough—geographically and culturally Puerto Rico was still too similar to the United States. In 1980 a Fulbright application to

Uruguay was rejected but hopes of visiting the Southern Hemisphere were not. Another attempt was initiated the following year, this time to Argentina. The effort resulted in a firm committment to visit Bahía Blanca, Argentina, in May of 1982.

As I sat in my warm room at the Hotel Italia in Bahía Blanca (on the Southern coast of Argentina) on a windy, cold, and cloudy late August afternoon several days after my arrival, I could not help but wonder about people, people of all cultures. I had finally achieved the opportunity to ask the "right" questions. After twelve months of planning and a previous rejection (to Uruguay), both commissions had finally agreed to support a series of seminars and to initiate a research program on brain functioning at the Instituto Superior "Juan XXIII." The first of the seminars was scheduled for May 1982—about the time that the Argentine military launched an assault on the Malvinas, as the Argentines call the Falkland Islands. From the Fulbright Commission in Buenos Aires, I had received the most cordial of invitations and the greatest of assurances for my personal safety as a U.S. citizen (especially a Latin). In contrast to this friendly reception and encouragement, the U.S. Information Agency initially suggested not to proceed with my plans to visit Argentina during the Malvinas crisis. Considering such events as the takeover of the U.S. Embassy in Tehran, their concern was not without merit. Soon the concern evolved to more of an edict. Their point was clear, the U.S. Embassy had been evacuated except for a skeleton crew and visiting scholars would only complicate matters. It was not until I called the embassy that a marine corps sergeant on sentry duty made it clear to me that unless I was willing to carry a gun, I had no business going to Argentina. Thus the war (and the Exocet missiles) came and went without me, of course. Distraught and disgruntled, I settled back to academic routine.

Two months later I received an early morning phone call at my home in North Carolina; the travel ban had been lifted and all appropriate parties encouraged the resumption of normal relations between the two countries. While I was not ready to carry a gun in May, I was eager to carry knowledge, questions, and enthusiasm as a means to repair relations. At worst it was a challenge; at best, it would not only allow me to ask important questions but it would stimulate the resumption of cultural and academic exchange between these two long-standing friends. Although I was not sure what to expect, it seemed best at the time not to consider the possibilities after such a disappointing end to my original plans.

What I did encounter was a paradox and no clear answers to any of my questions. A demoralized, almost ravaged country existing simultaneously with a mature, sophisticated culture and people. The loss of the Malvinas did not seem as important to the Argentine people as other factors, especially since Argentina had not occupied the islands for numerous years. What was disconcerting was the morale, the censorship, the uncertain future of the country and its citizens. One morning the Argentines had risen to the news that their armed forces had successfully landed on the Malvinas; next, they were dealing stunning blows to the proud and sterling British forces; and, then, just as quickly as it all had started, it was over. The island was briefly occupied, but the country had lost the Malvinas, the war, and the future.

How did it occur? I was fortunate to have met one of General Menéndez's (a ranking official who directed the war and is currently facing court-martial) chief aids who informed me that the media had reported an extremely censored version of the true account. Now that the war is history, the Argentines know how many of their young were killed, they know that the *Queen Elizabeth* had never been hit, and they know that the United States had become Britian's chief ally during the crisis. I found myself trying to convince them to put their emotions and the past aside in favor of cultural and intellectual exchange. Who knows, maybe carrying the gun may have been easier.

Life went on, we all knew it, and it was best for all concerned if the past and the emotions could be squelched in favor of a more acceptable common goal. How strange and unexpected an experience it was when this goal was embraced. For example, a Sunday drive proved beyond all doubt that the Argentines were striving for more. Unexpectedly, the father of one of the part-time faculty members at the institute's psychology department turned down a long, winding road only to be met by numerous armed naval personnel at a gate. After providing appropriate identification, we were off to Puerto Belgrano, where the Argentine Navy had launched its attack on the Malvinas. Not only was I surprised to see the battleships which just a few weeks previously I had seen on the nightly news, but I was surprised when I was told that I was the first U.S. citizen to visit the naval base since the beginning of the war in May. To commemorate the visit, I was presented with a beautiful plaque. It was time to activate my mind, since it was clear that answers to my questions were being provided.

It was unbelievable. The annual inflation rate after the war was over 200 percent officially and over 1,000 percent on the black market. Oddly, the devaluation of the Argentine peso was not a result of the war. It had existed prior to the war and may have been the actual stimulus for the conflict. But the important point was how could these people live under the circumstances? Research faculty earned an equivalent of less than U.S. $10 per month, or enough to buy a paperback published in the United States. Tenured faculty could earn up to $50 per month while the rector, or president, of the institute made approximately $75 per month. As an academic,

I had simply guessed that my university colleagues were being grossly underpaid, but I was surprised to find that all professionals earned salaries in the range between U.S. $10 and $150 per month.

During those few months after the war, it was a never-ending battle of rumors, speculations, and uphill battles. People were wondering about their jobs, their professions, and their country. Above it all, people were still moving forward with visions of new horizons. The hope of a democratic government, of political and personal choice, of academic freedom, was thick in the air. The assurance that Argentina would eventually regain world recognition and confidence was discussed by the population. During strolls in their many parks or during their late-night conversations at the cafés, Argentines questioned themselves and the future of U.S.-Argentine relations. What can you say to a people whom your country has fought against (at least on paper)? In spite of conditions and in spite of the lack of easy responses, their zest for living and questioning managed to linger on. While we in the United States strove for technological sophistication and consumer comfort, basic human needs were at stake during those few months after the war. My colleagues in psychology at the institute were not concerned with doing publishable research, they were worried about existence and basic human needs. Nevertheless, they were eager to embrace a questionable future with an enthusiasm I was not used to, with a concern for those issues which are truly common to people of all cultures (regardless of political affiliation).

As I prepared for another of my many afternoon siestas in Argentina—between morning and evening seminars—I hoped to find answers in one of my dreams. While I now do not recall what I dreamed during those siestas, I still hope that regardless of what one does, the answers will always be there simply for the asking. All we have to do is allow ourselves to become unbiased, to experience, and to search for the core of human behavior. Luckily for me, answers to my questions came as a function of a Fulbright award.

In retrospect, it appears to be such a shame that I ever questioned the importance of the concerns that I had formulated early in my life. The right questions are not going to be answered by North American and European psychologists testing white rats and college students. If the questioning of psychological phenomena and human existence is truly important, we owe to ourselves, to our discipline, and to society to expand our horizons and our minds.

References

Beach, F.A. "The Snark Was a Boojum," *American Psychologist* 5 (1950): 115-24.
Epstein, S. "The Stability of Behavior: Implications for Psychological Research," *American Psychologist* 35 (1980): 790-806.

PART VII
ON LEARNING FROM
OTHERS' MISTAKES

Introduction

The exchange process, like any other human endeavor, does not always proceed smoothly. And there are pitfalls of considerable diversity which confront every grantee. Irving Louis Horowitz, an experienced international scholar, discusses some of these pitfalls in relation to doing research in other countries.

Horowitz starts with a controversy over the value of Fulbright exchanges in the Soviet Union and uses it as a warning, suggesting that one need not accept the cultural assumptions of the host country nor should one develop cynicism toward disagreeable cultural constraints. He then moves on to provide pragmatic advice on maintaining a proper balance which will produce research of value to everyone. He concludes by pointing to one of the long-term consequences of the Fulbright Program that is often overlooked: It is possible to travel halfway around the world and to encounter people with shared problems and values which transcend the more obvious differences. That ability to locate and encounter such an international community is, in large part, a result of the continuity of the Fulbright Program and is perhaps its proudest accomplishment.

24

Reflections on American Innocence and Guilt Abroad

Irving Louis Horowitz

Just when the Fulbright Program is reaching the sort of commonplace acceptance characteristic of established agencies, a piece appears reminding everyone that the Fulbright effort, launched amidst a sea of controversy, still retains the power to excite and upset. Stephen C. Munson, writing in the November 1983 issue of *Contentions*, the publication of the Committee for the Free World, goes to work on Professor Robert Kelley, a professor of history at the University of California at Santa Barbara, who in a statement for the "Viewpoints" section of *Perspectives*, the publication of the American Historical Association, argued the merits of his Fulbright experience in the Soviet Union. This debate in its own way focuses sharply and brightly on the meaning of the Fulbright experience. Permit me to summarize the positions of Messrs. Kelley and Munson, and then reflect on the accuracy of their claims made in terms of my own three experiences (perhaps "encounters" might be a better word) with Fulbright assignments.

Professor Kelley's position is that the Fulbright semester abroad was noteworthy on several counts: (1) It allowed him to teach a course in American history that sharpened his sense of the essential and the trivial; (2) as a visiting Fulbright lecturer he escaped being treated with suspicion and distrust, which permitted him and his wife to live in a student-faculty dorm and in general share the everyday life with colleagues and students; (3) he avoided the plight of the normless tourist and in effect became an accepted member of the faculty at Moscow State University; (4) the topics and themes covered were unrestricted and, his being an American, permitted wide-ranging debate and discussion of comparative assets and liabilities of the two superpowers; (5) despite the political collapse of détente, he found that there was no corresponding breaking apart of intellectual détente—on the contrary, he found a wide overlap between himself and his Soviet hosts on a wide variety of historical problem areas; (6) finally, he argues that the Fulbright experience is a learning process accessible in no other way, making possible a clearer picture of America by seeing it at arms' length.

Mr. Munson's response to this position is that Mr. Kelley is a victim of delusion and illusion in some undigested admixture. He vigorously argues that the Fulbright experience in the Soviet Union at least, is essentially an experience in being hustled. It involves "going native," i.e., accepting uncritically the premises of the Soviets, including harsh criticism and caustic sarcasm about the United States, with no corresponding set of emotions tolerated or permitted about the Soviet Union. It legitimizes Soviet ideology as residing within the tolerable limits of good scholarship, instead of seeing it for what it is: a fraudulent ideology dependent for its authority on the power of the state, not the force of ideas. The Fulbright experience thus served, in this and in many other instances, to reinforce the anti-Americanism of American radical academics. The broadside concludes by bluntly warning that "that is what our academic exchange programs are all about."

We should be grateful to these two scholars for etching with great clarity the framework for serious discussion of the Fulbright experience. Each person will, or at least should, examine—seriously and critically—his or her own overseas encounters in the light of the presupposition and consequences of participating, for whatever length and in whatever capacity, in the life and culture of another people and culture.

My own experiences cover three distinct activities and three different periods in time. First, in the late 1950s, teaching a semester at the University of Buenos Aires in its then newly established sociology program—at that time still largely ensconced within the philosophy school. Second, in the late 1970s, as a senior visiting lecturer in India, in which the centerpiece was Indian-American relations in the light of larger East/West conflicts. And finally, in the mid-1980s, a special conference on the role of the university in the new information technology, underwritten by the Fulbright office at the American-Israeli Cultural Foundation. I should add that what follows is based not solely on Fulbright lectureships, but on a wide variety of overseas assignments. Still, given the high place of the Fulbright Program in our national public life, what I say may be viewed with particular significance to sponsors and recipients of the Fulbright Program.

I shall forego any lengthy discussion of the special learning processes involved in each of these three settings—that would form the backbone of an autobiographical profile far too long and opaque for present purposes. I should say that, in my personal encounters, the local, overseas administrators of the Fulbright Program were uniformly intelligent, thoughtful, and supportive. I doubt seriously that any of my stays overseas would have proven nearly as valuable or as memorable without such dedicated efforts by dedicated people—of a wide variety of backgrounds and nationalities. Indeed, oftentimes, this administrative support, contrasting sharply with local national conditions, spared me the agonies of encounters with local bureaucrats, who could sap the moral fibre of a saint if given half a chance. Fortunately and appreciatively, Fulbright overseas offices are staffed with people dedicated to their work who would not give the devil his remote due. This was true in Buenos Aires, New Delhi, and Tel-Aviv—which can only mean that Providence protects Fulbright programs and hence the Fulbright participants. Only clear-eyed administrative support makes it possible for an individual such as myself to offer these reflections on ideology and policy.

Quite simply, I do not think the role of the Fulbright Program is to provide quick fixes in Americanism; or for that matter, at the other end of the spectrum, to encourage grant recipients to "go native" by accepting the premises of the host country uncritically. What can be done, and perhaps with greater effectiveness than in the past, is to provide precisely the sort of educational guidelines and experientially grounded fieldwork techniques that Fulbright practitioners at their very best exemplify. The position of Professor Kelley borders perilously close on taking the host country orientation as plain truth, i.e., the "going native syndrome"; whereas Mr. Munson's critique involves the sort of cultivated cynicism and antagonism for overseas assignments that leads to conflictual situations, i.e., the "belligerence syndrome." The aim of the good Fulbrighter is to avoid either excess. The task of the commission is to provide mechanisms that permit navigation of the foreign rapids. The task of those who have benefited by overseas assignments is to provide moorings to make such navigational tasks meaningful.

The folklore of research is so much a part of academic life that the risk of saying the obvious is omnipresent. Field manuals and laboratory handbooks well describe the hazards of the research process. At the other end of the spectrum are a series of ideological tracts which so heavily emphasize the pains and pitfalls of research and overseas assignments that the net result is often intellectual paralysis. If every piece of data we touch and every person we instruct is filtered through biased lenses of a conquering imperium—How is objectivity in research possible in general, much less in alien contexts? Add to the manuals of research and tracts on antiresearch the organizational constraints set in motion by professional associations and their committees on ethics insinuating moral limits in work affecting human subjects, and we complete the triad that only the bravest can overcome. Yet manuals on how to, tracts on why not to, and codes on what cannot be, aside, the rush to fieldwork continues. Research in and on Latin America alone jumped six times between the late 1950s and the late 1960s.

The need to offer specific guidelines to beginning overseas research has increased correspondingly. With such standing needs in mind, these remarks are offered as a personal testament to problems of method, ideology, and ethics in doing overseas research. These comments shall be confined to the work process itself, the daily dilemmas endemic to overseas research, faced by everyone. Because Fulbright awards contribute a large proportion of such scholars, the sponsors of this program must be especially sensitive to what it is asking of younger scholars in particular. There are three stages to be considered: (1) before going overseas; (2) how to handle oneself abroad; (3) what to do and when to call it quits, or the protocol of leaving.

First, there is language preparation. It is an Anglo-American conceit that everyone who is important speaks English. And while Fulbright awards always specify language requirements, it provides no testing mechanism beyond the informal. The new researcher will find that even those who do speak English often cannot communicate as well as may have been anticipated, although it is usually better than an American's knowledge of the foreign language. Involved in linguistic limitations is a matter of studying elites versus masses. The failure to study the language(s) of a host country adequately confines and consigns the new researcher to a small elite stratum that knows the English language. As a result, the literature on development reveals ten times the information on elites as is available on ordinary people. There is abundant literature of economic data from bankers and industrialists, but little on how the poor live and labor, or the character of agrarian structure. This point is made to illustrate that language preparation is not merely a pedagogic or bibliographic advantage, but downright essential to avoid serious forms of biased reporting. Since it is at times a source of friction with explosive ramifications it becomes directly relevant to the Fulbright awards system.

Before going overseas the researcher should imbibe and digest all available travel books. Often they will be more important than the literature in his specialty. I know that this was and continues to be the case for myself. The researcher will need them more than the specialized scholarly literature. They will help get information required in terms of food, clothing, and shelter. The first layer of information upon going overseas must derive from travel books. Guides to hotel accommodations, travel, weather conditions, are often first-rate. Travel books are updated annually and well constructed. They sometimes exhibit a higher level of rational organization than many organizational handbooks. They are written in a manner that everyone can understand. And the overseas researcher begins his journey with the same biological, social, and personal needs as anyone else making a trip abroad. In the world of foreign lands, we are all tourists; and the fact that basic costs are not borne by Fulbright does not change this condition one iota.

One needs a good geography book to learn the topography of the area: terrain, elevation, resources, and demographic distributions. Good geography books tell you about the kind of social organization at the micro level. Mineral wealth, transportation networks, communication systems, can also be located either in geographic works or in statistical yearbooks. These latter are a goldmine of information, and often permit useful cross-indexing and correlations. When one has exhausted the geographic and statistical literature, and only then, immersion in the works of one's area of specialty is a plausible next step.

One should establish personal contacts before leaving, so that whenever the researcher or teacher gets to his/her destination there is someone to meet him/her and ease the burdens of those first days and weeks. Embassies, as well as local commissions, are the best source for reaching good people. This involves a veritable "who's who" in the area. Establishing a meaningful correspondence between teaching, research, and the human element in the intended field is a necessary precondition. Some cultures require formal invitations or statements for entry into a society. The young researcher will need a formal letter of introduction or a series of letters to indicate why he/she is going overseas. After all, the researcher is in the sovereign territory of another state and therefore must explain his/her presence. Overseas visiting rights are limited by law, custom, and tradition. Those arriving from advanced, often powerful imperial lands, should not forget such facts. The Fulbright offices in host nations can be the scholar's personal embassy office. Too few people use it for more than a place of reporting and receiving payments. Perhaps the local office should become more active in integrating the experiences and researches of Fulbright scholars.

This prepared, the researcher can now leave for the specific assignment area he/she is going to study. Travel light. Do not presume that one must carry all of Americana in a personal suitcase. This will force you to buy ahead, and have initial early contact with pharmacies, groceries, and other kinds of establishments. It will give the researcher a sense of the touch, sight, and smell of the country in which he/she is about to stay. One discovers differences in national brands and local tastes in everything from toothpaste to beer. All this is important because one begins with one's requirements, not with abstract theories. The more young researchers do for themselves and the less their dependency on the vision of others, the better.

Do not land and do research. To hit the ground running may be a good slogan in business but it makes for bad scholarship. Become familiar with the society. Establish permanent contact points. Do nothing for the first several weeks other than learn the local customs, culture, and idiosyncracies. Do not try to analyze. Enjoy the new environment. After being in the host country for several weeks the need to commence research will overtake the researcher. But the quality of that research product depends less on the translated survey research instrument in your briefcase than on what you learn in the ongoing process of living. Understandably, agencies like Fulbright want their money's worth; but perhaps in the process allow for an insufficient warm-up phase.

The most difficult recommendation with respect to overseas research concerns traveling itself. If at all possible, especially on short trips, do not travel with husbands, wives, children, or lovers. The purpose of overseas research is oftentimes diluted by returning in the evening to an English-speaking and culture-bound environment. Young researchers, because they are young, have an innate propensity to make friends easily. Becoming part of the world in which one is living makes research that much more feasible and manageable. Moments of pain and anguish will be part of such a "go-it-alone" procedure. But the ultimate rewards that result from deeper immersion in the overseas culture are well worth this personal sacrifice. This is an especially hard recommendation vis-à-vis Fulbright, since by making cash allowances for families and spouses it may be seen to encourage such practices. By resisting demand for increasing family allowances, Fulbright can take the lead in generating a work orientation rather than a purely personal orientation.

A good preliminary to the commencing of research is going to the local or national library archives and exploring every possible technical book-shop in the overseas area, especially if one is in an urban environment. One can and should learn an enormous amount of information about the local cultural scene. One of the great benefits of being in a foreign situation is proximity to new sources of information, often of enormous use to people accustomed only to reading standard sources in a given field within their own language system. Often the difference between good and poor research can be reduced precisely to the degree to which local sources are tapped. This has the added advantage of increasing language proficiency in a mini-mal amount of time, since the impulse to read abstract theory, readily available in one's own native language, is weak; whereas interest in a par-ticular area heightens the need to know—and that means to learn—what-ever it takes in the way of linguistic retooling.

There is an iron law of good social research whether one is in the United States or outside: Do not attempt the preliminary acquisition of data when secondary information of a high order is available. Just as we have a statis-tical abstract of the United States, many countries have similar yearbooks of basic statistical information which cover demography, stratification, and other related areas. Do not replicate what has already been done. A sample survey of fifty will never equal a total survey of five million. Only when one is familiar with the national statistical archives is it possible to be certain that one is generating information, not replication. To be sure, the quality of statistical information varies widely from nation to nation. Some areas, notably Canada, Western Europe, and even portions of Latin America, maintain excellent statistical abstracts. In other countries the information is more difficult to come by. Whatever the case may be, make sure that available sources of secondary data are examined before attempting primary research. Too many Fulbright research products I have seen suffer from a needless parochialism because of an erroneous belief that "original research" is the same as generating one's own data.

In terms of interview schedules, make sure that they are prepared in an idiom and level thoroughly understandable to the local culture. Too often, translations are ludicrous, given local nuances in the use of language. Prior to any administration of such interviews, the researcher should be certain of having authoritative permission to do this kind of work. Otherwise, the political fallout upon innocent researchers could be much heavier than any remotely anticipated at the start of a project, and such flack is especially damaging for policy-sensitive agencies such as Fulbright. The researcher administering the interview materials should make sure they are worded in such a way as to avoid arousing suspicion, hostility, or giving offense. The full disclosure of those providing funds is important, sometimes even necessary to be taken seriously. Soliciting the help of overseas colleagues in the administration of questionnaires and in data processing also provides assurance for the host nation that the purpose of the research is not only legitimate but willingly shared with the host population.

When one is abroad, it is wise not to pontificate about the host country. A serious anomaly of going overseas is that an ordinary person automatically becomes transformed into an important visiting personage by virtue of identification with a powerful nation and the degree of personal wealth as expressed in clothing and accommodations. The Fulbright researcher often appears to be intellectually sophisticated when in fact he might be quite ignorant politically, not to mention peculiarly naive about the institutional fabric of his own country. As a result, one who is staying in the host country with many expenses paid by the Fulbright award should have a sense of modesty, without any presumption of problem-solving in any large-scale sense for other peoples or nations. Politics is a risky business, and when one remembers the modest degree of involvement at home, one should then also take into account the similar, if not greater difficulties involved for scholars of other nations with respect to their own countries. The arrogance of power is matched only by the conceit of those who are in fact powerless. While political discussion is often the alpha and omega of personal contact and interaction, the conduct of that discourse should be the clear understanding of the outsider status necessarily retained by the overseas researchers. I have seen Fulbright recipients who at home would be graduate students of modest talents, hire chauffeurs and maids in foreign countries. The individual paid in dollars (or equivalent amounts in the national money) is wealthy within the confines of rural Third World countries. A good rule of thumb is: Do not flaunt what you have; and do not be overly critical of those who do not.

I would strongly urge all researchers to prepare preliminary drafts while overseas. It is very difficult to accumulate data in one country and perform the writeup process in another. The *Verstehen* that comes from being immersed in the overseas world vanishes quickly, and along with that goes a sense of literary urgency as well. The field process should include a writeup stage, and this should not be left for a return to quieter or more distant environs. The gain in dispassion is not worth the loss in urgency.

Either while in the host country or shortly upon returning home, preparations should be made for the research to be shared—if a demand for it exists. The purpose of doing overseas research is the performance of something useful and worthwhile to all parties concerned. Insofar as possible, the data should be deposited not only in the host country, but in the latter's language. Arrangements for joint publication should be made as soon as feasible, and here the Fulbright offices could play an important ancillary role. Full disclosure and sharing of information is important, not only on the face of it, in terms of the universality with which all information should be treated, but it assures the right to return by scholars. It is significant to maintain contact with people from the host country, not simply to do follow-up studies, but as a basic measure to determine the accuracy of the researcher's premises.

A significant series of problems for the researcher are related to personality changes arising as a result of a new cultural contact. Not infrequently, the young researcher or teacher develops either strong affection or animosity for the nation visited. This results in either romanticizing or needlessly denigrating the worth of others. One safeguard against this is to put some distance not only between yourself and the host country, but a good distance between the preliminary draft prepared overseas and any final draft prepared for publication. That is about the best safeguard available for maintaining a fair-minded, balanced view with a minimal amount of distortion as a result of strong feelings of either a positive or negative variety.

Research abroad is an ongoing experience. It is not a one-shot activity—at least not for those who take work in an international context as a primary scholarly commitment. The purpose of overseas research is ultimately the same as research at home: a contribution to knowledge, or at least to information. The techniques, methods, and theories applicable in one cultural context should be applicable in another. Variations will take place, and must be adjusted as well as accounted for. However, the needs of the human race for survival, growth, and autonomy are real throughout the world. Forms of human relations vary; contexts differ; but the content of human experience remains the same. This I take to be the philosophic rationale of the Fulbright system.

There is a special, if hard to detect, benefit from doing overseas research that only those who have done it systematically are aware of: To understand the United States, it is advisable to leave the country periodically, if not systematically. To work in an overseas context is a remarkably fruitful way to understand the costs and benefits of being an American. It permits a more realistic and sounder appraisal of American events, placing them in a world context which is at the same time more modest and yet more authentic. To the extent that the United States becomes itself an object of study, the researcher can have a profound sense of being "overseas." Marginality has always been more conducive to basic research than integration into the host culture. The exilic imagination prevents the excesses of patriotism, and hence refuge in national chauvinisms. Overseas activities are a central training ground for a better understanding of world affairs no less than of American society.

Scholarship is indivisible. As a result, interaction takes place at the level of scholarship per se. Exchange professorships, shared research designs, transfer of resources, and above all a dialogue on the nature of social reality that extends to variables beyond nationality—all take place. Without such a rich inner history to each discipline there can be no research per se and hence no overseas research in any geographic directions. This is not to deny the elitist and colonial potential of all asymmetric relations; nor is it to assume that knowledge is simply the cumulative mechanical outcome of scholarly exchange. However, if teaching research is to mean anything at all, it involves the commitment to evidence and reason. The particularisms frequently alluded to as obstacles in the conduct of research across national lines are real enough and cannot be overlooked or suppressed, but in no way does that signify the impossibility of intellectual exchange and scientific or humanistic endeavor. It only means that the tasks are somewhat more difficult than imagined by an earlier and more parochial generation of scholars.

The ultimate task of the scholar overseas and the ultimate worth of the Fulbright approach are identical: to remove the sense of the exotic, the strange, the alien; to make events and peoples in faraway places as real and as meaningful as events and people who are our neighbors, associates, and acquaintances. Nothing is more profoundly mistaken than to think that "they" are different from "us." The psychological wellsprings, the sociological taproots, the economic underpinnings—all must be made real; and that means connected to a larger world that displays unity in diversity. There are laws, norms, mores, traditions that illumine the human condition. The overseas researcher is merely the instrument for uncovering them in contexts largely unknown to most people, including most scholars.

The delicate thread of historical continuity and discontinuity, economic dependences and independences, sociological movements and political parties, each and every one of these tensions, contradictions, polarities, antimonies—or whatever rhetoric or grammar one prefers—must be reigned in, harnessed as it were, by living individuals. When the overseas researcher does so satisfactorily the results will be found useful by the community of scholars; new connections will be entertained and established. But more important, such results will be authenticated by the community of human beings who are the objects no less than the subject of the overseas research sponsored by the Fulbright Program.

I have herein attempted to distill and digest more than a quarter century of overseas research and teaching—sometimes with the aid of Fulbright, other times with other supportive agencies. The twin errors of overidentification with a host country and culture on one side, and overcritical reaction on the other can never be entirely eliminated. Hence, the kind of differences expressed at the start of my piece should be viewed as the ideological extremes through which every Fulbright recipient must navigate. Hopefully, these remarks are sufficiently representative of shared experiences as to provide a useful compass in this navigation of overseas research and teaching processes.

If one were to summarize the Fulbright experience at its most concrete and abstract levels alike, it turns out to be the degree to which intellectuals—men and women of ideas, drawn from all sectors of the academy—can communicate with each other as human beings. To travel halfway around the world and encounter people with shared problems, common premises, and similar values is no small achievement—one made far easier, far more rational by the Fulbright Program than perhaps any other single piece of legislation in U.S. history since the Morrill Act, which gave rise to the land grant universities. This comparison, so evident when drawn, says all that needs saying to justify the Fulbright Program's expansion and extension.

PART VIII
ON BREAKING NEW GROUND

Introduction

The forty years of the Fulbright Program have provided a span of time long enough to have affected careers of important scholars. Sometimes, that effect has a determining influence in the nature and direction of one's subsequent career. Richmond Lattimore, who was to become one of America's top classicists, indicates that, while his Fulbright was a "failure," it also was a time when he created some of the works which provided his initial reputation. His contribution, written shortly before his death, is an interesting comment on the meaning of failure.

Two other contributions suggest other opportunities. Elbert Smith was one of the early Fulbrighters in Japan. Twenty-one years later, he was one of the first lecturers in American history to go to the Soviet Union. Those Fulbright experiences served as an important base for the contributions he made as a member of the Board of Foreign Scholarships, which has policy responsibility for the Fulbright Program. Albert Yee had the unique opportunity to be the first Fulbrighter to go to the People's Republic of China. While the program had been in operation in mainland China prior to the revolution, the subsequent isolation of the P.R.C. from the rest of the world almost eliminated any scholarly and intellectual contact. Yee was able to make a trip to China soon after President Nixon's historic trip and some eight years later, he was able to go back as the first Fulbright scholar.

25

Research in Greece

Richmond Lattimore

My project was to study and reconstruct the campaigns of the Great Persian War, and, particularly, the battles of Marathon, Salamis, and Plataea. I had been teaching these matters in graduate courses and was thoroughly familiar with all literary sources and modern speculation. My firsthand familiarity with the topography was nil. I proposed to work back and forth between the sources and the terrain, the library and the field.

By 1951 I had been turned down at least once, and the Fulbright grant, which finally did come, came very late in the year, perhaps as late as June or July. It was thought impractical (and unfair), therefore, to ask for a whole year off from teaching, so we compromised on a half year. With my family I sailed for Athens about the middle of January 1952, and went to work, returning to the United States in mid-September.

As for the cause of the delay, it is possible that it was doubt about the merit of my project or my fitness to perform it; apparently, there is some reason here for doubt. But there were also, certainly, rumors to the effect that the delay had its origin in suspicions about my personal and political qualifications, on the part of those who were impressed by the attacks made by Senator Joseph McCarthy on my brother Owen. In any case, even if inconveniently late, I did get my Fulbright.

On returning home I finished writing up my battles and submitted the manuscript to the Monograph Committee of the American Philological Association. They turned it down; so did the University of Chicago Press. I gave up and turned to more fruitful projects.

My present considered view is that I was *not* qualified for my task. I was proposing to do an archaeologist's job on military sites without the necessary archaeological training or equipment. That was naive. But the idea was right, especially when the work was undertaken by a consummate topographer like Eugene Vanderpool, who ultimately, with W. Kendrick Pritchett, turned his talents to this material. I hope they have learned a little something from me, because I did enunciate, or stumble across, some important principles and truths.

Although the main project was then to be called a failure, my Fulbright year, truncated as it was, was nothing of the sort. My introduction on Herodotus's methods in composing his history was detached, made into an article, and published. On the side, as it were, I completed a translation of Euripides' *Helen*, got well along with the translation of his *Alcestis*, and wrote a number of poems. All of the above have been published. I greatly improved my knowledge of modern Greek, both for reading and speaking. I talked with farmers and herdsmen as I went about my sites and explained my reconstruction of the Battle of Plataea to a Greek army officer whom I fell in with at a *kapheneion* near the battlefield. I participated in field trips of the American School of Classical Studies, and also came to know many other classical scholars—Greek, British, French, German, Italian. Extensive travel by train and bus, with a good deal on foot, taught me and my family much about the Greek land. Led by a Greek guide and along with the famous archaeologist Homer Thompson, we ascended Mt. Cyllene, nearly 8,000 feet high; my family, unaided, did various peaks up to 5,000 feet. My wife and my two sons, fourteen and twelve, were all able to lend a helpful hand at the Agora Dig. I came away from Greece that year knowing far more about Greece in general than ever before, and I think all of my family found it an experience which enriched our lives.

26

Fulbright Experiences

Elbert B. Smith

In 1954, when the Fulbright Program sent me to lecture for a year at Ochanomizu University and the University of Tokyo, I was already the father of three young sons and was dedicated to the proposition that their world should be different from the atmosphere of violent cruelty and inevitable world war that had characterized my own high-school and college years. I had hailed the Fulbright Program as an instrument for the world's future peace, and I was delighted by the opportunity to participate in it.

Japan was still struggling to recover from World War II, and many of its citizens, understandably enough, had not yet forgiven the United States for Hiroshima and Nagasaki. Also, many Japanese felt threatened by the nuclear testing being conducted in the Pacific area. The blueprint of a new Japanese democracy had been created by the occupation, but it was still in a developing stage after more than a thousand years of dictatorship by a military elite. I saw my assignment as an opportunity to try to show my Japanese students the enormous opportunities and possibilities in a society like that of the United States, without minimizing the equally numerous pitfalls and opportunities for serious mistakes also inherent in our system.

I taught an American history survey, a course in international relations, and a graduate course on America in the twentieth century. For the survey, the American Embassy provided me with an excellent short text published in both Japanese and English, and a handful of excellent books relevant to the other courses were also available in Japanese.

Also, of course, we tried to make as many friends as possible in the hope that at least some of our personal relations could be transposed into friendly attitudes toward the United States. We soon learned that even when they disagreed strongly with official American policies, our Japanese friends were anxious for us to understand that this did not reflect enmity toward Americans or to America in general. I met a group of students each week for discussions of Japanese problems in English. I suggested the topics

211

and worked to improve the English of the participants. We also had col-leagues and many students to our home and went on various sightseeing tours and picnics with them. We shared a duplex house with a Japanese family consisting of a mother, three children, and the maternal grand-mother. The father had been killed during the war. Our "landlady" painted us a beautiful scroll, and we have remained friends through the years.

In the spring I toured several other Japanese cities, where I spoke on various topics to business, political, and academic audiences. My lecture, "The Making of American Foreign Policy," was published in Japanese and distributed as a pamphlet to the American cultural centers by the U.S. Information Service.

I cannot vouch for the quality of my teaching or lectures, but we came to love our students and colleagues dearly, and felt that at least some of this affection was mutual. For many years we corresponded with former stu-dents and took pride in their professional success. Also, we brought back a five-year-old Eurasian orphan boy (American soldier father and Japanese mother) to be adopted by a friend, and six months later we adopted a four-year-old girl of the same origin. The boy is today a wealthy and responsible citizen of California, and the girl is still our only daughter in a family of four sons. She attended the University of Hawaii and now lives in Maui. Two of our children attended the private American School in Japan, and Mrs. Smith taught there for one semester. This school experience with many different nationalities was invaluable in helping our children develop a proper appreciation for people of other races and nationalities. Also, we brought back hundreds of slides, and for many years afterward I did public lectures and occasional slide shows on Japan and its problems and policies. We felt that we had taken full advantage of every possible opportunity to learn and be useful.

Twenty-one years later, the phone rang and a voice asked if I would be willing to go to Moscow. In February 1976 we found ourselves, without the children this time, lecturing at Moscow State University. If we had thought our mission to Tokyo important, you can imagine the exaggerated signifi-cance with which we endowed our efforts in Moscow. I was only the third professor to have the American history lectureship there, and we felt like true pioneers. I was allowed to teach my own version of the American Civil War and Reconstruction with no interference. Students read the books I brought, and we enjoyed stimulating discussions and arguments. Two stu-dents were assigned to us each week, and a well-planned program of cultural enlightenment kept us busy visiting museums, churches, art gall-eries, palaces, historical sites, theaters, and sporting events. We often re-ciprocated by taking students, and sometimes their wives or husbands, to the Bolshoi or the Palace of Congresses for ballet, opera, and concerts. We also enjoyed dinner parties at the homes of colleagues, and a guided tour with students took us to the ring cities of Zgorsk, Vladimir, and Suzdal. In the spring we traveled with an American group to Odessa and Istanbul on a Soviet ship, and later we went unescorted to Yerevan, Armenia; Tbilisi, Georgia; Tashkent and Samarkand, Uzbekistan; and Leningrad. Most important, in all these places, and particularly in Moscow, we walked the streets, rode the buses and subways, and rubbed shoulders with literally thousands of people. We felt that we had taught a more accurate and realistic view of American history and society to a large number of highly intelligent young people, and that we had become qualified to present a much more realistic analysis of Soviet society than most Americans are able to see. Slides showing Soviet citizens looking like Americans and doing the same things Americans do at least reduce the Soviet people to human size.

In 1978-81 I served on the U.S. Board of Foreign Scholarships, and in this capacity we studied Fulbright problems and opportunities on a tour that took us to Moscow, Copenhagen, Bonn, Warsaw, and Budapest. The experience on this board strongly reinforced my previous convictions about the value of the Fulbright Program as an agency for peace. Most frustrating, however, was the fact that we could have expanded our exchanges with the Soviet Union and Eastern Europe, as well as with West Germany, much more than we did if the money to finance them had been available. It was sobering to learn that Germany and other nations were spending more money than we were on international academic exchanges.

Between 1976 and 1982 we were visited by several Soviet professors and graduate students, including most of those now teaching American history at Moscow State University. In 1982 we returned to Moscow for another semester of lecturing, and immediately resumed earlier friendships. We were royally entertained, and our relations with students and colleagues were much more informal than they had been in 1976. Again I taught the coming of the American Civil War as the "first Cold War," based in large part on misperceptions of each section's motives and intentions. I also brought a much larger collection of books, and was able to help several students with theses and dissertations. In 1976 we had traveled at our own expense. This time we were sent to lecture in Tashkent for ten days and in Leningrad for four days. From Tashkent we had side trips to Khiva, Bukhara, and Samarkand, as well as to two collective farms, and I later traveled independently to Tallin and Riga. Again we felt that we had been able to present a more accurate and realistic picture of America, and had learned a great deal more about the Soviets. Particularly useful were the opportunities we had for comparing 1976 and 1982.

The American professor lecturing in Moscow dreams that at some future date one or more of his students may achieve a position of leadership or influence and perhaps do something more reasonably because the professor was there. Whether any of our teaching efforts or strong friendships in the Soviet Union will ever have any such effect is problematical, but the Fulbright Program at least gave us the opportunity to try.

Meanwhile, I have delivered dozens of lectures in America arguing that while a balance of power may be necessary for peace at the moment, it cannot be the final answer. Our present situation should be an interregnum during which we and the Soviets should be doing everything possible to understand the origins and nature of our differences, to emphasize our similarities and common problems, and to dispel our mutual misperceptions. Our mutual survival requires us to live in peace, and this can be achieved without either nation sacrificing any of its more important principles. Our differences are the products of our differing historical experiences. Our similarities, of which there are many, stem from our common humanity, with all its potential for both good and evil. The task of survival may prove impossible, but the Fulbright exchange programs give people of good will in every country involved at least a chance to work for better understanding among young people who have the potential for future leadership.

27

The First Fulbrighter to the People's Republic of China

Albert H. Yee

How wonderful it was to receive the first letter of invitation sent in the winter of 1978 from the Institute of Psychology of the Chinese Academy of Sciences (Academia Sinica)! Yet life in 1978-79 grew hectic, so one delayed acceptance out of frustrating desire and uncertainty. The institute mailed several follow-up invitations and finally asked a friend in Minnesota to telephone. He explained in greater detail that I had been chosen to be the first American psychologist to be invited as a distinguished lecturer ("foreign expert") by the Chinese Academy and to be officially hosted by its Institute of Psychology and the Chinese Psychological Society. I insisted that the honor could go to any number of psychologists. With a new position and move, I could not leave very soon and begged that someone else go first. In November 1979, Professor Ching Chi-cheng, the first psychologist from the People's Republic of China (P.R.C.) to come to the United States and be honored as such by the American Psychological Association (APA), phoned me one evening and asked why I had not accepted their invitation. After listening to my explanation, Professor Ching suggested that I consider going to China with him when he returned in May 1980. With half a year to arrange my schedule for a month's journey, I took the suggestion and Professor Ching's plan prevailed most nicely. We arrived in Beijing on May 10, 1980 and were met by a large welcoming party. A week earlier, the Asian American Psychological Association, which I served as president, honored Professor Ching with a banquet in San Francisco attended also by P.R.C. diplomats. The 1980 tour took place eight years after my attempt to locate China's psychologists for the APA as a member of its International Relations Committee (Yee, 1973a, b).

In Tokyo with a Senior Fulbright Lectureship in 1972 while on leave from the University of Wisconsin-Madison, I received permission to visit the People's Republic after three applications through the P.R.C. Embassy in Ottawa, Canada. The P.R.C. did not have an office in the United States. This was only a few months after President Nixon's historic visit to China, plans for which I had had a hand in designing through the National Security Council. Although I had concluded my lectures at Tokyo University and Tamagawa University for the semester, the Fulbright director for Japan declined permission for my departure to the P.R.C. It appeared that there was no precedent nor policy governing Fulbright travel to the P.R.C. Fortunately, the dilemma of having a rare visa for the P.R.C. and not being able to make use of it was solved by officers of the U.S. Embassy in Tokyo who overruled the director. Elated that the first American had received permission to enter the P.R.C. from Tokyo, the embassy, however, sobered a bit when they could not answer the question of how one actually entered China, a nation that had been closed to Americans for twenty-three years. The visa simply said that I could enter China by way of Guangzhou or Shanghai and that the visa was good for three months. One embassy official who was particularly helpful, I believe his name was Norris Smith, formed the idea of asking Jack Reynolds of the NBC office in Tokyo for assistance. NBC-TV crews had accompanied President Nixon to Beijing earlier that year and Mr. Smith thought that they might be able to advise us. Inquiries to Japanese sources had provided no leads, and I wondered whether NBC could help. Within a week, NBC sent good news. The message said that Bob Green of the NBC office in Hong Kong had contacted the Chinese authorities there. The straightforward Chinese told him that "we know about Professor Yee's visa. Tell him to come to the China International Travel Service office in Kowloon, Hong Kong, as soon as possible. We shall take care of him."

Completing the commitment of a lecture tour of the American Information Centers (USIA) throughout Japan, I hastily prepared to comply with the instructions from Hong Kong. Francis Tenney, director of the State Department's China desk and somehow related to the Fulbright Program, and Harley Preston, the APA's director of external affairs, each provided travel grants of $500 as requested to help cover expenses. Everyone seemed to share in the excitement and anticipation of the trip; it was a marvelous spirit of cooperation and enthusiasm rarely experienced in a scholar's life and one which I shall never forget. To show how very scant knowledge of the P.R.C. was in those days and also to reflect the unwarranted fears that prevailed among Chinese Americans, I recall that as we packed my bags for the trip there was a tinge of concern whether the family and I would meet again. All of which seems so very preposterous today.

The information relayed by NBC proved to be letter-perfect. After a check of my papers and my signature (in Chinese!), the Kowloon travel office booked me on the first train to Guangzhou which was early the next morning. After resting overnight with a faculty friend at the Chinese University of Hong Kong, I walked to the deserted train stop in the bright blaze of the December dawn over the jagged mountains across the bay. In time, the train chugged its way to the campus stop. As instructed by the travel office, I sat anxiously on a bench until a man with a big red star on his dark hat approached me. He simply asked, "Are you Professor Yee?" I said "Yes," and he took my bags and placed them in a special car. Returning to China by train in 1972, the hour-and-a-half ride from the Hong Kong border to Guangzhou passed comfortably and without event. In 1947-48, bandits would raid the trains on the same route quite frequently, and that is why relatives had booked me on a British steamer on my first trip to Guangzhou in 1947. Occasionally, the train passed through villages with high watchtowers and turrets built during the days of banditry. In 1947-48, I read news reports of British military skirmishes out of Hong Kong against the bandits with Spitfire fighter planes, battalions of troops, and destroyers. The bandits must have been quite formidable in their day and an age-old curse that finally ended with the advent of the P.R.C. Riding that train, I became the first Fulbright scholar and APA representative to visit the P.R.C. For this fourth-generation Chinese American, the trip to the P.R.C. carried abundant memories and special meaning, for I had been disillusioned by almost all my experiences there in 1947-48. Starvation, deprivation, war fever, and corruption sobered the teenager's senses and gave him a dismal impression of his ancestors' land.

In Guangzhou, the Pearl River looked relatively void of craft without the mass of bobbing sampans and great barges lining the bund. Now well-paved instead of pot-holed and filthy, the streets seemed empty without the mobs of beggars, coolies, hawkers, and rickshamen milling about seeking one's attention. In 1972, twenty-four years after I returned to the United States, the general welfare of the people had advanced greatly since the old days. I could see food and other essentials in good supply and at inexpensive prices too. Less than four dollars covered a person's monthly food costs; a heavy overcoat that I purchased in Beijing for my son cost only $8.50. Though wages were low, the people earned enough from an average of about $40 per month to bank savings. However, patched clothing, common orthodontic problems, and crowded housing indicated that the Chinese standard of living compared favorably not with any Western nation but with its own past history. The quiet submissiveness of the people in 1972 versus the good-humored and often noisy, outspoken nature typical of the Cantonese gave the first clue to the chilling effects of the Cultural Revolution (CR), which had started in 1966.

Although material gains were obvious to see, those with university degrees, bourgeois backgrounds, foreign connections, involvement with

Western and traditional Chinese arts and crafts, and others suffered the brunt of the CR in 1972. With the support of the senile Mao Zedong, the radical leftist leaders (the "Gang of Four") attempted to overthrow Chinese and alien traditions that they thought prevented the progress of true socialism and the development of a classless society. They attacked foreign influences, such as Beethoven and Western clothing, and condemned philosophers, such as Confucius, and ancient works of art. Young Red Guards, released from studies, destroyed pianos, ancient paintings and statues, and treated intellectuals and all those targeted as traitors. The psychologists suffered punishment and recrimination for their "foreign orientation" and supposed lack of faith in the worth and powers of the masses.

After three frustrating weeks that frigid winter of 1972, I could track down only five psychologists, four in Beijing and one in Shanghai. The five conducted no teaching or research and were "undergoing transformation" to see how they could be of service to the masses. Tight-lipped about their precarious situation, I could obtain no information on the fate of their colleagues, especially those who had been educated in the United States and Europe. During meetings with the psychologists, they asked very little about psychological developments in the world and seemed to know very little about current events. For example, they did not know about the campus upheavals still active at that time in the United States over the Vietnam War, news of which they were happy to hear. Conversation livened when I suggested that I would pose questions for them and then answer them. We continued as proposed for hours at a time. However, each time that I interjected questions about the whereabouts of their former leaders in psychology, no one would answer and silence prevailed until someone changed the subject.

In university libraries, I found psychological journals from the United States and Europe and even showed them some of my own publications which seemed to please them very much. The journals showed no sign of use and the psychologists I met in 1972 exhibited little familiarity with the scientific theories and methodology of American psychologists. As I explained the nature of the Fulbright Program, which made it possible to lecture in Japan and to journey to the P.R.C. to visit them, I could see that such privileges for scholars seemed incredulous to them. Invited to meet some sociology students at Beijing University, China's intellectual center, I asked the students some elementary questions about methodology when they told me that they were conducting interview surveys of peasants. The students could not answer simple technical questions, and I began to see the other side of the CR policy of abolishing entrance examinations and giving the political acuity of peasants, workers, and soldiers priority in university admissions.

Following that visit and until the end of the CR in 1977 after the death of Mao Zedong in September 1976, I maintained correspondence with the psychologists through the Institute of Psychology and worked on their behalf through the Liaison Office established in Washington, D.C., in 1974 to represent the P.R.C. APA executive officer Kenneth J. Little and other APA leaders fully supported attempts to communicate with and assist the beleaguered P.R.C. psychologists. Attempts to obtain similar overtures of friendship from other professional bodies met with unexpected negativity based on "political problems." Such reactions, whether from individuals or professional body directors, surprised and disturbed me. They clearly implied that anything done for and with scholars in China meant "political" assent, a rationale that I rejected as arrogant and short-sighted. However, I always found reassurance at those times by recalling that the Fulbright Program had given assistance to my 1972 visit to the P.R.C. and had therefore furthered national goals by encouraging the establishment of U.S./P.R.C. scholarly relations.

The APA sent publications to the psychologists located in 1972. I sent news on psychological developments and continued to write, even though some propagandistic and hate mail came to me from the P.R.C. which I interpreted as adherence to the CR line. The first hate letter came in 1973, supposedly from the editor of the important *Peking Review*, to say that if I ever returned to the P.R.C. "your dog legs will be broken!" The letter accused me of "raising the Red Flag to pull it down," which meant that my true intentions were to harm the P.R.C. The State Department and the P.R.C. Embassy in Ottawa, Canada, expressed considerable concern and asked for copies of the letter. The embassy then asked for the original copy which I delivered. In time, I was informed that the letter was bogus and sent by persons unknown to create confusion among friends. Whether bogus or not, we shall never know for sure; either possibility is credible as we look back now. Seeing that the fragile line of communications with the Chinese psychologists continued and grew stronger remained the key objective amidst strong distractions. APA invitations to attend annual conventions drew repetitiously brief but polite declines. That is why Professor Ching's appearance at the 1979 APA convention in New York signaled the beginning of a new era in U.S./P.R.C. relations in psychology. Since 1979, many more psychologists have visited and studied in the United States. Through the auspices of the Ministry of Education in May 1981 and then the Kwangtung Provincial Bureau of Higher Education in October 1981, I revisited many of the psychologists who had hosted me in 1980 and met others for the first time. In 1980, I learned that there were 1,000 psychologists working in the P.R.C. and hundreds of new psychology students. The number had increased to 1,500 psychologists in 1981, a great gain but still only one per 670,000 people!

The psychologists that I met in 1980-81 impressed me with their enthusiasm to learn and promote psychology. The antiintellectualism and deprivation of the CR remained a cloud over the psychologists even in 1981, and its effects will take a long time to be overcome. However, the relative lack of negativism and remorse for their personal suffering during the CR drew my enduring respect. The psychologists and other intellectuals I have met express their regrets with the CR by saying how far behind they had become in research, study, and familiarity with developments abroad. Despite their past setbacks, their love of country, devotion to psychology as a science, and means to assist societal progress gave pause and made one reflect on one's own commitment to ideals and others. My several visits to the P.R.C. often brought to mind the freedoms and privileges scholars in the United States take for granted. I wondered whether Americans realized their precious advantages, such as the Fulbright Program, and were doing enough to preserve them.

Officials in the ministries of education and foreign affairs discussed with me the greater development of psychological training, the priority psychology should be given in research and social service, and government support for increased student/scholar exchanges. I also made it a point to recommend that the P.R.C. accept and work with the Fulbright Program. Although meetings with leading officials were always warm and encouraging, it remains to be seen whether psychology in the P.R.C. is given greater governmental support. Resources are limited and the P.R.C. has dedicated itself to modernize its science and technology, defense, agriculture, and industry, which are broad, general goals that could include the psychologists far more than in the past. I gave examples of research and study in the United States which supported such objectives. At least five departments of psychology are training students. The Institute of Psychology resumed publication of the journal *Acta Psychologica Sinica* in 1979. The CPS joined the International Union of Psychological Sciences at the 22nd meeting of the International Congress of Psychology in Leipzig, July 1980. For many years, I had called for this result urging IUPS secretary general Wayne Holtzman (University of Texas, Austin) as well as the Chinese psychologists to have the P.R.C. become a member of the IUPS.

One highlight of so many experiences which came about through Fulbright awards in 1972 involved the Blackfeet Indians of Montana in 1980. Before the two of us returned to the P.R.C., as previously discussed, Professor Ching Chi-cheng visited the University of Montana and gave two lectures which were well received. He gave a provocative history of China's psychology (Ching, 1980). We took Professor Ching to Browning, Montana, where the Blackfeet welcomed him warmly. In Beijing, a model tepee and other gifts from the Blackfeet Chief, Earl Old Person, were formally received as a gesture of friendship to the Chinese people. It was quite wonderful helping Professor Ching explain to his colleagues the friendship of Americans, such as the Blackfeet of Montana and the sincere sense of goodwill they presented. The gifts have been deposited in the Beijing University Museum. As more American scholars visit their counterparts in the P.R.C., such as through the Fulbright Program, perhaps some will come across the display of American-Indian artifacts and wonder how they ever got there.

The Institute of Psychology sent a commemorative scroll with the following poem written in classical T'ang calligraphy:

> *The spring flowers welcome a faraway guest*
> *to be compatriots surpasses being the best guest*
> *Our mountains and rivers are strengthened*
> *our emotions are similar to those of people of the*
> *same blood*
> *We try to increase our mutual scholarship*
> *at the same time to deepen our friendship*
> *We remember well your departure*
> *your image lingers freshly in our minds with wishes*
> *for your early return.*
> *Dedicated to the first American psychologist who*
> *came to China by invitation, Professor Albert H.*
> *Yee, the Summer of 1980, Beijing.*

Surely the Fulbright Program can be likened to Henry Adams's famous line: "A teacher affects eternity; he can never tell where his influence stops." The above experiences, which deeply and enduringly affected so many people and institutional and international events, would not have been possible or developed in the same positive form without the Fulbright Program.

References

Ching, C.C. "Psychology in the People's Republic of China," *American Psychologist* 35 (1980): 1084-89.

Yee, A.H. "Psychology in China Bows to the Cultural Revolution," APA *Monitor* 4 (1973a): 1, 4.

_____. "Schools and Progress in the People's Republic of China," *Educational Researcher* 2 (1973b): 5-15.

PART IX
THE OTHER SIDE
OF THE COIN

Introduction

The previous essays have emphasized one direction of the Fulbright experience—that of Americans working and learning in other countries. The other side of the coin is, of course, the opportunities for those in other countries to come to the United States to work and study. They have come from many countries, and we can illustrate only a small part of that range—Belgium, Norway, and Japan.

Belgium

Herman Liebaers was associated for over thirty years with the Royal Library of Belgium and he used his experience, including an early Fulbright, to further international library affairs. He served as an advisor to the governments of Belgium, France, and Iran, as president of the International Federation of Library Associations, and as a consultant to the Council on Library Resources in Washington. Based on his long international experience, he is able to observe, "In America, nothing is completely different from Europe, but nothing is completely the same."

Norway

Sigmund Skard provides a background of the Fulbright Program in Norway. He points out the importance of the program in the development of American Studies in Norway and his own important role in the continuity of the exchange between American and Norwegian scholars. Two other contributions exemplify the continuity of the program.

Orm Øverland points out the influence of the Fulbright Program in the evaluation of his career and in the development of quality in the American studies programs. He also comments on the importance of the development of a truly bilateral exchange program. Many countries in Western Europe, as well as Japan, have begun to institutionalize funding to support their share of the exchange process. Jan Egeland comes from the most recent generation of Fulbrighters from Norway, having completed a year at the School of Law at the University of California-Berkeley in 1983. He exemplifies the ability to be appreciative of his experiences without being uncritical.

Japan

Shigemitsu Kuriyama provides an interesting overview of the beginnings of the Fulbright Program through his participation in 1950-51. Now executive auditor for IBM-Japan, Kuriyama has had a distinguished career in the Ministry of Finance and the World Bank as well as being chief economist for IBM-Japan.

Hideo Kawabuchi provides an interesting account of the formation of the Japan Human Relations Association. Especially in light of the recent worldwide interest in the success of Japanese management ideology, his account of its origins is instructive. His account of his indebtedness for ideas from Professor William Foote Whyte of Cornell University Institute of Labor Relations and his encounter with him some thirty years later suggests the importance of "creative misunderstandings" as a result of cross-cultural experience. Mr. Kawabuchi is president of the Toa Koyu Company and Advisor to the Sumitomo Corporation in Osaka.

Kiyohiko Tsuboi's essay suggests that more than industrial human relations have been a by-product of the Fulbright experience for those in Japan. Tsuboi's account of the importance of F. Scott Fitzgerald for him will be surprising for those who might find Fitzgerald an unexpected choice for communicating "human" experience.

28

A Voice from Old Belgium

Herman Liebaers

Being a Belgian I have to give priority to the Belgian American Educational Foundation (BAEF) over the Fulbright Foundation. The first came out of World War I and its memorable Commission for Relief in Belgium (CRB), while the second grew out of World War II, and the organizational structure was consciously taken over from the older one. The main differences between the two foundations are obvious. The Belgian American Educational Foundation is limited, as its name indicates, to two countries, while the Fulbright Foundation covers many. Today the BAEF still operates as a purely private foundation and hence may be considered, from abroad, as more typically American than the Fulbright Foundation in which the government has a rather large finger in the pie.

However, in my case the Fulbright Foundation came first. I was granted a fellowship in 1950 to study library planning and building. In 100 days I visited 100 libraries over the country which seemed to me without boundaries. I even added a six-week consultantship at the Library of Congress. At the time I was a young librarian at the Royal Library in Brussels and my older colleagues did not appreciate my exposure to American librarianship. When I came back to the library I promised myself never to compare publicly any given situation with the United States, actually never to mention America, while privately my major professional point of reference was America. Not long after my return I was involved in a discussion about the number of hours that the library would be open to the public. I said that the existing system certainly went back to the time of gas light. Some baiting colleague asked whether it was better in the United States, and I made the unforgivable mistake of answering "yes." They made me feel like a traitor to the good old European civilization.

I did not come home when my Fulbright grant was over, because in New York I was offered an advanced fellowship by the BAEF and I went on another tour of the still too large United States, changing the field from librarianship to art history. For reasons still unknown to me today I found myself directing a summer art school in Brussels in 1950 before I left for the United States. The main sponsor of this art school was the BAEF. The dissatisfaction of the foundation with the way the Belgian Art Seminar had developed and the sudden death of its director were the main reasons that someone else had to be put in charge. Since it was me and since I was in the United States, the officers of the BAEF thought that I could try to familiarize myself with the American world of art museums and art departments of universities. Imagine how happy I was when my two fields of activity met in rare-book departments or in print rooms. In my country the national print room is part of the Royal Library.

Over the years the Belgian Art Seminar became the main focal point of my experience with Americans. Every summer I was granted a two-month leave of absence from the library to run the school. Some preparatory work had to be done before the students arrived and after the end some follow-up had to be carried out. I enjoyed every minute I spent with the seminar. With the 1950 criticism in mind I decided to focus the whole session on one glorious period of Belgian art and the first choice fell on the Flemish primitives. Later we reverted to Rubens and the seventeenth century.

Further, a drastic reduction of the ex cathedra lectures was agreed upon, most of the time being given to a direct contact with the works of art themselves. The staff and the subject matter were Belgian, the student body consisted of about fifteen American art historians and as many non-Americans, the Belgians being excluded. The American graduate students came over with fellowships from the BAEF, while the European students were selected through the mixed committees of countries with which Belgium had signed a cultural agreement. From time to time UNESCO added a Fellow from Asia.

This experience lasted for five years and at the end I had the feeling of knowing both in Europe and the United States, most of the top museum curators and leading art historians. This resulted mainly from my repeated visits to the major training centers where I asked the distinguished and elderly directors to send their best students or younger staff members to Belgium. The graduate school of New York University, the Metropolitan Museum, the National Gallery, and some palaces in Europe are names I recall with gratitude.

I could not avoid comparing the American students with the European participants, more particularly with the Italians. At the very beginning I was intrigued by the fact that nearly all these Italian students came to Brussels via Monaco and since they were always late, I tried to find out what mysterious links may have existed between gambling and Flemish paintings. I was ashamed to find out rather late that Monaco is Italian. My good American friends were always on time or even a couple of days early, but they were quiet, serious, and dedicated. They wanted to see as quickly as possible the real works of art of which they had heard so much at home and had seen only in piles of slides and photographs, while noting particular details for checking. Although I gradually discovered strong and outspoken personalities among them, the first impression was mostly one of evenness, which spread equally well over all the American students, those of Italian origin as well as those who were connoisseurs of Italian art. Completely different were the Italians themselves. They were certainly more interested in meeting their American colleagues, in discovering immediately those who spoke Italian, and they had a keen eye for good feminine profiles.

The group was dominated quantitatively by the Americans and Italians, but I should not be unfair to individual participants from other countries. I became an amused observer of these local idiosyncrasies. Differences, such as between Northern and Southern Europe or between the United States and Europe, have since stayed with me and have gradually compelled me to look for explanations. The homogeneity of the group from the point of view of professional interests proved to be a solid base for digging into national or regional peculiarities. I committed the classic mistake of considering the Americans as a monolithic group. I was encouraged, however, by the geographic mobility shown by their vitae.

After a couple of years I found myself in the middle of a group of Belgian art historians, museum directors and curators, art critics and collectors, for whom in turn it was curious to observe their reactions to these foreign art historians basically interested in the artistic expressions of the Low Countries. The Belgians found themselves at ease as Europeans among Europeans, with practically no language problems, but reacted very differently toward the American visitors whom they could not identify with the widespread caricature of American tourists. Some of my compatriots had an American experience of their own, some acquired it on the occasion of the seminars and, finally, some refused to go deeper into the problem of transoceanic relations, hiding generally behind the language barrier. Although I tried, I was not a neutral observer and I often had serious arguments with this last group of fellow countrymen, blaming them for refusing to see that the American art historians were often of Jewish origin and were as such citizens of the world.

Writing more than a quarter century after the end of the seminars I look upon them as a highly human experience where national antagonisms were transcended by professional dedication, where local idiosyncrasies enriched an international exchange of ideas and observations. At the time I was hardly older than the students, sometimes even younger, and I benefited most of all from the many individual contributions. I was also very proud when I discovered by sheer luck in one issue of *The Times Literary Supplement* three books written by former art students—an American, a Frenchman, and a Dutchman. I remember nearly all students. What is no longer clear in my mind is the group to which they belonged, except where friendships among two or three of them grew during the seminars or even led to a transatlantic marriage.

In 1954 I took a leave of absence from the library to become associate secretary of the BAEF, with headquarters in New York and an office in Brussels. I began to commute between the United States and Belgium and never stopped since. The Belgian Art Seminar remained my main responsibility, but I also spent part of my time writing up biographical notes on senior CRB Fellows to be published in the foundation's directory. I liked it as much as the seminar. I could constantly compare my own American experience with that of fellow citizens active in the various branches of academic life. There is no doubt that the common part in these very different experiences was the discovery in the United States of a boundless display of energy. "There was an eagerness to find new and better ways of doing things. There was more teamwork, more openness, frankness, and ease in meeting people than in Europe. There was a generally optimistic attitude. There was mobility," as one observer put it. The BAEF allowed me also to finish my Ph.D.

After two years there came an abrupt end to my formal association with the foundation, because I was appointed director of the Royal Library, a rather unorthodox move from the bottom of the hierarchy to the top. I remained director for seventeen years and tried to translate my American professional acquisitions into the reality of the Belgian library world. For thirteen years I was responsible for a new building, working with obsolete plans and forcing some new ideas into an architectural conception which owed nothing to the tremendous library building renewal in the United States during and immediately after World War II.

As soon as I was appointed I looked for able staff members to send to the United States. I scouted for all possible fellowships and finally had more offers than candidates. From time to time I even had to slightly twist an arm. It was not long before nearly all single staff members had spent a few months or a year in the United States. The fellowships which were available did not cover the expenses of married couples, but fortunately libraries generally have a good average of single persons on their staff.

Once I had two single librarians at the same time on the other side of the ocean, August Cockx who was spending a year at the Linda Hall Library in Kansas City, and Elly Indestege who was a fellow at the Folger Shakespeare Library in Washington, D.C. It was customary at the time that at the end of their stay visiting librarians were offered a trip through the United States. Mary Ann Adams at the Library of Congress organized these trips, and when she found two Belgians on her list, she decided to put them on the same planes and send them to the same cities. What was due to happen, happened. They got married as soon as they were back in Belgium, although both had been working previously for quite some time at the Royal Library without looking at one another.

The range of responsibility was wide indeed in the library and I even widened it by including scientific and technical documentation under the guidance of my man from Linda Hall. If someone asked me what the library exactly covered, I had a ready answer: "Everything that separates Mr. and Mrs. Cockx!" Mrs. Cockx was indeed working in the Rare Books Department.

After my first trip I published an unpretentious assessment of America and I opened it by noting that the United States was fortunate in having no ministry of education. Things had changed in Washington, but Belgium, which is 300 times smaller than the United States, is still abreast of America with four ministers, a Dutch-speaking and a French-speaking one for both education and for culture.

Some people think that we have two ministers without education and two without culture, as was quoted recently in the Parisian *Revue des Deux Mondes*. If I have learned one lesson in the United States it is confidence in people, individually and socially, and not to turn for everything to the government as we do in continental Europe, more in the southern than in the northern part, I admit.

In Belgium government interference grew worse year after year, and soon I was to forget the brilliant dedication of the new building by the king and the whole royal family on 17 February 1969, exactly thirty-five years after the death of King Albert I, to whom the library is dedicated. Reluctantly I had to admit that I lost my battle with the various layers of Belgian bureaucracy.

Parallel to this failure I found myself more and more involved in international library work. I was elected president of the International Federation of Library Associations the same year.

For the second time I left the library with the idea of no return and I started working in 1973 as a consultant to the Council on Library Resources in Washington, D.C. Though my consultantship was shorter than both the council and I expected, I am still connected with CLR as a board member, actually the one non-American board member. At the council I found again that American virtue: responsible citizens can decide for themselves and act according to their own ability.

On 1 January 1974 I left the council to join the Belgian court. This was a move that my American friends did not understand. It came also unexpectedly for me. When the king asked me to work for him I had my doubts about my ability to meet his expectations. He waved them off airily; "You only have to cross the street from the library to the palace." I was soon to realize that I needed more than a topographic knowledge of Brussels to understand what he meant. Not to mention the fact that like most of his compatriots the king ignored that I had been pushed out of the library by the Belgian bureaucracy and that I deliberately had put an ocean between my homeland and me. Were it not for the king I would not have returned to Belgium.

At home I inherited the prerevolutionary and hence pompous title of Grand Maréchal de la Cour—chief assistant to the king. I am not going to explain what such an assistant is supposed to do, but my experience over the years led to a rather simple conclusion: Whether the head of the state is an elected president or a king by inheritance, there were no major differences. In a constitutional monarchy like Belgium, the king had no personal power. As the leader of society he has to look after public morality, which in periods of societal transformation, as the one in which we live now, is extremely difficult. A quick look at the map of Europe shows that constitutional monarchies are the best safeguards of democracy. So, I did not plunge back in the Middle Ages, as some people in California thought.

The king traveled several times to the United States during my term of office. Generally these were private visits, but one was more official, when he opened the Belgium Today program organized in 1980 in Washington, New York, and San Francisco on the occasion of the one hundred fiftieth anniversary of our independence. That old Kingdom of Belgium which became more recently independent than the United States! The king had to fly home after the Washington party, because there was a cabinet crisis at home and the king is entrusted with constitutional powers to solve the crisis. The luncheon at the White House was sad: It was the very day the failure of the rescue operation in Iran was announced. In such circumstances grief is shared among hosts and guests. America is no longer large, Belgium is no longer small. One a republic, the other a kingdom. So what?

More than a hundred times I crossed the ocean over a period of about thirty years. I am afraid I did it more and more the American way: "If it is Tuesday, it must be New York." But however short the visits, they were always an occasion to reappreciate American values which had gradually penetrated my way of life, first professionally and later just humanly. I never lost my European roots, my local idiosyncrasies. I remain even proud of my Brussels connection, with one foot in Germanic Europe and the other in Latin Europe. What a wealth and what a privileged position to understand the European origin of the American civilization. I said after my first trip: "In America nothing is completely different from Europe, but nothing is completely the same." I repeat it today.

29

Killing Myths and Prejudices:
Bridging the Atlantic Gap

Jan Egeland

I came as a visiting Fulbright scholar to Berkeley exactly ten years after joining, at fifteen, the Norwegian groups protesting U.S. involvement in the Vietnam War. It was some nine years after doing a high-school specialization on Che Guevara, the Latin American revolutionary, and five years after my first brief visit to the United States on my way to work with a Catholic aid organization among the rural poor in Colombia, South America.

I knew a lot about the nature and consequences of U.S. foreign policy, about its political system and economic power. I knew considerably less about American domestic lifestyle, academic institutions, national and local public debate, and strikingly little about the multicultural and multiracial vitality and dynamism in U.S. society at large.

It was certainly good for me to learn and understand a great deal more about this, the world's most important society, through the only contact I had not had: direct and human participation for a full year. Maybe it also was useful for my local social and academic environment to have somebody there with a different background when debating everything from peace movements and human rights to winter sports and languages.

Certainly the wise method of the Fulbright Program for building cross-cultural understanding and eliminating misunderstandings worked in my case: I appreciate more the difficult U.S. superpower position, I have a clearer picture now of how much I do not really understand of American society and therefore should learn from a society which is very much alive and very much in transition and formation.

This does not mean that I changed my value systems or my political and ethical views in the course of the nine months in California—which was never the purpose of these exchanges in the first place. I *still* believe U.S. interaction with Central and South America is fundamentally and trag-

235

ically wrong, and I still believe the Washington administration at this writing is dangerously wrong in its arms race against "the other side" (which lies far away from Washington, but happens to be bordering my own country).

Forcing peoples' minds is just the opposite of Senator Fulbright's vision: The Fulbright Program or the Scandinavian-American Association (my other sponsor) *never* directly or even indirectly tried to influence my opinions. On the contrary, they were interested in having, for what it is worth, *my* opinions about the environment I met. This is, of course, part of why the program always worked so well, and why the quality of the Fulbright label stands undisputed in so many different countries.

For the same reasons, the big "Project Democracy" of the Reagan administration, with all its exchanges, publications, and seminars, may *not* be the best format for increasing international acceptance of Western and American values. If a program for greater international understanding and cooperation is seen in the context of an international "battle of ideas" it defeats its own purpose.

The greatest value for me while studying and traveling in the United States was the absolute direct and indirect freedom to judge for myself: When I visited the San Quentin prison I was, for example, struck by how open and honest everyone was toward me as a student and journalist considering the very severe problems California and the United States has in the treatment of law offenders. I was taken on a "guided tour" by some of the inmates serving life sentences who fiercely criticized the inhuman system with no interference from the guards. I was, in short, more free to investigate the situation than I would be in my own country, where bureaucracy and official and private institutions are much more reluctant to face the media and the public. This relative secrecy is there even though I know that the kind of inhuman and degrading conditions in San Quentin would not be found in our punitive systems.

Being young, a liberal social democrat, Scandinavian, and an academic, I certainly carried to the San Francisco Bay Area my share of myths and prejudices about the United States and Americans at large. It was also, therefore, where I so much wanted to go for a period of time: to test some of these myths obtained as an observer from Europe and Latin America against reality. I wanted to meet that diverse mixture of people who represent the dominant political and cultural influence in my own country's postwar history.

"If your Scandinavian welfare state is functioning as well as you seem to think, why is then the suicide rate so high up there?" a friendly student asked when I was telling a law class about the Norwegian social and legal context. It is a question I have been asked as many times as I have met the standard remark about "Finnish lack of independence" due to Soviet interference. In isolation such viewpoints would certainly underscore one of my original "American prejudices": that an American's rudimentary knowledge about faraway countries does not decrease his willingness to have easy solutions to their complicated problems.

One year with the University of California, visiting other academic and social institutions and meeting with countless Americans representing as many different opinions, quite effectively killed such a myth. If, on average, there is less knowledge about Europe in the United States than vice versa, the willingness to listen and the interest for understanding the opinions of others was refreshingly higher (and less arrogant) than among most of us on the other side of the Atlantic. And herein lies the magic of the Fulbright Program: It gives us, with "no strings attached," the opportunity to see the human inside, sympathetic and diverse, of the monstrous superpower we observe and simplify as one giant actor in the international arena.

It is much more difficult to judge the benefits of the exchanges on the "other side." What could Berkeley, with academic and material resources much greater than anything I know of in Europe, gain from having us, the Fulbrighters and foreigners? One easy way to avoid answering would be to say that "now it is the turn of Americans, having at this point in history the richest universities, to organize the international meeting place for academic work." But hopefully, there is an added positive element for vital U.S. educational institutions to have this source for frank and direct debate with an outside world in which the United States has been a superpower for such a short time.

Being part of one of the big American universities did away with another old myth about the United States: that everything in this country is politically as right-wing and conservative as much of its political leadership appears to be. American universities are not only the world's richest educational institutions, they are in many ways also among the most flexible, dynamic, and liberal. For a Norwegian student having always specialized in one single topic at a time, it may seem a bit "loose" when American students in the same term may combine studies in political science, astronomy, computer science, and tennis. But this freedom to choose, combine, and specialize in the intellectual marketplace is fundamental. I would have liked to see us adopt some of that academic flexibility and maybe for the United States to take some of our less competitive and more cooperative atmosphere among students.

It is forty years since the first Fulbrighters crossed oceans and borders to live in and learn from another society. At that time the world lived through one of its most difficult periods with a maximum of political tension and human misery. The program proved to work. The experiences and friendships from these thousands of individual projects in transborder understanding, have been an important contribution when trying to fight fundamental global problems.

My experience as a Fulbrighter is still not a year old, and we cannot claim that our generation of the exchange program has been able to do anything of measurable importance for the ideals the program originated from. However, I would risk this opinion: It has never been more important than now to continue the program, as tension is mounting between military alliances and between the unjustifiably rich and the untolerably poor nations. We need forty-times-forty more years of the Fulbright Program which has killed so many myths and built so much trust and understanding in a world so much in need of exactly that.

30

On Realizing the *Exchange* in the Fulbright Program

Orm Øverland

The Fulbright Program deals with individuals, facilitating their move-ment from or to the United States and other countries all over the world. It is thus a decisive influence on thousands of lives and has directed and shaped not only careers but personalities. These individuals, however, function in societies and take part in the forming of institutions, policies, and culture in general. Consequently, my essay is concerned with the per-sonal as well as the general, and moves back and forth between the bio-graphic and the historical modes. Hopefully all is informed by the belief that interest in what we have been should be generated by a concern for what we may become.

I inhabit two lands and owe allegiance to both. One is the small northern kingdom of Norway with clearly demarcated national borders and with a language, culture, and traditions which set it apart from other nations. From this land I am often separated by great distances, as now in Seattle, in the extreme West of the United States. From the other I am seldom far away. This is the land of academia, an amorphous internation that only recently has received a lexicographic recognition, but with a code, culture, and traditions that set it apart from other contenders to internation status. My awareness of the formative impact and strength of both these ties surfaced after a travel grant from the Fulbright Program in 1964 helped me to embark for three years of graduate work at Yale University.

Certainly it is a common experience that travel, and in particular pro-longed stay abroad, teaches us as much of the country we left behind as of the country we visit. This experience was particularly acute in my case, entering a graduate program in American studies where the ubiquitous question of "American uniqueness" made the concomitant question of the significance to me of my own nationality all the more pressing. During my second year I found myself unable to respond to a question put to me in

239

class: "How can you possibly teach Robert Frost to Norwegian students? His poetry is so uniquely American." Having met, or so I believed, so many of Frost's characters on Norwegian farms, I had not been conscious of a problem in communication. Later I realized that national uniqueness should not be confused with incommunicability: it does not mean separateness; nor does it mean self-sufficiency. During those three years I developed the conviction that you can only learn to appreciate what a country, its culture, and traditions mean to its people through understanding what your country means to you. This sense of national identity is the necessary foundation for internationalism: Without the *national* we are left merely with the *inter*, a piece of flotsam with no port of departure and no direction. This conviction has deepened through the years of travel that have followed. As an *exchange* program, the Fulbright Program rests on the same conviction: belief in the value of exchange assumes value in what is exchanged. For me, then, the Fulbright Program became an introduction to nationality and internationality, not merely to the United States.

In 1964, however, going to a different and more prestigious university seemed even more exciting than going to another country. Nationality did not interest me overly much at the outset; I looked forward to an academic experience different not only in degree but in kind. I am certainly not the only European scholar for whom the American graduate school has been a crucial intellectual experience. In that respect my greatest expectations were not only fulfilled but surpassed. But as I came to see the experience of nationality as a basis for different yet interdependent attitudes to the world, I came to see the universities that are rooted in these different soils also as part of one large transnational community. It is not only that the pursuit of learning and understanding is a shared aim, nor that communication within the community is so international that a Norwegian may teach American literature in Hungary and Japan, but also that the members of this land of academia have so many cultural traits in common and, more important, share a set of values that remain as standards of behavior however difficult they are to live up to.

But then universities developed in medieval Europe before nations and nationalism as we now know these concepts. The language of learning (as of the church) was international and scholars were wanderers. (Fellow Fulbrighters from other continents must not only forgive but appreciate my Eurocentricity just as I can only justify it in my own appreciation of other complementary views of the world.) The rise of nation-states and their rivalries, however, served both to create boundaries for the migration of scholars and to corrupt the sense of dual allegiance that is essential to scholarly integrity. I am not suggesting any fall from a golden age of academia, but merely pointing out that the demands of nation and of academia often may appear to be in conflict with each other. Regret it as we may, scholars have always stood ready to serve aggressive and repressive regimes, lending their learning to misguided nationalism and the subjugation of other nations, creeds, or ideologies, and thus denying their allegiance to the international community of science and scholarship. When the Fulbright Program was conceived, free movement in academia had come to a virtual standstill. Not movement as such, of course, since the great intellectual vitality of the best American universities at the time in no small degree was the result of the forced migration of so many of Europe's best minds. In the years immediately after the war the one-way migration of intellect continued westward, now not so much for preservation of life or pursuit of freedom as for better material conditions and rewards than those a ravaged Europe could provide. At the receiving end of this migration, the United States would at least not seem to have had any immediate selfish need to promote mobility in academia.

With the initiative that created the Fulbright Program began a new international migration of scholars that has continued to grow and that has led to consequences in the lives of institutions as well as of individuals that defy simple measurement. These migrations have been a significant influence in the shaping of my life.

When I was a student of English at the University of Oslo the department was fortunate in having a yearly turnover of visiting Fulbright professors who brought with them their specific scholarly insights and learning as well as intimations of a different and exciting culture. The Fulbright Program may not be primarily concerned with promoting the study of American culture, but this is certainly the area where it has had the most obvious impact on the universities of my country. This could come about because both universities and the school system were committed to the development of the study of American culture as part of the study of English before the Fulbright Program made itself felt. In sending visiting professors in American studies to the English departments, the Fulbright Program was thus not foisting intruders on reluctant or indifferent institutions but offering assistance in developing a fledgling academic program without sufficient human and material resources. American studies at Norwegian universities consequently never depended on the Fulbright Program but have benefited greatly from it. Without the Fulbright Program the study of American culture would hardly have had the quality and standing it has today. The program's unqualified success in this particular case was brought about by a shared interest and common effort.

But the most significant impact of the Fulbright Program has not been in such intangibles as academic program development or specific research projects but in the attitudes and outlook of the many prominent scholars who spent a formative period of their careers at American universities. Not all of these were sponsored by the Fulbright Program, but the channeling of other American resources into the funding of academic exchange was surely influenced by the existence and successes of the program. One way of measuring the impact of the exchange experience on the many who were exposed to it is to look at the importance given to exchange at our universities today.

I have been using the word *exchange* as if unaware that in reality there was no true exchange to begin with. It was a one-way operation, a gift, a spilling over of American abundance; and for a while this annual gift seemed a permanent feature in the life of our universities: Professors and students, coming and going, all provided for by an act of the U.S. Congress. But the budget priorities of governments do not have permanence and the Fulbright Program was, if not reduced, at least given other directions that meant reductions to Europe. And this change in policy in Washington gradually restored meaning to the word *exchange* in the Fulbright Program by introducing the concept of reciprocity. The fact that European countries and Japan in varying degrees now contribute to the funding of various aspects of the Fulbright Program speaks not only of the economic growth of these countries but, more importantly, of the success of the program in having demonstrated its value as something far more than a free ride. And other developments in academic exchange speak further of this success.

The growing number of bilateral exchange programs between American universities and universities abroad are the most interesting and promising offspring of the Fulbright Program. In recognition of the value international exchange has had and has for them, the generation of scholars and administrators now influencing the governance of universities has realized that local initiatives must be taken to ensure continued scholarly exchange independent of the health of the parent Fulbright Program. The avenues of exchange had been built for us and had become indispensable for the intellectual quality of universities on both sides of the Atlantic: It was therefore natural that maintenance of these avenues should become a major concern. My university is small by international standards and our programs are correspondingly modest. Each year a group of American students from the University of California system and from the University of Oregon come to stay with us, contributing to the diversity of our student body and receiving the enriching but often unsettling experience of exposure to a foreign way of life. And each year a corresponding group of Norwegian students goes the other way, to contribute and to receive. With the University of Washington we have a faculty exchange program that has given impetus to academic programs and research projects on both sides.

All such exchange programs testify to the lasting influence of the Fulbright Program.

This fact has been recognized by the same government that initiated the Fulbright Program, in that U.S. federal grants have been made available for the support and strengthening of such bilateral exchange programs. The logistic advantages of university-to-university programs are obvious. They may also more easily lead to long-term cooperative projects and organized faculty development. It is to be hoped that governments and foundations on both sides of the Atlantic will see the importance of encouraging them. However, the true measure of their value will be that the universities involved continue to give them support and that they thus can survive and perhaps even thrive independently of the fickleness of government budgets.

The Fulbright Program and its immediate relatives and offspring, however, are radically different in their implications for the United States and for the other countries involved. Throughout this essay I have used the term "international" about programs that, for my country, only involve the United States, and I have written about "the two sides of the Atlantic" not merely as if this were the extent of my world, but as if this were synonymous with Europe and the United States. For my American colleagues in academia the Fulbright Program has been a truly international program, opening up avenues of exchange between the United States and countries on all continents. However, the effect of the program on the universities in these other countries has been to tie an incommensurately large part of their academic exchange to one country, not by creating barriers to other exchange but simply by doing such an excellent job of smoothing that one road back and forth to the United States. There was a point in my career when it became a stumbling block that I had virtually no contact with colleagues from other nations and knew more of work being done in faraway America than I did of work done by next door neighbors, not to speak of more distant parts of the world. This realization forced me to reconsider the benefit of merely being on the receiving end of beneficence.

The ultimate test of the impact of the Fulbright Program would therefore seem to be the degree to which the recipient countries recognized the value of the international exchange of scholars, and thus recognized the internation status of academia, by funding similar programs themselves. The initiative and the responsibility for such programs will have to come from the universities, and I am glad to see a growing commitment to international exchange at my own university, expressed both in the establishing of bilateral exchange agreements with universities in other countries, like the Sudan and Canada, and in a university-sponsored program making it possible to invite scholars from abroad to work with us on projects of common interest. Thus the Fulbright Program after four decades of activity is bearing all manner of fruit by which the tree may be known.

Having benefited so greatly from this fruit, I find myself serving the two lands of my allegiance as chairperson of my university's committee for international exchange, working actively to improve the roads leading to other regions of academia and thereby making Norway a better place to live. In this work I feel that I, however modestly, am helping to keep alive the ideas given such eloquent expression in the program that carries the name of Senator J. William Fulbright, and find that I am still exploring the implications for my own life of that 1964 Fulbright travel grant.

31

Fulbrighters in Norway

Sigmund Skard

This volume of essays is intended to bring together testimonies concerning the importance of Fulbright grants to the writers' own lives and careers. In my case, personal experiences seem inextricably intertwined with the more general effects of the Fulbright arrangement in Norway.

The American impact on my nation dates far back. As we know now, Norsemen from Norwegian-settled Iceland and Greenland were the first Europeans to put foot on the soil of the New World, some five hundred years before Columbus. After that, connections long remained tenuous, as Norway became a powerless province of the Danish realm. But the memory of past exploits endured and, in the eighteenth century, strengthened a rising patriotism, which was also encouraged by the libertarian ideas of the American Revolution.

In 1814, when Norway withdrew from its union with Denmark, enthusiasm for free America became a force in the growth of Norwegian democracy. Ties were further strengthened by an immense emigration to the United States; the percentage of the emigrating population sometimes was only equalled by Ireland. This closeness reached its height in the fellowship-in-arms during World War II. In 1949, it was natural for Norway to join NATO, a military alliance with the United States. The only foreign statesmen to have public monuments in the Norwegian capital are American presidents Abraham Lincoln and Franklin D. Roosevelt.

The educational system of Norway, however, only showed small signs of similar attitudes toward the United States. In the study of modern history the United States, of course, could not be completely ignored. But in secondary schools and at the university the study of English was completely focused on Great Britain—its language, literature, and culture. As late as World War II, one could still pass any examination in English at the University of Oslo without having read a single American book or displaying any knowledge of the history and life of what had become for many the greatest English-speaking nation.

World War II made this situation intolerable. Soon after the conclusion of hostilities the Norwegian government established a full professorship in American Literature at the University of Oslo, then the only university in Norway. This professorship was the first of its kind in the Nordic countries. I was appointed to the chair. Somewhat later study of America was made obligatory in secondary schools, on a par with that of Great Britain. In 1957, after considerable resistance, similar requirements were introduced in the English Department at the University of Oslo, to be imitated in time by the three universities established in Norway after the war.

Turning this program into a reality was, however, no simple matter. Systematic American studies had hardly existed in Norway before. Moreover, the country was facing enormous problems with reconstruction after the war. The task could not be performed without substantial assistance from sources outside Norway. Such assistance was, however, willingly afforded, initially by the Rockefeller and Ford foundations. With support from the former institution I was able to spend the year 1946-47 in the United States, preparing for my new post and building up a research library for a prospective American Institute at the University of Oslo. But the real problems were waiting at home. Fortunately, however, from 1949 onward, the Fulbright arrangement came into the picture.

As of 1951, American studies was to be taught in all Norwegian secondary schools, but by a staff of teachers who, during their university education, had acquired little or no background for such work. This situation had to be met with extraordinary measures. From 1950 to 1961, with the assistance of Fulbright funding, the American Institute at the University of Oslo arranged eleven summer school sessions for American studies, where secondary-school teachers were prepared for their future work. Some of the courses were also frequented by teachers from other Nordic countries.

The problems were even more pressing on the university level, for qualified native teachers as yet were hardly available. The decisive importance of Fulbright support could be clearly seen in this connection. Through grants from the Fulbright Foundation, several American scholars of top rank taught American studies at the University of Oslo in the early 1950s. From 1957 to 1969, when our needs were even more demanding, we had a Fulbright visiting professor of American studies each year, thirteen scholars in all, which was most unusual at a time when such visitors were in great demand in many other countries.

Fulbright professors also taught in other departments of the University of Oslo, but perhaps not as regularly as in our English Department. Each scholar, in his field, helped develop our contacts with the United States. Most of these American visitors were at the beginning of their university teaching careers. They were accepted as ordinary staff members, and were well treated. I think most of them enjoyed their pioneering experience in Norway thoroughly, and in their work set a high professional standard. Similar Fulbright visiting arrangements were eventually set up with the other new universities in Norway.

No less important was the movement westward across the Atlantic, which was also made possible through Fulbright funding. By 1968, a total of 1,685 Fulbright fellowships had been granted to Norwegians, many of them within the various fields of American studies; grants have also been numerous after that year. Some of these grants went to Norwegian university teachers of American studies, whose numbers were now finally on the increase. For a year of study in the United States, I not only had Fulbright travel grants, but the salary for my American substitute in Oslo also came from the same source. The scholarly value of the studies thus made possible is incalculable.

Perhaps in the long run, it meant just as much to the great number of young Norwegian students who were able to visit the United States under these fellowships, preparing for their future careers in secondary schools and universities. If, in the 1980s, the various fields of American studies are as solidly entrenched in the educational system of Norway as anywhere else in Europe, and now almost exclusively taught by Norwegian scholars, this is in no small way due to the Fulbright arrangement.

To me personally, the growth of American studies in Norway has been a source of great professional satisfaction. Fulbright grants have widened my own scholarly horizons on both sides of the Atlantic, and have given me invaluable contact with people from various fields of learning. But the Fulbright Program also came to mean much to me on a far more personal level. At the University of Oslo my wife (a colleague from the Psychology Department) and I both worked in fields which necessitated wide international exposure. Guests to our home from abroad were numerous. In our younger years we quite naturally fell into the role of academic innkeepers. Fulbrighters made up so large a percent of these guests to our home that for many years the U.S. Educational Foundation even paid our entertainment bills. Some of our most fruitful and pleasant academic memories are connected with these social events and with the changing crowds of exceptional men and women who journeyed across the ocean. To a great extent these experiences, too, were due to Senator J. William Fulbright and his farsighted initiative more than forty years ago.

32

Japan Human Relations Association and Cornell University

Hideo Kawabuchi

Hiroshi Yamada was once an efficiency engineer at the Osaka Industrial Efficiency Association (OIEA), whose board of directors was headed by Tsuneo Ohuchi and my boss Seiichi Matsumoto, senior managing director in charge of the labor relations and personnel departments at Sumitomo Metal Industries (SMI), Japan. I used to attend board meetings in place of Mr. Matsumoto and that was why I came to be acquainted with Mr. Yamada. It was he who asked me to write something about the personnel administration of the defunct Japanese navy and about practices of labor unions—elections, training of rank and file, and collective bargaining at the time of "Sturm und Drang" after World War II.

Even during my Fulbright stay in the United States, Mr. Yamada and I corresponded and surely OIEA's monthly magazine *Industrial Efficiency*, edited by him, was a good reference for my study at The State School of Industrial and Labor Relations (ILR) at Cornell University.

In 1952 I returned home to resume work under Mr. Matsumoto. Mr. Yamada asked me to write a report about industrial relations in the United States and organize a seminar sponsored by his association. I had written a report of my academic life in the United States under the title of "Personnel Administration Note Book," published by the Institute of Japan Iron and Steel Industry and with an introduction by Professor Emeritus Enjiro Awaji of Tokyo University. So I sent a copy to Mr. Yamada and he proposed that I hold a series of studies with my book as a text. This was the beginning of our Human Relations Association which was formally founded in April 1956 with a membership of over 4,300 companies totaling 360,000 employees. I was elected chairman, Hiroshi Yamada, senior managing director, and his younger brother Kenjiro Yamada, managing director of the association.

The Yamada brothers have an aggressive and extraordinary talent together with an enthusiastic spirit of inquiry. Hiroshi wrote some twenty books and countless articles in his chosen area while Kenjiro helped his brother compose a supervisor's handbook, publish the monthly magazine *Man and Management* and many kinds of standardized forms used for each step of practices of industrial and labor relations, and organize several seminars at home and abroad for executive training and development. These references and forms are all invented from brain-stormings, seminars, and panel discussions held under their auspices. Small and medium-sized organizations particularly appreciate them for the daily administration of employees. Some of the books and pamphlets are best sellers.

The Yamada brothers and I used to talk about the modest but unique activities of the Japan Human Relations Association for further development and came to agree about the huge impact of our leading principles from the very beginning of its establishment: (1) give-and-take; (2) discard the shadow for the substance; and (3) single representatives from each category of business line.

Under these slogans, many a young and old businessman and their successors would get together to discuss, analyze, reconsider, and adjust to their organizations, being refreshed and brain-stormed. Thus a quarter of century passed with slow, steady, and satisfactory steps.

In the process of development, our association has been strongly influenced by two sorts of philosophies: religious and pragmatic. In 1905 Tenko Nishida founded Itto-en, an ethical society in Yamashina, Kyoto, with a peaceful world through service and prayer as its platform.

Late president Seiichi Suzuki of Daskin Co. was one of the followers of T. Nishida and has resuscitated his former organization of Kentoku, a Polish chain-store venture which was taken over by an American and which made Daskin a prosperous company in turn. Mr. Suzuki was a very close friend of Hiroshi Yamada and asked him to be a board member.

It was probably in the early 1950s that Messrs. Suzuki and Yamada introduced me to Mr. and Mrs. Melvin Evans, founders of Democracy in Action, Inc. (Chicago), and also the editors of a magazine on human engineering with the same title. I met them at a businessmen's club in Osaka and remember that the enthusiastic participants listened to an evangelical approach to business leadership which was greatly admired by the managerial people, who were convinced that the American way of thinking and business management excelled others. I assume that Mr. Konosuke Matsushita, founder of "National" Group, has had no personal relation with Mr. Evans, but they share nearly the same business concepts and views of life. Mr. Evans believed creative leadership had deep roots in four life areas of work, home, hobby, and faith, which are always present in the numerous books written by Mr. Matsushita on his belief in PHP (Peace, Happiness, and Prosperity), and published by PHP Laboratory.

We have learned from Mr. Evans that "the beginning of leadership is an alert, open mind, courage, force of personality, and finally persistence" in "The Cutting Edge of Leadership" (May-June 1954 issue of *Democracy in Action*), and this philosophy seems to have been fully achieved thereafter in Japan.

Japan Human Relations Association celebrated its twenty-fifth anniversary in July 1981. Its board of directors decided to have a special program to remember its functions and to renew its goals. One of the big events in commemoration of its foundation was the seminar with Dr. G. Hofstede, professor at the European Management Research Institute, Holland, as the guest speaker on value analysis of the industrial and labor relations concept of the Japanese. There were over three hundred participants, and the frank discussion of various aspects of businessmen's activities as they are involved in international relations elicited much interest.

The actual records of prosperous members' activities, however, have been proven in each edition of its monthly magazine, *Men and Management*, its bi-monthly booklet, "Self-development," and several training aids. Several institutes organized both at home and abroad, are also popular among the member companies. So we are satisfied with the thus far fortified foundation of business expansion which shall last in harmony with the needs of the members in the rapidly changing world of business and industry.

As for the foreign scholars interested in our common subject of industrial relations, I wish to express my sincere appreciation of three other experts in the United States. They are Dr. William Foote Whyte, Mr. Aaron Martin Cohen, and Professor Harold Oaklander. Dr. Whyte was professor of human relations at ILR School, Cornell University, to whom I owe my own personnel policies and practices at SMI since I returned home. *Street Corner Society, Human Relations in the Restaurant Industry, Pattern for Industrial Peace*, etc. were books that moved me deeply. Though his scheduled visit to Japan with Mrs. Whyte in 1974 did not materialize, we exchanged correspondence to organize a program to make his visit efficient. Japan Human Relations Association was naturally enthusiastic to receive this prominent scholar on several occasions, not only to meet his needs but to impress the member organizations with updated knowledge of the United States and Latin America.

What a delight it was when we received information on his visit to Tokyo and Osaka in the spring of 1982! The reason he visited the People's Republic of China first and then came to Japan on his return home was explained by Dr. Whyte himself later. According to him, China was a teacher of Japan for the past thousands of years. In this respect, the United States has been a teacher of Japan only for a short time. In order to understand Japan better his visit to China was indispensable.

He gave a series of speeches in Tokyo and Osaka not only for the academic circles but for the management and labor unions. His concerns were related to quality control circles (QCC), worker participation in management, and comparison of efficient management of the two countries.

His repeated words that the United States needs to learn from Japan surprised the participants of the JHRA seminar. I told him it was he who taught me HR philosophy; 6,000 Japanese students learned updated theories and practices for the past thirty years under GARIOA (Government Appropriation for Relief in Occupied Areas) and Fulbright exchange student programs. The economic reconstruction of Japan achieved after World War II is mainly due to U.S. assistance and encouragement.

In response to my words, he said to us, "It is a creative misunderstanding, Mr. Kawabuchi!" I gazed at him and he kept on speaking very quietly. In the 1940s the United States found it necessary for management to communicate with the employees of all organizations and through the 1950s the United States became the superpower in the world. So it was quite natural that Japan recognized American management, its theories and practices as the best and did their best to learn American views and know-how. The student caught up with the teacher and overcame him to some extent.

Dr. Whyte showed us an example of participatory systems of leadership in industry. "It appears that Japan picked up the ideas from the United States, adapted them, improved on them, and implemented them on a large scale. Now the United States is trying to catch up to Japan in developing a participatory system of management, and it might be useful to compare the models developing in our two countries."

So he put a word. "The Japanese misunderstand the whole situation. It was a creative misunderstanding, though."

I have another story to add to our appreciation of Dr. Whyte's visit to JHRA. I have been acquainted with Mr. Aaron Martin Cohen, ILRer (1959) and an officer of Cornell Club of Japan. He has been in Japan for many years and a lecturer at Sophia University, Tokyo. Martin and I were present at the party to welcome Dr. and Mrs. Whyte at Cornell Club and discussed QCC and lifetime employment systems. His views on these problems are very interesting and I know he sent some of them to Dr. Whyte. By and large, Martin seems to be pessimistic in expecting significant results from the introduction of QCC into the United States because of the difference of individual workers and his view of life at a workshop as "a coherent, integral set of cultural embodiments." JHRA reported the gist of the lecture and discussions raised at the seminar by Dr. Whyte in the *Men and Management* issue of August 1982.

With these discussions and comments in mind, Dr. Whyte and JHRA have cooperated to organize the first institute at the Cornell campus. The first one was held in the summer of 1983 for executive development programs. Our common subjects so far discussed were taken up there in more detail and as anticipated we obtained good results for a better understanding of the business circles of the two countries. Both the Cornell staff and the Japanese participants were fully satisfied and we are now planning the second institute either at Cornell or at a proper place in Japan in 1984.

The theme of "Look East" or "Learn from Japan" is said aloud in some other places in Asia. But we have to be so humble that we may listen to their true motives for the sake of our mutual dependence and prosperity among the countries of Asia.

Dr. Oaklander is also an ILRer and a professor at the Graduate School of Business, Pace University, New York City, and he spent his academic years during the same time as I. It was in early summer 1979 that I heard from him regarding his visit to Japan in the fall. His main purpose in visiting Japan was to gather much important information about lifetime employment from interviews with many executives, union officials, government experts, and college professors. My trips at home and abroad unfortunately interrupted our meeting, but our common interests and careers shall bring us to cooperate with each other. Again, our association will be a help to Dr. Oaklander, who has been doing research on employment, layoffs, and productivity in comparison with U.S., Swiss, and Japanese labor practices.

Thus, our Japan Human Relations Association has grown to respond to the wider expectations both at home and abroad. One of its activities is concerned with productivity improvement through communications. For one thing, the association has emphasized the suggestion system and the merits of the member companies which participated in the campaign in terms of profit, mechanical trouble, safety, absenteeism, etc.

33

U.S. Educational Grant Programs in Japan

Shigemitsu Kuriyama

I went to the United State in 1950 as one of some three hundred Japanese students selected to study under the GARIOA (Government Appropriation for Relief in Occupied Areas) educational grant program that year. This U.S. Army-funded program was the predecessor to the Fulbright Program, and provided educational grants to Japanese students during 1949–51. From 1952 onward, the Fulbright Program took over, as a result of the conclusion of the San Francisco Peace Treaty the preceding year.

The timing of our stay was auspicious, for conditions in the United States for receiving foreign students had never been better in the past, and will probably never be as good in the future. In the course of my year of study, I became totally convinced that Japan should ally itself with the United States, and I have remained in this conviction to this date.

The timing was auspicious, for the totality of U.S. society was in a mood particularly fit to receive foreign students. Confidence and generosity were in the air; the United States had been victorious in war, undamaged by hostilities, and had emerged as the most powerful economy in the world. The U.S. dollar was literally equated to gold in the Charter of the International Monetary Fund. Charles Kindleberger had diagnosed that the world was doomed to a permanent state of "dollar shortage": No other major country could ever expect to attain the high productivity level of the United States.

In my view the people of the United States, by historical tradition, are among the most friendly and generous in the world. This characteristic is reflected in the history of U.S. diplomacy which, compared with others, has probably been among the most humane and idealistic, although I realize that some hold different views on this point.

Underpinned by this characteristic, aware of the supremacy of the United States in the world, and bolstered by the abundant and increasing material comforts in life, the social ambience in the United States at that time was such that almost any ordinary man on the street was eager to extend a helping hand to the war-impoverished citizens of other nations, allies and enemies alike.

The timing was auspicious for another reason. The Japanese were also in a state of mind that was favorable for the program. The GARIOA educational grant program had fortuitously combined the above-mentioned receptive mood in the United States with the traditional Japanese mentality of "On." "On," as is widely known by now, is a concept of moral indebtedness cultivated over hundreds of years of Japanese history. Under "On" a person who receives a favor becomes subjectively obligated to the benefactor (his "On-Jin"), usually for life. The greater the need of the recipient at the time he receives the favor, the stronger is his feeling of "On."

This is why the timing of the GARIOA program was favorable, for it was started at a time when the poverty in Japan was steep, and the gratitude of the recipient that much stronger. So poor were we that the grant recipients received a few yards of cloth to make clothing, so that they would have at least one decent piece to wear to the United States. I remember one of the students I traveled with exclaiming, "It's almost as if we've come to heaven!" when she saw the variety of meats, vegetables, fruits, breads, dairy products, and beverages at the cafeteria counter of the International House in Berkeley.

There was no end of good will among my many encounters with the U.S. people during my stay. Naturally there were exceptions. But by and large the American people, each in their different ways, were friendly, generous, considerate, and helpful. With few exceptions, I am convinced, the GARIOA grant recipients returned loaded with fond memories of good friends, warm families, pleasant meals, merry parties, and thoughtful advice.

The favorable effect of postwar U.S. educational grant programs on U.S.-Japanese relations, in my view, has been literally invaluable, i.e., too valuable to be measured. For one, the recipients, who had to compete in a nationwide examination, were by and large good human material. For another, virtually all returned to Japan with a deep feeling of "On" toward the U.S. people. In the decades that have elapsed, some have occupied key government posts, others top business positions, and still others influential educational posts. These grant recipients, with few exceptions, have favorably influenced Japanese public opinion toward the United States to an extent disproportionately great to their limited number. For they not only held leading positions, but knew the United States well, and were sentimentally oriented toward friendship with the United States.

I believe, for the above reasons, that U.S. government money spent under the GARIOA educational grant program in Japan was well spent, probably placing it among the most cost-effective government programs in U.S. history. The program, subsequently replaced by the Fulbright Program, and its surrounding environment, have changed a great deal over the years. Regrettably these have on the whole worked to erode, rather than enhance, the effectiveness of the program.

The effectiveness of the program has been eroded, first by its reduction in scale. The number of Japanese grant recipients each year was counted in the hundreds under GARIOA. Under the Fulbright Program this was scaled down and at present only some seventy Japanese students are being funded per year. Although the more rigorous screening process this entails probably has meant better qualified recipients, the reduction in numbers was nevertheless there. In the program's earlier years this was especially to be regretted, since it happened to be, as stated earlier, the "golden age" for Japanese student programs in the United States.

A more important reason why the effectiveness of the program has been eroded, however, lies in Japan's relatively better economic performance compared with the United States in the ensuing years. As Japan grew more affluent, the feeling of "On" on the part of Japanese grant recipients diminished. At the same time, the U.S. people became less inclined to generosity toward the increasingly richer Japanese: They had their own problems, not the least being the stubbornly large unemployment, while "quality" Japanese products flooded U.S. store displays and discount shops. Now that Japan had become the world's second largest economy, the U.S. people found the behavior of Japan unacceptably unmindful and "childish": The Japanese were not behaving as a grown-up should.

Cultural difference has worked to reinforce this nascent ill-will among the two countries. As has been extensively discussed in recent years both in the United States and Japan, there is a vast gap between the two cultures. The gap is wide, possibly unbridgeable, and it is probably undesirable that it be fully bridged. What is needed is a better understanding of each other's culture, not a full bridging, and perhaps more importantly, a basic feeling of trust between the two nations.

Since we cannot expect the entire population of the two countries to undertake the foregoing, I consider a Fulbright-type program as the most promising practical alternative. By selecting potential leaders of each country, exposing them to the other's culture, and establishing a firm bond of trust between them, we can certainly hope to reduce, if not eliminate, future friction in U.S.-Japanese relations.

Here I must refer to the flow of U.S. students to Japan being supported by the Fulbright Program. At the inception of the GARIOA-Fulbright programs the flow was entirely one-way: from Japan to the United States. Starting in 1954 it became a two-way flow, albeit a lopsided one. This continues to be the case today, with some seventy Japanese students going to the United States in 1983 and some thirty-five U.S. students coming to Japan. The U.S. population being twice as large, the ratio should probably be in reverse.

Nevertheless, thanks importantly to the Fulbright Program, the number of Americans speaking fluent Japanese, which could be counted on two hands thirty years ago, is probably now in the hundreds, if not thousands. Even so, the number is small compared with the number of Japanese speaking fluent English today.

Since 1980 the Japanese government has been contributing annually to the Fulbright Program in Japan an amount roughly equal to the U.S. contribution. It is true to Japanese tradition and heartening that the GARIOA/Fulbright alumni in Japan have been conducting since 1982 a fundraising drive mainly to provide educational grants to American students coming to Japan. The drive, proving to be highly successful, is true to Japanese tradition because it is an effort by the alumni to repay their "On" to the U.S. people. It is heartening because it is an effort to get the U.S. people to know Japan better, not vice versa. The flow of students, for long lopsidedly in one direction, is now being corrected by the program's Japanese alumni, three decades after its inception.

34

The Road to Princeton:
In Quest of the Naked Soul

Kiyohiko Tsuboi

It was already dark when our limousine pulled up to the entrance of the Nassau Inn. This must be located along Nassau Street, I thought, where Amory Blaine in *This Side of Paradise* loitered down when he first came to Princeton, investigating displays of the stores along the street, and dropped in a "Jigger Shop" to eat a "double chocolate sundae." But we could hardly see the street. It took almost one hour from Newark along Route 1 in the cold, bleak dusk of March 1979. After settling down in the cozy Room 210 of the hotel, my wife and I went down to the restaurant to eat supper, looking out into the shadowy lanes, "where Witherspoon brooded like a dark mother over Whig and Clio, her Attic children, where the black Gothic snake of Little curled down to Cuyler and Patton." Then I began to think of the journey we made.

It was a long way to Princeton from Okayama, Japan, a countrified city, about 500 kilometers west of Tokyo: Okayama to Tokyo, four hours by a bullet train, then an overnight flight from Narita, the Tokyo International Airport, to Los Angeles, then to Columbia, South Carolina. I was to see Dr. Matthew J. Bruccoli, professor of English at the University of South Carolina, who is the indisputable authority on F. Scott Fitzgerald, a poet laureate of the Jazz Age in 1920s America. And on his advice I had come up to see the Fitzgerald papers housed in the Harvey S. Firestone Memorial Library at Princeton.

I do not remember exactly when I first read Fitzgerald. It must have been sometime in the mid-1950s when I encountered his writings. This encounter was certainly a great experience in my life. It was as if I had been struck with a thunderbolt through the mountainous clouds of cultural barrier between Japan and America. And after the first shock was gone, I found the old familiar face of an old friend. His message came straight to the core of my heart. And I have never regretted my meeting with him in his books and my devotion to reading his fiction thereafter. At first his style seemed a little old-fashioned compared with contemporaries such as Hemingway and Faulkner, but something young, honest, earnest, and candid exposed in his novels must have attracted my aesthetic sensitivity. One, and perhaps the greatest, reason why I was so moved by his novels was his way of writing, an honest description of his feelings. Somehow I could understand his urge to tell us all the secrets of his mind.

In modern Japanese literature there is a literary genre called "Watakushi Shosetsu," or "I" novels, which mainly deal with novelists' own lives and their personal feelings and thoughts. In the latter part of the nineteenth century French-born naturalism found some enthusiastic followers among Japanese writers. Reflecting the predominant mood of those days the Japanese naturalists tended to depict the bleak side of society and man. Then some of the radical naturalists began to explore deep into the human mind by being utterly honest and faithful to their feelings. They exposed their hidden secrets to the public frankly and unashamedly: Toson Shimazaki (1872-1943), Katai Tayama (1871-1930), Zenzo Kasai (1887-1920), Koji Uno (1891-1961), Naoya Shiga (1883-1971) are a few examples. Their self-exposing, self-abusing, and confessional tendency is possibly due to the Japanese national character of hypersensitive self-consciousness, the tradition of which could be traced up to Basho Matsuo (1664-1694), the great Haiku poet in the Edo era.

Since I had been quite familiar with contemporary Japanese novels as a boy, especially the "Watakushi Shosetsu," whose expressing manner is quite the same as Fitzgerald's (which must have been rather odd to American readers), reading *The Great Gatsby* and *Tender Is the Night* caused a great emotional joy but at the same time a familiar sensation in me. And I felt as if I had heard the novelist's own voice.

A novelist has an innate urge or desire to write, to express and reveal his inner self and his deep-rooted emotions, but at the same time he has as much worldly desire to be rich and famous as ordinary citizens. In other words, he inevitably possesses a split character: the one side to expose himself and the other to cover and hide his weakness under earthly splendors.

Fitzgerald too had such a split character that critics called him a novelist of "double vision": a tendency to see the object from two different points of view at once. He tried to see himself from inside and from outside, contrary to Hemingway who had built walls around himself and covered his true face with a mask of masculine bravado, to which he was faithful to the end. When he found that he could no longer keep it, he collapsed and killed himself.

Consequently, Fitzgerald was obliged to lead a tragic life, though romantic superficially, which he had exposed to the public and confessed his tragic self in his novels and essays, especially in *The Crack-up*. No wonder Hemingway attacked, condemned, and ridiculed him for his weakness in *The Snows of Kilimanjaro*. There are rather few American writers who have been so true both to themselves and to the world as Fitzgerald (Thomas Wolfe is another self-confessing American writer, but of a different type). He is one of these American writers with whom the Japanese could empathize, if only we could read his beautiful English, even though the physical aspects of the world that he created are quite different from us, and they are sometimes beyond our comprehension.

The language was the greatest barrier I had to overcome. Because my schooling unfortunately coincided with World War II and Japan fighting with the United States, the language (English) education in my secondary school days was limited to such an extent that we had practically no classes in English. And only after the war my true English learning began at the age of fifteen, which was definitely late for language study. When Japan was defeated in 1945 and occupied by American troops, it was as if we had been invaded not by American armed forces but by American civilization. Only a week before we had been taught how cruel and hateful Americans were, and this week we found that fair-skinned young soldiers were all but kind and intelligent. They were ambassadors from the great affluent United States of America. They were all teachers and benefactors. Almost all the Japanese young men of my generation had more or less the same puzzled curiosity, which has driven me and others to American studies in search of the identities of Americans and ours. Thus, in the course of my study of English and American literature I happened to meet F. Scott Fitzgerald and his works.

Next morning at the Nassau Inn we woke up early. After breakfast at the warm coffee shop, with many green potted plants hanging down from the ceiling, we stepped out onto Nassau Street. We found ourselves in the hard-blowing, icy wind, as predicted by Professor Bruccoli, who had kindly advised us to take our winter coats before we left South Carolina. On the way we asked a passing girl about the location of "the library," but somehow she directed us to the public library and on to a cemetery. We knew there was something wrong, and immediately turned back. After walking a block or two we found the Firestone Library without further difficulties. Professor Bruccoli's letter of introduction to Professor Richard Milton Ludwig, who was in charge of rare books and collections, miraculously paved our way to Fitzgerald's papers.

In one of the simple and austere rooms of the special collections we sat at a desk with Fitzgerald's handwritten papers spread before us. The next moment it seemed that I was talking directly to him. Reading his delicate handwriting in pencil on yellowing paper, some words erased and rewritten with colored crayon, I almost spoke to him aloud. Here you are! I have been looking forward to this moment for a long time. Then I thought I saw his sad smiling face, with his arms stretched out to the "green light." "I saw him. I was him." There his naked soul was beating on "against the current, borne back ceaselessly into the past." His unfulfilled desire, his never-ceasing quest for the meaning of life, and his unhesitant commitment to the truth under the cover of "the greatest, gaudiest spree," all of Fitzgerald was before me. I felt as if I stood on the top of a high mountain, finally face to face with the man I had long sought.

After some strenuous research we left Princeton, exhausted but with pleasant memories, for Washington, D.C., to attend the meeting for Fulbright grantees. Even though the red-carpeted reception in Washington, D.C., by the International Communication Agency was more than we had expected, it was a sort of anticlimax after the great experience. However, all this was made possible by the Fulbright grant, for which I am ever grateful.

PART X
A VOYAGE TO THE MOON

Introduction

It is ironic to suggest that when Senator Fulbright was able to implement his magnificent vision embodied in the cultural and educational exchange program, the scope of his aim was too narrow. At that time, the exploration of space had the ring of science fiction, not scientific reality. However, Harrison Schmitt heard the news of Sputnik I while a Fulbrighter in Norway. Later, he became the first civilian astronaut, the sixth man to walk on the moon, and then, subsequently, like Fulbright, a U.S. senator (N.M.). Joining Daniel Patrick Moynihan (N.Y.), they became the first two senators with Fulbright experience. So, both in the halls of government and in the expanse of outer space, the influence of the program continues.

35

The Fulbright Experience

Harrison H. Schmitt

It was cool in the parlor of the neat, postwar farmhouse as I settled down for my evening's ritual dose of static, news, and Willis Conover's *"Jazz from A to Z"* beaming out of North Africa on the Voice of America.

It was October 4, 1957, and I was a Fulbright geology student working in the magnificent fjord country known as Sunnmøre in western Norway. The historic news breaking upon the world seemed totally at odds with the age-old struggle my new friends waged to scratch out an existence. The thin soil covering the narrow coastal "strand-flat" of this glaciated land had been farmed by their Viking forebears, but nevertheless, offered little support to life, much less comfort.

"That sound you hear is the beeping of Sputnik I, the first artificial satellite of the Earth, launched earlier today by the Soviet Union." That was it. The professional, aseptic tones of the Voice of America's newscaster announced the event that began a new era in human history; an event that not only redirected my life but redirected the course of human evolution away from Earth and into the new realm of space.

The late Ian Campbell, my faculty advisor at "Caltech" and later president of the California Academy of Sciences, first brought up the idea of applying for a Fulbright Fellowship during my second year at Caltech. He obviously was wiser and more clairvoyant than I, as I struggled through the "sophomore slump." My only thought was, "He has got to be kidding! I'm going to be lucky to still be here in two years, much less have the grades necessary for any graduate fellowships."

However, I survived. Ian persisted, and I applied. My only strength in the Fulbright competition was a close working and personal relationship with the Caltech faculty, men like Ian, the late Dick Jahns (later dean of Earth Sciences at Penn State and Stanford), and Bob Sharp (then chairman of the Earth Sciences Division at Caltech). Probably, by stretching the truth to no small degree, their recommendations convinced the selection board that I and the country would benefit from a year of activity in Norway.

You may legitimately ask why would a "Schmitt" from New Mexico choose Norway as his host country? Two reasons: first, I am terrible at languages and no working knowledge of Norwegian was required; and second, the glaciated, ancient geological terrain of Norway is a geologist's paradise, populated in part by geologists of international stature. Thus began a year-long adventure in education, science, and politics, an adventure which brought new thoughts that ultimately changed the course of my life.

One could sense the change the morning after Sputnik, as Martin and Ida Jakobsen and their families in the little coastal farming settlement expressed their wonder and fear to this young American student. As had been the case with the troops needed to integrate the Little Rock schools a few weeks earlier, my command of the Norwegian language was barely up to the task of understanding their questions, much less explaining the event.

A few weeks later, back among the international students in residence at the University of Oslo, the same wonder and fear was expressed in English with Slavic, French, German, and Asian accents as well as those of Scandinavia. There was wonder at what man's mind and technology had done; there was fear at what their protector, the United States, had *not*.

Even this naive Fulbright student "from a small mining town in the West" could not miss the profound impact Sputnik was having on my student friends from around the world. I also could not help but conclude that Sputnik and the space age it heralded would have a profound effect on human history. Thus, the philosophical seed of interest in spaceflight was planted in my mind:

> On the second night spent on the way to the Valley of Taurus-Littrow on the Moon, I took one more glance at home before covering the windows for sleep. The feeling then was, "If there ever was a fragile-appearing piece of blue in space, it's the earth right now." Let me tell you more about our generation's new view of earth.
>
> The Apollo explorations of space and the Moon which we have watched and lived on were man's first halting, but clearly personal look at his universe. Our unique character among the living species of nature is carried forward in many ways. One outward reflection of this character is that we have had the audacity to try to understand our place in this universe and in its future. We have had the further audacity to try to use understanding to alter the universe and to more fully understand the Earth using in large measure the corrected vision from space. [Excerpt from "New View of Earth," presented at the First Annual Tyler Awards Dinner, Pepperdine University.]

My isolation as a youth had never become apparent to me until I was exposed to the diversity of individuality in new friends at the American summer school in Oslo, at the Geologists' Museum in Tøyen, on the International Students' Association ski trips to Rondone, and among the Norwegian farmers of Sunnmøre. This exposure prompted many new thoughts, a few of them poetic:

The Collector
I am a collector of many things,
The reminders of the long past springs,
The summers, falls and winters spent
With otherwise forgotten friends who lent
A day, hour, and then some slender strings.

These attachment strings in later years
Have broken bringing some hidden tears,
Leaving only the places there
In a book, a box, for none to share
But the mind with hope that memory clears.

Who knows but some day we'll meet
Walking down some new but unknown street,
And there relive those treasured moments,
Their brief, forgotten joys and comments,
Without which my book is incomplete.

Yet I collect these many things,
The tickets, clovers, the bits of strings,
All of which are but a dent
In a past I can ne'r repent,
Its many joys have masked the many pains.

(Oslo, Norway, late summer 1957)

One did not have to spend many weeks in Norway to recognize that its preuniversity educational system was vastly superior to that in the United States. This realization, indeed shock, catalyzed a continuing involvement in the struggle to create an educational system for young Americans that is compatible with their future responsibilities to themselves, their country, and to freedom.

Although we seem to have made little progress since 1957 in providing an educational system that matches the accelerating rate of increased need, my personal efforts have steadily expanded from the emphasis placed on this issue in my report to the U.S. Educational Foundation in Norway: a continuing commitment to share our space experiences with young people, the chairmanship of two Senate subcommittees responsible for educational legislation, and currently writing and lecturing throughout the country on this critical issue.

I summarized some of the thoughts on education germinated as a Fulbright student in a recent lecture at the College of Santa Fé as follows:

> The minds of people are a resource that can be renewed only through education. The nation is not meeting the challenge of this renewal which our rapidly moving economic world creates.
>
> Education is one of the *most difficult* immediate problems the nation must solve in its search for economic growth. It also is the *most critical* long-term issue facing us.
>
> Through education, we learn to recognize our economic and esthetic opportunities. Through lack of education, we fail to benefit from those opportunities. Through neglect of education, we limit our ability to understand our problems and their solutions.
>
> There is no more compelling foundation for democracy or for the survival of freedom in a hostile world than education.
>
> So far, I cannot imagine anyone disagreeing with the statements I have made here about education. However, when one starts suggesting improvements to education, we find that politics and special interests have a way of preventing needed reform.

The formal justification for a year of graduate study in Norway was to enhance my background and experience in the earth sciences. After discussions with my Caltech advisors, I left for Oslo with the intent to study the remarkable and beautiful coarse-grained rocks of southern Norway called "pegmatites." However, as a service to another professor and still close friend, Lee Silver, I planned to go to the "bowels of the earth" in western Norway to get some rock samples for his experimental work at Caltech. These rocks, called "eclogites," are formed at very high pressures deep within the earth and are of great interest in studies of the earth's mantle.

After arriving in Norway, I soon ran into a remarkable character, Tore Gjelsvik, a geologist who had used his geological studies of the rocks of Sunnmøre in western Norway as a cover for resistance activities during World War II. Through his farm relatives, Tore arranged for a late summer visit to Sunnmøre in order to collect samples of eclogite.

Once in the beautiful and friendly fjord country, I was hooked. In addition to collecting samples for Lee, I began a research project that brought me back the next spring, again in 1960 for six months, formed the basis of my Ph.D. dissertation at Harvard, and stimulated an interest in the planet Earth that was satisfied only by geological studies on its dwarfed twin, the Moon.

In the fall of 1973, newly returned from the Moon, I returned to Norway to visit my old friends in Oslo and Sunnmøre. Thirteen years had aged us all, improved our lives, but in no way dimmed the memories of good times and good friends. I shared with them new memories like the following paragraphs delivered to the House of Representatives a few months before:

> I would like first to tell you about a place I have seen in the solar system. This place is a valley on the Moon, now known as the Valley of Taurus-Littrow. Taurus-Littrow is a name not chosen with poetry in mind, but, as with many names, the mind's poetry is created by events. Events surrounding not only three days in the lives of three men, but also the close of an unparaled era in human history.
>
> The valley, however, has been unchanged by being a name on a distant planet while change has governed the men who named it. The valley has been less altered by being explored than have been the explorers. The valley has been less affected by all we have done than have been the millions who, for a moment, were aware of its towering walls, its visitors, and then its silence.
>
> The Valley of Taurus-Littrow is confined by one of the most majestic panoramas within the view and experience of mankind. The roll of dark hills across the valley floor blends with bright slopes that sweep evenly upwards, tracked like snow, to the rocky tops of the massifs. The valley does not have the jagged youthful majesty of the Himalayas, or of the valleys of our Rockies, or of the glacially symmetrical fjords of the north countries, or even of the now intriguing rifts of Mars. Rather, it has the subdued and ancient majesty of a valley whose origins appear as one with the sun.
>
> The massif walls of the valley rise to heights that compete well among other valleys of the planets; but they rise and stand with a calmness and unconcern that belies dimensions and speaks silently of continuity in the scheme of evolution. Still, the valley is not truly silent; its cliffs yet roll massive pages of history down dusty slopes; its bosom yet warms the valley floor and spreads new chapters of creation in glass and crystal; its craters yet act as the archives of their sun.
>
> The valley has watched the unfolding of thousands of millions of years of time. Now it has dimly and impermanently noted man's homage and footprints. Man's return is not the concern of the valley . . . only the concern of man.

It was the atmosphere of the early 1960s at Harvard that finally crystallized my commitment to enter politics at some appropriate future time. However, the earlier Fulbright exposure to an international view of the United States, building of a familial interest in history and current events, formed the emotional foundation for that commitment which was finally consummated with entry into the race for the U.S. Senate in 1975.

Seeing our crises in space technology, in the Little Rock schools, and in the developing world through the cultural insights and biases of others constituted a crash course in political objectivity. It also accented the basic and continuing values of our society based on both individual diversity and individual freedom. The continuing political impact of my Fulbright experience is perhaps best illustrated by these paragraphs from another recent College of Santa Fé lecture:

> The challenge before us today is to decide that the United States *will* embark on a program to sail the ocean of space, to develop its economic potential, to protect our assets and interests in space and on the Earth, *and* to establish our own sovereignty and the sovereignty of freedom. Just as Great Britain dominated world politics for four centuries because of its technology and the sovereignty its empire established throughout the world, the United States and freedom could dominate the future, if only we have the will to do so. Our "empire" will not be that of territory, through conquest, but that of services through technology in which all the world can join and benefit.
>
> It cannot be overemphasized that the presence of citizens of the United States in space for both defense and nondefense purposes is in itself a deterrent to aggression. As in Europe, Korea, and elsewhere, such presence simply raises the ante for any potential aggressor. It shows we are serious about freedom and that space will *not* be a sanctuary for oppression.

Within the international student community in residence at the University of Oslo in 1957-58, were a number of students from developing countries. Our many conversations persuaded me that these countries and the United States would be well served by the creation of an American corps of technical experts that could live, work, and teach among the people of these aspiring nations. I proposed such a corps in my report to the U.S. Educational Foundation in Norway. Needless to say, I could not have been more pleased than when his independent insights resulted in President Kennedy establishing the Peace Corps a few years later.

More recently, the urgency of the transfer of information and know-how to the people in developing countries has increased markedly. In my recent lecture series, I concluded:

> Information systems technology, in the broadest sense, makes it possible to rationally imagine the gradual elimination of hunger, disease, poverty, and ignorance in underdeveloped portions of the world. These four horsemen of disaster are rushing down on mankind and freedom at unparalleled speeds. However, for the first time in human history, we can consider technically realistic means of stopping their onslaught and using that capability as the foundation of our foreign policy toward these underdeveloped nations.
>
> The foundations for this new foreign policy lie in the gathering, analysis, distribution, and use of information. There is no present indication that our institutions and their leaders have any conception of what that statement means.
>
> The collection and distribution of information on a worldwide basis via satellite has provided a distinct change in the course of human history. The most graphic demonstration of this change came when, on Christmas Eve

1968, hundreds of millions of human beings throughout the world simultaneously had a new thought about a familiar object in the night sky—the Moon.

The men of Apollo 8 were there, and the moon would never be the same for anyone. Now, we realize that the world will never be the same; that there are solutions to those age-old problems of the human condition on earth. There are solutions, *if* we are wise enough to reach out and grasp them.

Through information technologies, we can and should create programs aimed at permanent, eventually self-financing, services for worldwide communications, weather and ocean forecasting, earth resources discovery or monitoring, societal services such as health and education, and prediction of natural events of disastrous human consequences or broad-scale economic impact.

Through technology and know-how we can and should help underdeveloped nations create agricultural, health, resource, and educational systems that permit their entry into the twentieth century. As I have traveled as an astronaut in Africa, Asia, and Latin America, I have heard one message from those who do not want dictatorships of either the Right or the Left: "Send us know-how, not dollars. Dollars just go into the pockets of our leaders; know-how will go into our minds."

The Fulbright Program is many things to many fortunate people. For me, the Fulbright experience clearly shaped the broad framework of my life.

PART XI
KALEIDOSCOPIC VIEWS

Introduction

It is obvious by now that the Fulbright experience is diverse and complex. To try to convey that experience, it is often useful to make contrasts. Contrasts often highlight cultural differences. Since many Fulbrighters are involved in teaching, it is not surprising that the classroom provides the awareness for such contrasts. John Freear came from the University of Kent to the University of New Hampshire and that prompted certain contrasts between British and American students. Michael Gunter faced another contrast in Turkey. While the University structure was modeled on the typical American university, student behavior was rather unpredictable, reflecting in part the unsettled political situation in that country. Connie Huning found that Western logic did not provide a culturally appropriate solution to "overbooking." Her initial exposure to Taiwan provided the beginnings of greater understanding of Chinese culture which she can communicate to Asian-American high-school students. Runhild Wessell found that her Fulbright experience changed her method of teaching a foreign language to generations of high-school students in Hicksville, New York. Richard Knoll discovered the importance of cultural differences in Korea in attempting to communicate the universal message of music.

Sara Turner was conscious of the importance of understanding cultural differences in social work education. In particular, her interest in gerontology provided a unique focus on the care of the aged in Taiwan and that lead to the production of a videotape which she produced and has since shared with American students. Jenny Johnson had to struggle with the problem of how to respond to criticism of the United States in Nigeria. This promoted her to try to learn more about her country.

For Terry Lacy, the Fulbright was the opportunity to rethink her future, to explore what people are and what culture means. For Arthur Steinberg, the year provided an opportunity to build a case for a new dental school in Ireland which a number of years later was realized.

There are other results. Walter Klein describes the activities of the Exchange Teachers Club of St. Louis, which provides a mechanism of continuing the Fulbright ideals. Finally, Jeanne Smoot, currently director of academic programs at the U.S. Information Agency, comments on her experiences as a grantee in Mexico. Now that she is in a position to influence future programming, Dr. Smoot has the base of her own Fulbright experience among her resources.

36

On American Students

John Freear

We had not known what to expect when we arrived in the United States. We were not so naive as to expect it to be just like the America depicted in the detective serials shown on British television. Years of listening on BBC radio to Alistair Cooke's weekly "Letter from America" had prevented that. We were, however, quite unprepared from the warmth of our welcome in Durham. We already knew one or two of the faculty at the Whittemore School, where I would be teaching, and they, of course, were most welcoming.

In my teaching at the Whittemore School, I found myself having to make some adjustments. One occurred on about the ninth week of the 15-week fall semester, when my subconscious was still expecting the imminent end to a 10-week term. Perhaps a more significant adjustment was to the fact that courses generally lasted for only fifteen weeks. The number of contact hours was much the same as in England, but there the courses were spread over at least twenty teaching weeks with a month-long vacation in between. In consequence, at least in the basic courses, I felt under constant pressure to keep up with the syllabus and thus try to avoid the temptation of discussing more peripheral, though relevant, topics as they arose during the course. In some ways this was a very good discipline for me, but I had sufficient vanity to believe that the students may have missed a rewarding educational experience!

I was astonished at the number and frequency of interim examinations—usually three or four per course—and at what seemed an excessive reliance on the multiple choice form of testing, although I recognized that the large number of students in the Financial Management course made its use almost inevitable. After about six weeks, I decided that I had to set the students an essay question, just to reassure myself that they could string a few words together in a comprehensible and grammatical way. By the end of the year's teaching, I had concluded that my students were more knowledgeable about the detail of a course than they would have been in England, but that they had suffered by being so constantly under the pressure of time and examinations that they were somewhat inhibited from standing back from their learning and from seeing it in perspective.

In terms of demonstrated academic ability, there appeared to be little to choose between my students in the United States and England, although there was probably a slightly lower proportion of weaker students in my classes in England. At this time (1979–80), I was struck by a noticeably greater degree of motivation on the part of American students. (However, since then, I have noticed an improvement in the motivation of my students in England, no doubt partly due to the poor employment situation.) This greater American motivation I attributed largely to the fact that most of the American students were having to take a more active part in financing their way through school than their equivalents in England, and so were more concerned to ensure that they received value for money in their education. This could be carried to extremes, as in the case of the student who arrived one morning to take an examination, looking particularly exhausted. He was financing his schooling by flying a freight aircraft around New England for most of each night.

37

On Turkish Students

Michael M. Gunter

In early September 1978, I arrived in Ankara, Turkey, with my wife and two children to become a Senior Fulbright Lecturer in International Relations at the Middle East Technical University (METU). We were met by the executive director of the Fulbright Commission in Turkey, who quickly cleared us through customs and whisked us off to our prearranged, furnished apartment.

The university itself proved to be an excellent example of ambivalence between the old and the new. METU was specifically modeled after the typical American university. This meant it lacked the rigid formality of the European institutions, and sought to cultivate the more relaxed U.S. atmosphere. Young Ph.Ds. who had just joined the faculty taught their own courses and participated in departmental and university-wide decision making, just as their senior colleagues did. Class sizes were small and student-instructor relationships informal. Unlike other Turkish universities, most instructors at METU did not wear ties. For a country that often practiced strict protocol, this lack of formal attire proved pleasing indeed.

METU was established in 1956 to provide higher education to students throughout the Middle East. English was the official language of instruction. A grading system based on the same five-point scale of A, B, C, D, or F that I was familiar with in America was used. Books were supposed to be in English. I found the names of political science courses, in many cases, identical to those in the typical American university.

Realistically, however, a very different situation existed. The official language, English, had not really been mastered by many of the students. Most of my students spoke virtually no English at all; occasionally I met a student who was fluent in the language. The result was as might be expected—most of the Turkish professors conducted their courses in Turkish and also used textbooks in that language. This, of course, caused difficulties for the students who were not Turkish (about 10 percent). I struggled to find the vocabulary that was simple enough to be understood in my lectures, but still sophisticated enough to say something meaningful.

The politicization of the students and associated violence represented another marked contrast to contemporary America. Because of the violence, METU has been closed almost as much as it has been open in recent years. Rumors of impending closings occurred frequently. Classes were often cancelled at the last moment to protest this or that. At my predominantly Marxist university (METU was reputed throughout Turkey as a leftist or Marxist bastion for both students and faculty), the student leaders and their organization were as powerful as the university's administration.

The gendarmerie (a national police force in regular army-type uniforms) literally occupied the campus, searching all who entered and often those who left. This proved time-consuming since the campus was located outside Ankara and thus had to be reached by free buses which ran about every half hour from a few central points within the city. When the crowded buses reached the campus, the occupants usually had to file out and sometimes the males were searched. Females were not frisked, which made it fairly simple to smuggle weapons or other contraband onto the campus. When I pointed this out and suggested that there should be female gendarmes to search the women, my students had a good laugh. Despite Ataturk's attempt to Westernize, women definitely had not achieved equality with their male counterparts.

Once my lecture was interrupted by two student leaders who entered and began to harangue the class. Grasping the situation, I left the classroom. My colleagues accepted this kind of behavior and advised me to take up where I had left off, without alluding to what had happened, when class met again.

On the day the Egyptian-Israeli Peace Treaty was signed in 1979, the U.S. Embassy sent a message advising me not to go to the campus that day. It was one of the few times I heard from any of the numerous, but usually aloof, American officials in Ankara. One of my Turkish colleagues advised me to ignore the warning, and doing so was appropriate. It was business (confusion?) as usual at METU.

At my first meeting with the thirty-four, fourth-year (senior) students, I learned that now we would decide when to meet, the previously published schedule of classes notwithstanding. The student leaders had their ideas about this, and since I had no specific time demands, this was not a problem.

Since the course had been planned late, there was not enough time to order textbooks from abroad. Later I discovered that even if there had been enough time, the books still would be *yok* because of the hard currency problems. Turkey did not have the money to order foreign books. From the

METU and TAA libraries, as well as from my colleagues, therefore, I obtained a few dated texts on American, British, and Soviet government. This situation continued during the second semester when I taught two of the originally planned courses: International Relations (to seventy-two students, the normal maximum was forty, but I wanted to meet as many Turkish students as possible) and a seminar on the Peaceful Settlement of Disputes (for seven graduate students). The graduate students were mostly members of the Turkish foreign ministry, although one was the French cultural attaché, and thus spoke good English.

The UN Information Center in Ankara proved useful for the seminar because it distributed free pamphlets and booklets concerning the United Nations in general and peaceful settlement in particular. For the most part the students were eager to investigate the holdings of the UN center. Surprisingly, however, none of them seemed aware of its existence until it was called to their attention. The UN officials probably publicized the center's existence, but apparently with little success.

The primarily Marxist students signed up to hear what the "Imperialist" (as I was sometimes affectionately, sometimes critically, called) had to say about world politics. Although their Marxism prevented them at times from fully trusting or accepting my remarks, this situation improved considerably until about mid-term examination time. Their demeanor, questions, and comments during and after class substantiated this. These were my halcyon days at METU! However, about a half hour before the midterm examination, a delegation of about ten students suddenly entered my office to announce that because of the arrest of some other students by the gendarmes the previous day, they were not prepared "psychologically" to take the examination. Several then elaborated on their reluctance. One told me there was a cross-country race that day they wished to attend. In addition, added another, they had only received my notes the previous day. (The student who understood English best had drawn up and distributed mimeographed copies of my notes.)

I suspected that long, unsettled, and irregular academic conditions had sapped them of their sense of academic duty and schedule. They simply had been too lazy to prepare for the examination and now were grasping at anything for an excuse. This attitude was somewhat cultural in nature. Accordingly, I told the student delegation I would confer with my colleagues. They all advised me to give the examination, and pointed out that two other professors in the department had done so that very day.

Then began the examination to which nobody came. I sat alone in a large lecture hall, while outside the student leaders haggled with two or three Turkish professors who had been sent to help me as proctors. Finally, after almost an hour, all seventy-two students quietly and politely entered the room and took their seats. My colleagues told me to make no comments but to simply proceed with the administering of the examination. After the materials had been passed out, twenty-six students rose and handed in blank test booklets as they left. The remaining forty-six took the examination. Later I was told this showed that only a minority had opposed taking it. These "radicals," however, were effectively able to disrupt the schedule.

My previously announced policy had been to give an automatic "F" to anyone who missed the examination without a legitimate excuse. The department ostensibly backed me on this issue, but privately advised me to relent. After mulling the matter over for a few days, I finally announced that I would give a make-up examination to the twenty-six, but lower their grades on it one-half a letter. Nobody missed the make-up exam, although one month after I returned to the United States a half dozen or so make-up examinations arrived via air mail from students who had been in the martial law prisons for various offenses and thus had missed my final.

My final week at METU was particularly moving. One evening my colleagues gave a banquet for me at the Faculty Association, a faculty club on the campus. The food was decent, the drinks plentiful, and the conversation amazingly easy and frank. After formal speeches of gratitude as well as gifts had been exchanged, a group of us visited Ankara by Night. A Turkish nightclub tends to be dense with cigarette smoke as almost every Turk learns to smoke by age twelve.

The final farewells to my students were perhaps even more touching. A reception was held for me by the student organization, and several individuals presented me with little gifts and letters of thanks. Afterward I left with a few special student friends to go to a pleasant *cay* (tea garden) on the outskirts of Ankara. In my graduate seminar, the one female student gave me a bouquet of flowers. When I spoke spontaneously to my sometimes delinquent International Relations students about peace and their role in achieving it as the leaders of the future generation, several of the girls cried, and I nearly shed tears myself.

Returning to America did not sever completely my relationship with Turkey. I helped one of my former undergraduates obtain a graduate assistantship to pursue her studies in international relations at an American university. To a lesser extent, I also helped several others come to the United States to pursue their careers.

Since returning to America, I have sent several timely monographs and current texts to my Turkish colleagues. Owing to economic problems, such materials have been virtually impossible to obtain in Turkey. Occasional letters from former colleagues and students continue to keep me abreast of events taking place in what was my home for one academic year.

38

Taiwan: Only the Beginning

Connie Huning

The old cliché that "times change and education needs to keep up with change" applies particularly to me and my Fulbright experience. My high-school and college education reflects the trends of the late 1950s and early 1960s where emphasis was placed on Western civilization and its contributions to American culture. My early high-school teaching reflected my academic training and specialization within the framework of European culture. However, as the years passed, times changed with the growing concern and interest in Third World countries. With these changes came the need to educate young Americans about the culture and importance of Third World countries within the dynamics of world politics.

My original Fulbright application was to go to the Middle East, an area close to my academic training, experience, and interests at that time, but a combination of circumstances led later to my application for a Fulbright Summer Seminar to the People's Republic of China and ultimately selection as a participant in the 1981 Taiwan Fulbright Summer Seminar. In 1980, my husband, also a high-school social studies teacher, traveled to the People's Republic of China and became enamored with the Chinese people and their culture. At the same time, I had a growing personal contact with Asian students in the classroom and was becoming aware of some of their educational needs, as well as the need to establish understanding, if not mutual acceptance, among all the students. Independence High School in San Jose, California, has a student body of over 4,000; approximately one-third of the students are Asian, many of Chinese descent.

The door to Chinese culture began to open for me during the six weeks spent in Taiwan, and the lure of the Orient became a real experience. I was soon to learn that Asian concepts and logic are a bit different from Western ones.

One of the experiences where cultural differences stands out vividly in my mind was a situation at the airport at the beginning of the tour of

285

Taiwan. The meeting we had been attending lasted longer than planned, and we arrived at the airport too late to board the flight for Haulien. It was possible that there would not be room on the next flight to accommodate our whole group. So, in true Western democratic fashion, we drew lots to see who would go on the flight and who would make the five-hour train journey. We were pleased with ourselves for having solved the problem so efficiently and democratically. However, our solution was not acceptable to our hosts. In fact, they were somewhat shocked at our solution. We were politely informed that it was not proper. The older men, then the women, were to be given the available seats. The younger men, oldest to youngest, would fill the remaining seats. As it turned out, the two youngest men in our group and one of our escorts made the trip to Haulien by train.

The Taiwan Fulbright was only the beginning of my exposure to Chinese culture and its people. I left Taiwan with a curiosity and need to see and experience more. A whole new and different world had opened up.

As the times changed, I too changed. I have gone from a traditional Western civilization orientation to becoming somewhat of a Sinophile, reading as many of the newest works on China and its people as possible. Yet at the same time, I find a blending in my own mind of the best of both worlds. As a teacher, I have become more professionally active in developing and sharing curriculum materials on China at the local, state, and national levels. In the classroom, I try to help bridge the cultural gap between East and West through providing a base to recognize differences and to promote a general cultural understanding among a variety of ethnic backgrounds.

39

Teaching German

Runhild E. Wessell

Two experiences have been of deep and lasting influence in my life: my graduation from Mount Holyoke College in 1930 and my Fulbright scholarship to the Goethe-Institut in Germany in the summer of 1956. The first shaped my life and career as a high-school teacher of German and the second changed my whole method of teaching a foreign language. My debt to both institutions is incalculable.

Total immersion in the language, life, and culture of Germany was the goal of the Goethe-Institut. Fulbrighters from the United States and teachers from other countries observed the institute's classes in which the students were young people from European and Middle Eastern countries who were planning to enter a German university. The faculty held discussions with us on these methods, gave special lectures, and also took us on trips around Bavaria. In the summer of 1956, the courses were given in five small towns. I was sent to Bad Aibling. The forty Americans were divided up among these towns and like the students, were housed one or two each with a German family. Students, Fulbrighters, and faculty all ate their meals together in the local inn. Everything possible was done to make our stay pleasant and memorable. It soon became evident that there was no one language that everyone could understand except German. Four weeks were spent learning and observing methods, and then all forty Americans and the other foreign teachers were reunited in Munich where a comprehensive three-week lecture course was given in methods of teaching, linguistics, instructional materals, literature, art, history, and contemporary problems. A one-week trip through Western Germany capped the climax on an enriching experience, the likes of which I had never before known.

The text, *Deutsche Sprachlehre für Ausländer*, written by Schulz-Griesbach, two of the institute's faculty members, was used in the beginning classes. Although glossaries in thirteen different languages accompanied the text, the vocabulary progression was so skillfully planned that a glossary was hardly necessary. The reading selection in the first lesson was on maps, starting with a map of Europe, but included the names of nine countries in Asia and South America. Such words as *ein Kontinent, ein Land, eine Stadt,* were easily understood by pointing out specific places on a wall map and using them in sentences. Students could therefore easily speak German from the first day in class, decisively establishing confidence from the start between teacher and student.

The Goethe-Institut also taught that the culture of a country is inseparable from its language. Since breadth of outlook and depth of scholarship were second nature to me as a Mount Holyoke graduate, I readily and eagerly accepted this new concept. Whenever a geographic term occurred in the reading or the name of a famous person, whether statesman, artist, writer or composer, that name was to be identified. *Bonn ist die Hauptstadt der Bundesrepublik, Goethe ist der grösste deutsche Dichter, Bach war Komponist* are examples. If the student was advanced enough, additional facts could be supplied. After any geographic term had been identified, that place was pointed out by the student on the wall map.

A teacher must, of course, add continually to his own knowledge through advanced study, reading, and travel. It was the Fulbright experience, however, that provided the new ideas that fired the enthusiasm and deeper understanding that led to an ever-broadening curriculum.

How does a teacher know how well he has succeeded? Former pupils returning home for visits frequently told the story. Their reports caused me great joy: continuing the study of German in college, successfully using German for an advanced degree, traveling to Germany, studying abroad, getting government positions. I always passed these success stories on to my classes. One day, a boy said to me after class, "Miss Wessell, you're a ham, always bragging about your former pupils." Still, from year to year, the light from the Fulbright summer threw its beams across the United States and the Atlantic Ocean.

Nostalgia overcomes me. I take out my diplomas. "Praeses et Curatores Collegi Montis Holyokensis. . . . Runhild Eugenia Wessell ad gradum Baccalaureae in Artibus. . . . cum laude." "Goethe-Institut. . . . Hiermit wird bestätigt, dass Fraulein Runhild E. Wessell . . . an einem Fort-bildungslehrgang für Deutschlehrer und Germanisten teilgenommen hat . . ." My heart stands still. Tears come to my eyes. How could I have been so fortunate in my life and career!

40

A Fulbright Experience: Korea

Richard C. Knoll

It did not take long to learn that Korea is a kind and generous nation involved with many trials and tribulations. This is a nation that loves to sing, dance, and tell all about its ancient heritage. I remember a quotation but not its author, pertaining to the way of learning all about a foreign country: "To learn all there is to know about a country, one must study the music, dance, culture, but not the government." I followed that advice and have had two full years of exciting and interesting excursions, both physical and mental.

Being a concert singer and a professor of music, I seemed to fit into their scheme. Many firsts came my way naturally, such as first singer to sing with the Seoul Philharmonic in a television film, first American to sing Handel's *Messiah*, Beethoven's Ninth, and Haydn's *Creation* with the Taegu Symphony Orchestra, and Rossini's *Stabat Mater* with the Pusan Symphony. The concert of Haydn's *Creation* was sung in Korean. Koreans enjoy vocal recitals and I have given many throughout Korea to capacity audiences. All performances were received enthusiastically and were very rewarding for me.

My main reason for coming to Korea was of course to teach voice and do as much concert work as possible. Teaching in Korea is indeed a new experience. My first day at Keimyung University I auditioned the graduate students assigned to me. As in the United States, there were good ones and mediocre ones. They were very enthusiastic about studying with a foreign professor and worked in a diligent, rewarding way. I had a little trouble communicating with them as I thought I might, but actually enjoyed the direction the lessons took. In the course of study, the same vocal problems that occur in American students were apparent with the Koreans; however, new and interesting challenges became obvious. One basic problem in their normal tone production is a throaty quality. It is directly related to their speech which uses many back throaty sounds and gives them a wide expressive vocalism but also causes many problems in singing. To deal with this required patience and discipline. It meant explaining and making diagrams to relate the principles and wisdom of the bel canto school of singing. The most reliable tool I could use and depend upon was that I could demonstrate exactly what I wanted to do. In this way, I was able to win their confidence and successfully improve their singing technique.

The next difficult problem was trying to cope with diction. Koreans have problems enunciating *Rs, Ls, Ps, Fs,* etc. In English, German, Italian, and French, one must be able to pronounce all the consonants and vowels clearly. The only way I could improve their pronunciation was to repeat time and again words that were problematic. This was very tiring and difficult; however, persistence paid off and obvious improvement occurred. Now many of my students are singing all over Korea, with much success. Some professional singers have traveled over 200 miles from Seoul to study with me, so I feel that my teaching has been effective and filled a need.

41

Taiwan Serendipity

Sara Turner

A social work practitioner is expected to act independently and with good judgement; most of my adult life had been spent thus; only in recent years had I been teaching full time. I plunged into my teaching assignments with vigor, but heeded the chairman's admonition not to accept an offer of a ride on the back of anyone's motor bike—the most common mode of private transportation. Fieldwork students often suggested a bike ride, rather than the slower public bus transportation. These initial contacts, certainly tentative on my part, were appreciated by the agency supervisors I met. Not many American social workers came their way, and I soon learned that my words were accepted as "expert" despite my careful efforts to disclaim their being so.

Keenly aware of the hazards of teaching social work methods which might be inappropriate in a culture quite different from a Western society, I became a learner in the truest sense of the word in a class which I taught— Human Development in the Social Environment. Using a text which described lifespan in age-experience sequences, I was able to draw from my students their own personal observations for their own (and my) greater understanding and insight. One is often warned that Chinese are quiet and unresponsive in classroom discussions, preferring that the teacher lecture while they take notes. This was not true for me, after they realized that I expected and would wait for some oral response, and whatever it was, I could support or elaborate on it. Perhaps they wanted to help me save face, but they could and did make class discussion an active part of learning.

A particular area of concern for me for many years has been gerontology, and one course taught at Tunghai was Social Work with the Aged. Considering that the proportion of people over the age of sixty-five who live in Taiwan today is 4 percent, comparable to the United States at the turn of the century, we must recognize that it is still a young country. Concerns are apt to be focused on the problems of youth, education, and employment opportunities. Yet there is increased concern for the problems of elders who there, as throughout the world, are living longer and are likely to need more in the way of social services. One of my colleagues lamented on the lack of audiovisual material for classroom use, saying that most that was available came from Western countries where people not only looked different, but had different resources for support as well as societal expectations. This remark served to ignite a spark that culminated in my production of the videotape "Old Age Has Many Faces," made in and about old people in Taiwan—an experience that affected me in both subtle and obvious ways.

Students had prepared for class assignment in-depth stories of older people they knew, and from some of these and others I came to know independently, we selected and filmed vignettes. As with all complex projects, things can and did go wrong. As we watched the footage accumulate it became apparent that none of our subjects met any of those commonly held stereotypes of age, that is, those obviously poor or in ill health. We recognize that developing countries do not have the resources to provide a universal money payment for social security. Thus it is no surprise to find people who continue to work actively as long as they are physically able. But it was a surprise to find those doing so with good spirits and vigor, in some cases contributing to the good of their community on a volunteer basis.

I had long been aware of the age integration in Chinese society and the respect and veneration shown to elders within one's family. It had a significant impact on me intellectually and emotionally to see so many visual vignettes of this in those eighteen months I lived in Taiwan. I recall visiting the small grocery store on our campus. It was about 20' x 20', with a smaller annex for meat, fish, and vegetables. It was run by two women, one in her twenties and one in her forties. An afternoon visit would frequently find both, along with an elderly grandpa and an elementary-school-aged grandson playing a hilarious card game, laughing with such abandon that the infant tucked at the end of the counter could not possibly sleep! It was a scene I mentally photographed and shared with students at home many times later.

42

Point of View

Jenny K. Johnson

I was surprised and very pleased to be chosen for the Fulbright Program at the University of Ife, Nigeria, in 1977. I thought Nigerians would prefer one of the male applicants, and I found to my further surprise that several of the department chairs at the university were women.

A very important feature of the Fulbright Program is the inclusion of family. Our three daughters, who were college students in the United States, took a year off and went with me. They attended classes at the university. Their father could not leave his job, but did come to visit. Getting acclimated in a rural West African university community could have been easier had we had an orientation program. Now there is such a program and I am especially pleased to have a hand in developing it at USIA. My daughters and I often refer to the remarkable and wonderful experiences we shared that year which, unfortunately, included a very serious auto accident that required my evacuation to the United States, leaving them to conclude my affairs.

My particular work with the School of Education was to design the first curriculum in educational technology for the University of Ife including the graduate degree programs. I began by gathering information about the part the new curriculum could play in the larger education curriculum through meetings with each of the department chairs in the School of Education. Often my perception of the situation was different from that of Nigerians. It occurred to me that I should try to look at events from a Nigerian's point of view. I believed the Nigerian point of view preferred a curriculum exactly like that of an American university. I felt strongly that the curriculum should be Nigerian and the similiarity to that of any other country should be coincidental. To support this view, I visited several organizations and institutions that would hire the graduates of the new Educational Technology Program. Because the use of technology was just beginning in education there were few job descriptions. I did identify a range of skills that would be needed by the new educational television stations planned for each state. My advisory committee agreed that practical subjects with labs and workshops would be needed most. By this time I had begun to realize that I could never really look at an issue from their point of view nor they from mine; but I did not stop trying. As the culture shock began to wear off, I became less of a missionary about the point of view question. Then my advisors told me the chief shortcoming of the curriculum was its lack of sufficient courses in history and philosophy of education and theory of instruction. They pointed out that the best U.S. programs included those subjects. There were many revisions and discussions and finally the School of Education approved the curriculum in educational technology. It went on to be approved by the University Senate on the first try. At the time, I still believed there was too much emphasis on imitating U.S. curricula; but since then I have decided that a curriculum taught in Nigeria, by Nigerians, to Nigerians, cannot be American, at least not for long. Implementation of the curriculum would certainly change it.

The Fulbright experience has helped me learn *when* to ask, "Do you see what I see?" and to avoid getting on a soap box. The University of Ife had quite a large international community with faculty from most European, American, and Eastern countries. When anything American was put down, I was expected to defend it, as was each expatriate according to his particular home country. There were those from the United States, however, who made a practice of supporting the critical remarks and even adding further condemnation of the United States. There was a certain cosmopolitanism about poking fun at one's homeland, but sometimes it was carried too far on certain issues, such as integration. I place great importance on being able to appreciate opinions different from mine without adopting them as my own. I also discovered I was not nearly as well informed as I thought on U.S. politics. One daughter sat in on a university graduate course on international relations; she called our attention to some other points of view too. We all make an effort to keep better informed now.

43

Present Challenge, Future Growth

Terry G. Lacy

The Fulbright year had an impact. It was just what I wanted when I most needed it: a chance not only to think but to rethink. I went to Iceland to learn; I did. The experience pulled together the threads of my past and opened the door to a productive future that could never have been without it.

A professor in the social sciences once asked me: How can we find the key moments in a person's life and predict what they will mean? He had no answer. Are these not the source of real education? And should our efforts not be directed to forging key moments for others? That is exactly what Senator Fulbright has done. The original question is philosophical and personal, though no less an educational concern. It is also precisely what these essays are about: one prime event in each of our lives, easily identified—but not so easily explained.

And after Fulbright? The ancient Icelanders went west to Greenland and east to Finland in expectation and adventure. This account instead is the saga of an American—and a woman at that—who came east to Iceland for all the same reasons, and found just what she was looking for. There were times in the beginning when the challenge was too great and the opportunities too few, but that has all changed. I have long since gotten used to the fact that the light switches go the wrong way and all the spoons have either shrunk or grown. I still thrill to the landscape and never tire of the clean air, even though the wind velocity often means we have it in large doses.

I am an opportunist. I joined the ranks of Teachers of English as a Foreign Language, benefiting from the training I had had in social sciences and my experience teaching technical journalism. Both at the University of Iceland and elsewhere, I have been challenged by Icelanders' problems with a different thought system, and mine in reverse in seeing the world through Icelandic eyes. Professional opportunities have broadened for me. My Icelandic partner and I have written the first *English-Icelandic Dictionary of Business Terms* (over 9,000 terms) and are presently working on the *Icelandic-English* version.

And what of our original question about prime events? A year in another culture is predictably a prime event, a lever to growth where, quite often, we least expect it. My youngest came to live with me and go to Icelandic school: *his* prime event. I watched him grow. The tourist comes expecting sweaters and Vikings. He sees sweaters because all the other tourists are wearing them. Unless he returns, he may not realize how much else there is. The Fulbright gave me a chance to explore more fully what people are and what culture means. I was fortunate and was able to return to deepen what I learned as a Fulbrighter and go forward. Ironically, while gaining what is Iceland I also have found a better milieu for expressing my Americanism.

44

Our Irish Year

Arthur I. Steinberg

On arrival at Shannon, we were to meet the individual who would prove to be my Irish counterpart, friend, and the basic reason for my successful Fulbright year, Mr. Louis Buckley, who at that time was chairman of the Conservative Dentistry Department of the Cork Dental School and Hospital. This school is one of the graduate schools of University College, Cork, a portion of the system of the National University of Ireland which encompasses colleges in Dublin, in addition to Trinity College in Dublin, Galway, Cork, and the seminary which prepares for the priesthood in Maynooth. In addition, the professional schools for medicine, dentistry, and the law are present in Dublin and Cork.

My own particular efforts at the university were comprised of classroom lecture and clinical teaching with student participation. The director of dental studies was, and is, my dear friend Professor Brian E. Barrett, at that time a dynamic man in his early forties possessing both a medical and dental degree with particular interest in histology and the clinical science of endodontics, better known as root canal therapy, wherein diseased nerve and pulp tissue of the crown and roots of the tooth are removed, the pulp chamber and canals mechanically cleansed and sealed, thereby preserving the life of the tooth. All this is described because it imparts the scientific interest and clinical acumen that Professor Barrett possessed, which allowed me great academic freedom in instituting my periodontology and oral medicine teaching program.

The Cork Dental School and Hospital on John Redmond Street, not far from the River Lee, served as a teaching and treatment institution for all the southern counties in the Irish Republic. Patients with rare orofacial disorders would be seen there to receive treatment. The school's facilities were somewhat antiquated and overworked because it did not enjoy the glamor and facilities possessed by the school at University College, Dublin, which was in a cosmopolitan environment. Yet the quality of teaching and research, despite lack of proper facilities, was of an outstanding caliber, possessing dedicated teachers in all disciplines. In addition, there was a degree of snobbery on the part of the Dublin professors and practitioners regarding the dental institution in Cork. Professor Barrett undertook the gigantic, if not impossible, task of bringing the current status of the school to the attention of the government in an attempt to gain support both spiritually and financially. It was hoped that a new teaching and treatment facility might be built in Cork City. Feasibility studies undertaken proved that such an institution could and should be built and should become part of the public policy of the prime minister, Jack Lynch, and his party, the Fianna Fail (Feena Foil). The Taoiseach Mr. Lynch was a Corkman, being native to County Cork, and did show an interest in Professor Barrett's plans.

To my amazement, it was announced that the Taoiseach would be coming to Cork one evening soon to meet with school officials regarding their plans for a new school. Professor Barrett asked me to speak on the school's behalf as an impartial observer from the United States. The evening arrived and the meeting was held at a restaurant in the Glanmire section of Cork. I was introduced to Mr. Lynch, a largish man who had been an all-Ireland hurling champion as a youth. He was quite interested in my work at the university and in the Fulbright Program. He later asked me whether I thought that a new dental facility was worthy of the government's attention. I proceeded to give a number of reasons in the affirmative. Mr. Lynch pointed out that the Dublin professors proposed a new and enlarged facility in Dublin thereby closing the school at Cork. I promptly denounced this idea, pointing out how many people from all over the southern counties of the republic—from Tralee to Rosslaire Harbor—would be denied proper oral health care. The prime minister charged me to prepare a brief on behalf of a new dental school and hospital to send to him within a few days. This I did, and sent him the arguments at his special address by special delivery mail. From that time on, Mr. Lynch became my friend. We corresponded over the years until he resigned his position as prime minister due to the pressures of Irish nationalism and Northern Ireland. However, his interest in medical and dental education was great and he was amenable to an exchange program between the Harvard School of Dental Medicine (my alma mater) and the Irish schools. Unfortunately, before a working program could be instituted, Mr. Lynch resigned.

Several months ago, we received an engraved invitation to attend the official opening ceremonies of the New Cork Dental School and Hospital. The invitation was sent late by a university official, thereby preventing our attendance. However, a transatlantic phone call to the Barretts could not have been more full of love and pride.

45

Exchange Teachers' Club of St. Louis

Walter G. Klein

In 1962 a small group of grateful Fulbright returnees and others who had had the experience of teaching in a foreign country organized the Exchange Teachers' Club of St. Louis. The purpose of the club was twofold: to share their experiences and enjoy each other's company and, even more important, to continue to promote the Fulbright exchange idea by welcoming and providing a ready circle of friends for teachers assigned to our metropolitan area, to our state of Missouri, and within a reasonable distance in the state of Illinois. Each year returning American Fulbrighters from this area are also invited to join our ranks.

Normally we have three to four meetings in the homes of our members plus a sightseeing outing in the spring to bid a "forget-us-not" farewell to our foreign friends. Our contacts and assistance, however, have also extended to advice and counsel about school problems, loan of furniture, linens, and household articles, and overnight lodging for those who come to St. Louis from elsewhere for a weekend cultural or shopping excursion. At Christmas time we maintain contact with our exchange friends by means of a round-robin letter. As a result we have had several return visits from them. Indeed, one lady teacher came back to marry a St. Louisan, settle here, and join our group permanently!

We are also willing to provide short-term hospitality in our homes for foreign Fulbright exchange teachers anywhere in the United States who would like to visit St. Louis or for those who may be traveling through to other destinations. All our activities are intended to show our appreciation for the hospitality and good-will shown us during our exchange experience and to acknowledge our debt to the Fulbright and other exchange programs for enriching our lives.

46

Ambassador Unaware

Jeanne J. Smoot

When I took my Fulbright grant at the National University of Mexico more than twenty years ago, I was not thinking about being a diplomat or an emissary for the U.S. government. I had barely turned twenty-one, and there I was—off for the first time in my life to live away from home. There had been an orientation in Washington—some talk about the disruptiveness in Latin American universities—but somehow it all seemed remote from me. I was going to Mexico—things like that did not happen in Mexico . . . but they did! There were some strikes, or hints of same, and the students overturned some vehicles. There were also questions about my academic credentials (the Mexican authorities at the time insisted that U.S. degrees were not the equivalent of Mexican degrees), and so I could not receive a Master's degree without first repeating the baccalaureate. This would have been a repetition of work and would have retarded my academic progress by four years. I soon realized that my advancement toward the doctorate I desired in comparative literature depended very much on my returning to the United States where my undergraduate credentials would be accepted by any major research institution and where I was assured that classes would not be suspended. When I did return to the United States, I went back with the feeling that my Fulbright had not been a success.

Friendships that I formed as a student in Mexico, though, were rewarding and have continued through the years. This is true to such an extent that it was with much anguish that I read of my Mexican friends in the capital who suffered through the recent earthquakes. Letters told of the daily aftershocks, the recurrent nightmares, the children still in schools where the water was contaminated, and the growing despair over corruption and mismanagement at high levels. One friend even wrote that he did not see Mexico surviving as a nation into the twenty-first century.

It was at the reading of these letters that I truly realized what my

Fulbright had meant. It was not the academic activity per se. That part of my Fulbright, while producing some very interesting classes and some excellent grades, had not netted me the master's degree I sought. From a pragmatic professional perspective, my Fulbright had been a failure. True, I came back fluent in Spanish and at the University of North Carolina did well in all my Spanish courses and ultimately earned that Ph.D. in comparative literature, but to this day I do not hold a master's degree.

What I do hold is infinitely more valuable. I hold and cherish friendships of more than twenty years' duration. The people I met while studying in Mexico are important to me. When a shock hits Mexico, it affects me, too. Their suffering is my suffering. And, while I cannot hang that kind of learning on my wall, I can hold it in my heart forever. It is infinitely more precious than a diploma.

Because I do care about Mexico, I want to do everything reasonably within my power to try to help the Mexican people, and, because of the language enrichment I gained there, my horizon is not limited only to Mexico: I have known and corresponded with other Spanish-speaking people, both in Latin America and on the Peninsula, for more than twenty years. Many of the scholarly articles I have written as well as the book that grew out of my doctoral dissertation are direct results of the heightened awareness of Hispanic culture that came from my Fulbright experience. This vital linguistic and cultural resource has enhanced my life and my administration of the academic component of the Fulbright Program.

It is not the degrees granted but the friendships forged that render infinite value to the Fulbright Program as a power for peace. Like the more than 150,000 persons who have participated in the program since its inception in 1946, I became an ambassador unaware, an ambassador almost in spite of myself and of the purely pragmatic goals I had originally set. On us, the ambassadors unaware, the strength and success of the Fulbright Program ultimately depends.

PART XII
THE FULBRIGHT
DIFFERENCE

Introduction

The value of the Fulbright Program over the last forty years should not be taken for granted. Like many innovations, when the initial novelty and excitement dies down, there is always a tendency to seek other novelties and new fashions. Ideas that work are rare. The values of the program, which have been chronicled in the preceding pages, are one reminder of its impact.

The impact is somewhat disguised, since most Fulblrighters "fade" back into the ongoing social landscape of American life—in high schools, universities, in professional life, in artistic and cultural affairs. They have been changed, but that change is hard for others to see. They are likely to remain loyal to the Fulbright ideals, but find it difficult to find any concrete way of expressing that support.

In the final selection, Michael Cardozo tries to identify the Fulbright "difference." Cordozo, former executive director of the Association of American Law Schools, is an apt choice for such a closing comment. As a young Washington lawyer, he played a role in formulating some of the original legislative language for the Fulbright Program in 1946. Later, he played a major role in the formation of the Fulbright Alumni Association. That association continues to be concerned with furthering the Fulbright Program and protecting it as a national "resource."

47

The Fulbright Difference

Michael H. Cardozo

Fulbright alumni are different from other people. Before they become Fulbrighters, they are about the same as other scholars, students, professionals, and similar seekers of an international experience. All those kinds of people, of course, are likely to have certain special qualities: more than average education and scholarly interest, extra measures of curiosity and energy, proven reputations for integrity, reliability, and diligence. These qualities are the soil in which the Fulbright experience can take root and grow into the Fulbright difference.

The Fulbright difference is not worn on a sleeve, nor does it keep people slimmer, their skin smoother, or their hair darker or more plentiful. The difference cannot be seen with the eyes. A way of thinking about people, societies, and governments in countries other than one's own makes the difference. An informed way of thinking about those things may be the simplest definition. In a world where actions, events, and words in one country are promptly known and heard everywhere else, reactions and responses based on knowledge and understanding are needed. Only thus can there be rational and peaceful relations among people and nations.

Examples of the consequences of the absence of an informed way of thinking abound in recent history. No example is more persuasive than the decision in 1943 that Turkey should declare war against the Axis. The leaders of the Allied world, Roosevelt and Churchill, had met in Cairo to plan grand strategy for winning the war. One of their decisions was that Turkey, then neutral, should become a combatant against Germany in the next few months. They had assurances from Turkish leaders that the sympathies of the Turks were on the Allied side, although the Axis was continuing to acquire substantial amounts of strategic materials from Turkey. Starting in 1941, when the lend-lease program began, weapons and other military equipment and civilian necessities had flowed into Turkey from American and British sources. The Allies wanted to assure the Turks that their military strength would be well supported if they displayed a resolve to deter an Axis invasion.

After the Cairo Conference, the military shipments, despite the needs elsewhere, were increased. At the same time many lower-level American and British representatives of various operations in Turkey, those who had social and official contacts with representative Turks in public and private life, were warning their superiors in offices and agencies in Washington and London that (1) the Turks were not going to declare war on Germany as long as the Germans had the power to attack, and (2) if war between Turkey and the Axis should start while Germany still controlled the air over the Bosphorus and neighboring waters, the ensuing destruction of Turkey's access to oil and coal would bring every wheel in Turkey to a halt, would cause power sources to grind to a halt, and light and heat to disappear—and we allies would be unable to prevent the disaster. Those were informed opinions, derived from knowledge and understanding about the Turks and their country. Roosevelt and Churchill had formulated their strategy in reliance on their own knowledge of how Americans and Englishmen react to conditions in the respective countries and reasoning by their leaders. They were surprised and angered, therefore, when the Turks, reacting as knowledgeable people would have expected them to react, refused to declare war. The added deliveries of arms, vehicles, and other equipment went to waste.

A significant difference existed between the personnel in policy positions in Washington and Ankara. Close to the top government leaders in Turkey were a number of officials who had been students in American universities, having first attended the American-sponsored Robert College near Istanbul. They understood Americans and their values; they were able to assure their superiors that U.S. war aims were bona fide what we said they were: to achieve a lasting peace in a world of freedom from war and oppression. That understanding helped them to convince Turkish leaders that their national interest lay with victory by the Allies over the Nazis. As a consequence Turkey actually helped our side in every way they could without invoking a disastrous Axis bombardment. If we had had people in Washington with as much understanding and knowledge of Turkey and its people, derived from an extended presence there, we might have adopted more rational and effective policies for dealing with the strongest power in the Middle East.

A lack of knowledge of Japanese customs and values caused an American television producer to encounter delays and embarrassment during the filming of *Shogun*. The consequences were described by Robert Garfias in his talk at the Third Annual Convention of the Fulbright Alumni Association in 1980:

In 1980 an American television producer and film crew in cooperation with a Japanese film crew and historical experts completed a lengthy and expensive television treatment of James Clavell's novel *Shogun*. The Americans relied heavily on the Japanese experts for the technical requirements of the film set in seventeenth-century Japan. They were not always prepared, however, for the level of historical accuracy which the Japanese considered absolutely essential. For example, in a Japanese room it is unthinkable for anyone to sit on the seams of the rush mats covering the floor. This seemed to the Americans like an unnecessarily burdensome convention on which they eventually succeeded in persuading the Japanese actors and crew to compromise. However, it was more difficult to persuade the Americans that they could not walk on the indoor sets with their street shoes on. Anyone who has lived in Japan can appreciate the shock and disbelief the site of an American walking on the Tatami with his shoes on might arouse.

A further difficulty in the procedure of filming occurred whenever the director gave orders for a certain task to be carried out. The message was relayed to the Japanese crew by one of the translators, at which time the director was frequently dismayed to find that rather than carrying out his orders immediately, the Japanese crew would all enter into a discussion of the order and only after all understood the instructions and its implications and there was consensus on the procedure, would the task be performed.

My own interpretation of this particular misunderstanding draws on two important Japanese cultural precepts. One is that it is considered rather crass to draw attention to the fact that someone should carry out a task merely because he is being paid to do so. Mutual respect requires that the task be carried out because of an understanding of the importance of the action itself and not because of the superior/subordinate relationship of those involved. Second, it is my assumption that the Japanese crew would have regarded their part in the filming of *Shogun* as an opportunity for international cooperation. Therefore in order to attach the requisite gravity and respect to the enterprise, all directions from the producer and director would need to be thoughtfully and respectfully explained and considered before the action could be appropriately carried out. To execute any task without such respectful discussion might have been deemed insulting to the professional status of the American guests.

Dr. Garfias cited his example to demonstrate his conviction that we need an "international perspective" because we cannot divest "ventures, be they in teaching, business, or industry, from their cultural contexts." He suggested that "every Fulbrighter can recall an incident which in some way parallels the cross-cultural misunderstandings which occurred during the *Shogun* filming."

Those misunderstandings can be particularly calamitous when they affect relations among nations. Today in many parts of the world we suffer from the absence of rational policies, guided by Americans with knowledge and understanding of the other people and their culture. Our relations with Iran are a shambles. We are on the way to a similar result all over Latin

America. Who can remember when we were less liked in Greece, where every citizen has a relative in the United States regularly sending money with goodies to the folks back home?

As for the Soviet Union, whose enmity is the most dangerous for us, "worse" moves further toward "worst" every day. That is one country where mutual understanding is going to be the only way to achieve mutual trust. Exchanges of students, scholars, scientists, artists, and even political leaders, are essential to achieve that kind of understanding. Both peoples must learn that the others are also human beings, with government departments and planners from multinational commercial enterprises. They might be joined by experienced scholars with other relevant specialties. Each seminar would deal with a particular country where the Fulbrighters spent their grant year. In this way the knowledge and understanding derived from the Fulbright experience would become available to those making government and trade policy. The purpose would not be to propose foreign policy positions. Rather, the Fulbrighters would be helping policymakers by describing and interpreting the values, culture, and society of the people and countries that were their hosts. While the seminars could be the often urged "constituency for the State Department," their function would stand on a higher level. Their deliberations could result in the highest fulfillment of the puposes of the Fulbright Act and its successor, the Mutual Educational and Cultural Exchange Act:

> ... to increase mutual understanding between the people of the United States and the people of other countries ... and thus to assist in the development of friendly, sympathetic, and peaceful relations between the United States and the other countries of the world.

A way must be found to organize and finance a program of seminars of the kind that will make that contribution. The Fulbright difference is such a valuable national resource that a program that takes advantage of it must be achieved.

About the Contributors

Harold B. Allen is Professor Emeritus of English and Linguistics at the University of Minnesota. (Egypt)

Richard Arndt served as Cultural Attaché at U.S. embassies in Beirut, Colombo, Tehran, Rome, and Paris. He was Director of Plans, Policy, and Evaluation in USIA's Bureau of Educational and Cultural Affairs. He retired in 1985 as Program Coordinator of the USIA Office of Near Eastern, South Asian, and North African Affairs. (France)

Kariamu Welsh Asante is with the Department of African-American Studies, Temple University. (Zimbabwe)

Molefi Kete Asante is Professor of Communications and African American Studies, Temple University. (Zimbabwe)

James F. Becker is Professor of Economics, New York University. (Italy)

John C. Blair is Professor of American Literature and Civilization, University of Geneva. (France)

Michael H. Cardozo is an attorney in Washington, D.C. He is a former Executive Director of the American Society of International Law and the American Association of Law Schools. (Belgium)

Alfred Maurice de Zayas is Human Rights Officer, Center for Human Rights, United Nations Office, Geneva. (Germany)

Arthur Power Dudden is Professor of History at Bryn Mawr College and Founding President of the Fulbright Alumni Association. (Denmark)

Russell R. Dynes is Professor of Sociology at the University of Delaware and a past President of the Fulbright Alumni Association. (Egypt, India)

Jan Egeland is at the International Peace Research Institute, Norway. (U.S.A.)

Mary Lee Field is with the Weekend College Program/Humanities, Wayne State University, Detroit. (Greece)

Marshall W. Fishwick is Professor of Communications Studies, Virginia Polytechnic Institute and State University. (Bangladesh)

John Freear is an Associate Professor of Accounting and Finance, Whittemore School of Business and Economics, University of New Hampshire. (U.S.A.)

Albert R. Gilgen is Professor of Psychology, University of Northern Iowa. (Ireland)

Andrew Gordon is Professor of English, University of Florida. (Spain)

Michael M. Gunter is Professor of Political Science at Tennessee Technological University. (Turkey)

Jay P. Gurian is Professor of American Studies, University of Hawaii, Manoa. (Turkey)

Julia Gurian is a public health specialist and shared her husband's Fulbright. (Turkey)

John Hancock is in the Department of City Planning, University of Washington, Seattle. (Japan)

Marga Rose-Hancock is Executive Director, Seattle Chapter, American Institute of Architects.

Irving Louis Horowitz is Hannah Arendt Professor of Sociology and Political Science at Rutgers University and Editor-in-Chief of Transaction/Society. (Brazil, India)

Connie Huning is Director of the CIES Fulbright advisory office in San Francisco. (Taiwan)

Chester L. Hunt is Professor Emeritus of Sociology at Western Michigan University. (Philippines)

Jenny K. Johnson is a curriculum development specialist most recently in Saudi Arabia.

Hideo Kawabuchi is Advisor of Sumitomo Corporation and President of Toa Koyu Company. (U.S.A.)

Wallace G. Klein is the longtime head of the St. Louis Exchange Teachers' Group. (Germany)

Richard C. Knoll is Professor of Music, University of Missouri, Kansas City. (Korea)

Shigemitsu Kuriyama is Executive Auditor of IBM-Japan. (U.S.A.)

Terry G. Lacy teaches English as a foreign language at the University of Reykjavik. (Iceland)

Otto N. Larsen is Professor Emeritus at the University of Washington, Seattle, and Senior Associate for the Social and Behavioral Sciences at the National Science Foundation. (Denmark)

Richmond Lattimore was Professor of Greek, Bryn Mawr College. (Greece)

Herman Liebaers was associated with the Royal Library of Belgium for over thirty years and was President of the International Federation of Library Associations. (U.S.A.)

Ray Marshall is a University Professor at the University of Texas. He was U.S. Secretary of Labor, 1977-81. (Finland)

J. Jeffries McWhirter is Professor of Psychology, Arizona State University. (Turkey)

Orm Øverland is on the faculty at the University of Bergen, Norway. (U.S.A.)

David Paletz is Professor of Political Science at Duke University. (Denmark)

Antonio E. Puente is Professor of Psychology, University of North Carolina-Wilmington. (Argentina)

Peter I. Rose is Sophia Smith Professor and Director of the American Studies Diploma Program at Smith College. (England)

Harrison H. Schmitt is a former Apollo 13 astronaut and U.S. Senator from New Mexico and currently a consultant on space exploration. (Norway)

Sigmund Skard is Professor of American Literature at the University of Oslo. This professorship was first of its kind in Nordic countries. (U.S.A.)

Elbert B. Smith is Professor of History, University of Maryland–College Park. Professor Smith is a former member of the Board of Foreign Scholarship. (Japan, U.S.S.R.)

Jeanne J. Smoot is Director of the Office of Academic Programs of the U.S. Information Agency. She is also Professor of English and Comparative Literature at North Carolina State University.

Arthur I. Steinberg is Clinical Associate Professor of Periodontics at the University of Pennsylvania School of Dental Medicine. (Ireland)

James L. Thorson is Professor of English Language and Literature, University of New Mexico. (Yugoslavia)

Kiyohiko Tsuboi is Professor in the Department of English at Okayama University School of Letters, Japan. (U.S.A.)

Sara M. Turner is Professor of Sociology, Anthropology, and Social Welfare, Humboldt State University, California. (Taiwan)

Chad Walsh is Professor of English, Beloit College, Beloit, Wisconsin. (Finland)

Runhild E. Wessell is a former President of the Greater New York Chapter of the Fulbright Alumni Association. (Germany)

Albert E. Wilhelm is Professor of American Literature, Tennessee Technological University, Cookeville. (Poland)

Robin W. Winks is Master of Berkeley College and Professor of History, Yale University. (New Zealand, Malaya)

Albert H. Yee is with the Chinese University of Hong Kong. (Hong Kong)